A Fulfilling Journey Through Conflicts and Contradictions

A Fulfilling Journey Through Conflicts and Contradictions

Mengesha Kebede Tessema

THE RED SEA PRESS
TRENTON | LONDON | NEW DELHI | CAPE TOWN | NAIROBI | ADDIS ABABA | ASMARA | IBADAN

THE RED SEA PRESS
541 West Ingham Avenue | Suite B
Trenton, New Jersey 08638

Book design: Dawid Kahts
Cover design: Ashraful Haque

Library of Congress Cataloging-in-Publication Data may be obtained from the Library of Congress.

ISBNs: 978-1-56902-774-5   (HB)
       978-1-56902-775-2   (PB)

"The book is dedicated to the resilience of refugees and displaced populations in Africa and elsewhere. May their plight find a durable resolution sooner than later!"

Table of Contents

FOREWORD

There is currently a positive trend of professionals deciding to record, for posterity, the challenges which they encountered and the achievements they registered in their lifetimes. This is a welcomed development. Autobiographies have historical and inspirational value, whether motivated by a family's strong urging to record, in print, the "successful" life of a relative, or an individual's own desire to provide firsthand information about the contributions made to family, community, and institutions.

I was pleasantly surprised and honored when approached by Mengesha to prepare the foreword for this autobiography. He had intimated to me on an earlier occasion that he was contemplating writing about his life experiences, essentially taking his storytelling to a higher level. This document must have been well in the making at that time. We have known each other since my first assignment with the United Nations High Commissioner for Refugees (UNHCR) to Addis Ababa in November 1983. Over the years, a professional friendship was nurtured and views mutually valued.

Mengesha's storytelling skills were impressive. He seemed to have above average knowledge of many subjects, down to the most minute detail. My usual comment was that he had the memory of an elephant. His book is informative and will no doubt allow many who shared his previous work environments, including at

UNHCR, to connect the dots and obtain deeper appreciation of the experiences that molded him from a young age, shaped his character, and even sharpened his survival instinct, such that he was able to surmount the challenges of university life in the midst of a civil war in Beirut, Lebanon.

Through his vivid recollections in the opening chapters of this book, we gather insights into his parentage; the political, social, and cultural environment of his formative, junior and high school years in Addis Ababa; the rigor and regality of life in the royal court of the emperor; embodiment of Ethiopian traditions and culture, specifically those related to the nobility; expectations and implications of proximity to the Ethiopian royal court in a highly stratified society; the excessively violent transition of political power in Ethiopia, and the era of the Derg and its leader Mengistu Haile Mariam. The book clarifies and demystifies information that had surrounded the Kebede family's relationship with Mengistu during that period.

The early chapters of this book also reveal the source of Mengesha's uncommon knowledge about guns, aircraft, arms and ammunition. It was mesmerizing for some of us to hear him speak with ease about the types of aircraft and arms that one group or the other was deploying in a conflict situation, or which country produced what. I concluded that he was just an avid reader of magazines on these topics. Reality check discloses that he had taken a strong liking to these instruments, and hunting, through a childhood friend, and through his frequent accompaniment of a military relative to an air force base. So strong was his attachment that he aspired to become a pilot. Evidently, this interest was sustained through adulthood, which explains why he was always so knowledgeable and current in his information.

The chapter on his pursuit of higher education at the American University of Beirut is also interesting and revealing of his character as an extrovert. He expanded his circle of friends, such that even with a high level of insecurity, they were able to undertake leisure travel out of Lebanon.

This autobiography speaks to selected high points in Mengesha's career as a staff member of the UNHCR. The reader follows his career path from recruitment as a general service staff member to his elevation to the national professional officer category; the transition to the international category and assignment to his first post in Malawi; higher level assignments and promotions up to the highest level of the international civil service. The highlights of his contributions to the organization are by no means exhaustive; those mentioned focus on accomplishments made under his leadership, and policy orientations that he was able or unable to influence.

It is true that Mengesha left his imprint at all locations in which he served. These are the indelible markers of his leadership, and I believe, his preferred management style, as exposed in this book. Those of his works which stand the test of time may have his name inscribed in the annals of the organization. As a former colleague, I would say that, even where there was some semblance of arrogance and bullying, his intelligence and confidence were always admirable attributes.

I commend Mengesha for a job well-done. Now, it is left to the rest of us to draw inspiration from here to leave behind a written testimony of our lives on planet earth. It has been a real pleasure doing this, and I invite you to read this book.

Ambassador Marjon V. Kamara
Duport Road, Paynesville, Monrovia, Liberia

FOREWORD

I n this aptly entitled *A Fulfilling Journey Through Conflicts and Contradictions*, Mengesha takes us on an epic journey, and with his eloquent, vivid, and graphic prose, he carries, engages, and immerses us in his childhood and upbringing, the Lebanon Civil War of the 1970s, the Ethiopian student movement in the Middle East, conflict and civil war and refugee camps across the African continent.

He also introduces us with the inner workings and dynamics of UN agencies, particularly the UNHCR, and makes complex and highly technical details intelligible and indeed enjoyable, even to the layman who is not familiar with the organization and its activities.

Mengesha has not only offered us his autobiography, but also a piece of history captured in a time capsule, that will transcend generations to come.

Bekure Herouy
Law Office, Addis Ababa

FOREWORD

The Story

It is often acknowledged that at times of crisis, strong and courageous leaders emerge. Having worked as Mengesha's deputy during his assignment as UNHCR's representative in Pakistan, I can confidently say that he was no exception to this rule. Throughout that tumultuous period, Pakistan continued to face challenges arising from hosting a large and protracted population of refugees from nearby Afghanistan. On top of these challenges came, also, widespread floods that stormed the country, devastated its economy, displaced millions of its people, and damaged much of its rural areas. UNHCR, as the refugee agency with significant responsibility to assist forcibly internally displaced persons, and Mengesha, as its representative in Pakistan, were in middle of it all.

Addressing these problems required immediate humanitarian interventions that were unconventional, costly, and beyond what the regular budget of the operation could allow. Funding was barely available to run the regular refugee aid programs, but not for a response to widespread floods that generated large destruction and massive displacement. Quickly, we switched to operating under emergency mode—a way and mentality of work UNHCR staff know all too well. In no time, a funding emergency appeal was prepared and launched to the world. The aim was to quickly buy and deploy tents, hygiene kits, shelter materials, and many other essential supplies to meet the immediate needs of the displaced population and help them to regain some parts of the lives they lost.

Luckily, many of our traditional Western donors responded positively to our appeal. But Mengesha knew that in order to meet the massive needs on the ground, we needed to secure as much funding as possible from non-traditional partners as well.

Our offices in the Gulf got in touch and conveyed an initial but strong desire from the UAE Red Crescent to assist. This was a welcomed gesture from a neighboring nation that shared many commonalities with Pakistan, including regional proximity, historic political alliance, and the Muslim faith. Knowing that every donation, no matter large or small, counts and could save lives, Mengesha warmly welcomed the UAE's offer to help, and did his utmost to make it materialize and translate into a large shelter project that provided tens of thousands of displaced Pakistanis, nearby Peshawar, a roof to sleep under.

Driven by Mengesha's determination to finalize the project in a record time, UNHCR teams in Islamabad and Peshawar worked tirelessly day and night with suppliers, contractors, and local community leaders to purchase and set up tents in the villages most impacted by the floods in the vicinity of Peshawar. At the same time, our colleagues from the Gulf accompanied the UAE Red Crescent leaders who visited the sites and saw first-hand the positive impact of the project they were about to fund. It was all teamwork, with the sole aim to assist those whose lives and livelihoods were destroyed by the floods.

But perhaps Mengesha's leadership was evident to me the most when he did not hesitate to take responsibility as the team leader, waiving much of the administrative hurdles that would have otherwise slowed the implementation of the project or rendered the negotiations with the UAE delegation unsuccessful. I still vividly remember a late evening meeting, at the residence of the UAE ambassador in Islamabad, with Mengesha finalizing the terms of the project agreement with the delegation from Abu Dhabi delegation when the negotiations were about to collapse over a minor but necessary clause related to the overhead cost of UNHCR. In order to save the project, and consequently save the lives of displaced Pakistanis, he made an unusual decision, yet without hesitation, to waive much of that cost for the sake of reaching an agreement and striking a deal. Because of that decision he made on the spot, weeks later, tens of thousands of needy people around Peshawar villages had a temporary place to call home. That is what I consider leadership.

Khassim Diang
Director of Executive Office of the UN Secretary-General
New York

PREFACE

E very time I share my story or my recollection of an event based on my experience with friends, colleagues, and family members, the usual reaction and feedback I received was their hope that one day I would document it all, and that I would share it more widely. Some would find what I had recited as being interesting, amusing, and educational. I was thus convinced that I had stories to tell and reflections to share.

The COVID-19 stay-at-home offered me the opportunity to put my recollections on paper. I started jotting down the various events and developments, chronologically, that had an impact on my life. I did not go out to do research, as the purpose was not to prepare a well-researched thesis, but simply to share my story of those things that have been enshrined in my memory as both good and bad.

However, in order to make my writing as factual as possible, I have reviewed documents in my possession, including my archives, and accessed UNHCR files electronically, directly, or through serving UNHCR friends. I have consulted and sought the views of family members, colleagues, friends, and partners directly or through electronic exchanges.

My long service within UNHCR, my upward movement from the General Service category to National Professional Officer, International Professional category, and ultimately retiring at the highest possible promotion grade level to be granted by the high commissioner was said to be inspirational for the new generation.

ACKNOWLEDGEMENT

I am indebted to all who encouraged me to produce my own biography. I am grateful to my former work colleagues and mentors, particularly Mr. Nicolas Bwakira, George Okoth-Obbo, and Marjon Kamara, who have all encouraged me to write this autobiography, and offered me their wisdom and encouragement. I am also grateful to Getachew Mahateme Selassie of the Ethiopian Red Cross, and Ayalew Awoke, former head of administration of the Agency for Refugee and Returnee Affairs of Ethiopia.

I am especially grateful to my two daughters, Natena and Helina Mengesha, who both extended encouragement and support by repeatedly reminding me that they "just can't wait" for its completion; as well as my brother Ayalew Kebede, and my nephew Bekure Herouy, who both encouraged me all the way, and read the first draft and offered me their invaluable comments and suggestions. I acknowledge the encouragement of my friend Dr. Dawit Zawde of the African Humanitarian Action, whose own initiative triggered my action. Thank you to Thowath Pal Chay, head of security in Gambella, and active leader in the Ethiopian Unity Patriots' Front, who shared with me his recollections. Thank you as well to my long-time friend Ayalew Awoke.

I would like to thank Ms. Charlotte Ridung, serving UNHCR colleague, for reading the first drafts and undertaking initial editing.

My gratitude goes to Adey Makonnen for her valuable edits and comments. Muna Sheriff, serving staff member, for sending me documents by email; and Bruno Geddo for his encouragement and for sharing his recollections.

When discussing my life and the biography, the journey would not have been possible without the support of my family, mentors, and friends. To my family, particularly my father, mother, and twin sister, who are not here with me in person, I thank you for encouraging me in all of my pursuits and inspiring me to follow my dreams. I am especially grateful to my father and mother for supporting me emotionally and financially.

Throughout my career with UNHCR, I recognize the tremendous support I received from my sister-in-law, Mrs. Adera Tsegaye. Adera, who worked in UNHCR Addis Ababa when I was recruited, helped me get settled in the organization by facilitating the induction process. During my assignment in Malawi, and the delivery of my second daughter, Helina, in Blantyre, Adera took leave and came out to attend the delivery, and provided support for a couple days thereafter. She extended to me all the support I needed during the turbulent time I was experiencing at home, leading to my divorce. Until her retirement and departure from Geneva, she was there for me, no matter what I needed.

I am also grateful for the friendship and support extended to me by Mrs. Ejigayehu Tesfaye. And upon my return to Ethiopia for retirement, I appreciate my nephew Bekure, his wife, Elsi, and his family for offering me initial accommodation and easing my reintegration.

INTRODUCTION

This autobiography is divided into four sections, linked with my recollection of major happenings that are presented mostly in chronological order, with some flashbacks or move arounds to complete a story. The first part deals with my upbringing and formative years at school in Addis Ababa, Ethiopia, and Beirut, Lebanon. The second part deals with my experiences as an international civil servant at UNHCR, spanning over thirty-three years. The multiple themes and many vignettes have been organized in a linear timeline chronicling where I started my personal and professional life, and where I closed the chapter. All have been lumped together to make the point that every international civil servant working for the UN—or any other organization, for that matter—had a life before joining the organization, and after.

Developments in the country of origin of serving international civil servants affect them directly or indirectly despite not being given recognition, or simply being downplayed. The change of government in Ethiopia had consequences that impacted my professional and emotional life, and this needs to be acknowledged. I always put my predicaments into perspective by comparing them to what happened to my Somali colleagues, who, when the state collapsed, ended up without passports, and were therefore unable to travel anywhere in the world. A few acquired Swiss citizenship, while, years later, High Commissioner Guterres secured travel documents and asylum for them in either Canada or Australia. I keep my fingers crossed that ethnic politics in my own country do not lead down the same path of Somalia.

Obviously, life continues after retirement. As I turn the leaf of a new chapter, I conclude my biography by sharing my final thoughts as a reflection of the autobiography.

In terms of substance, I have tried to capture my upbringing as a privileged young boy living in two worlds. My upbringing and adolescence was marred by political and social turmoil, with an attempted coup, a creeping revolution in Ethiopia, and civil war in Lebanon. Not divine intervention, but being brought up in a conflict-ridden environment, I assume must have been behind my prolonged involvement in humanitarian work in support of conflict-displaced populations in Africa and beyond.

After being protected from the outside world, sudden exposure to radical ideology led me to avoid conflict in Ethiopia and search for peace and education in Lebanon, only to be engulfed in civil war, political contradictions, and the mushrooming of Ethiopian ethnic liberation movements in the Middle East. The situation, in turn, resulted in relationship difficulties. The PLO and foreign friends assisted, and gradually life started improving, and I got out of poverty.

I returned to my country of origin to start an exciting life and career with UNHCR. Unexpected things that occurred on the way are noted. Being assigned to functions due to considerations that have nothing to do with my perceived career trajectory was my faith. Conflicts and obstacles with my government of origin kept cropping up along the way, and I became a witness to the resilience of refugees and internally displaced persons (IDPs) throughout my journey. I was able to observe the inside story of UN coordination. I also experienced the lack of coherence in oversight mechanisms in the UN and the Machiavellian considerations related to decision-making. Retirement and a new page turned for life to continue along its unexpected trajectory.

CHAPTER ONE

Formative Years

I was born in Addis Ababa, at the Adventist Seventh Day Hospital on the June 17, 1954, to my father, Dejazmatch Kebede Tessema, and my mother, Weyzero Yetateku Kidane. My twin sister, Turunesh (Turuye) came into the world some five minutes ahead of me, which technically made her my elder, with all the associated privileges of seniority I was reminded of while growing up. I am one of twelve children, the eldest being Woderelesh, then Assegedetch, Kassa, Yilma, Asfaw, Tenna, Ayalew, Turuye, Tegnagne, and Ayahelushem. Two more boys, Sishuh and Bizuneh died upon delivery.

I attended and graduated from our own private Amharic church school, having become proficient in literacy and biblical studies. The school was situated within the family compound and taught by the resident priest, Aba Degu. Turuye and I initially attended the Nazareth Primary School for Girls, which accepted boys at the kindergarten and grade one levels in those days. In grade two, I attended Saint Joseph School for Boys. After a year, I transferred to Sanford International School, where I was once again enrolled with my twin, and my other sister Ayahelushem, or Mame, and completed secondary school there.

Mame, Turuye, and Tenagne, my younger sister who attended the French School together with my niece Manalebish Mekonnen, ate at the same table, which meant they belonged to the same age group. Bekure, my nephew, joined that age group ever since he came to live with us. Roles and responsibilities were segregated along gender lines, where the girls had to undertake house chores such as cooking and sewing, while the boys did not have traditional household chores, but would play football. This arrangement extended to our stays in Chefebuki, Debre Zeit, or any other leisurely outing.

My immediate family could be stratified into different age groups. Etye Wodereyelesh and Etye Assegedetch were born before the Italian Occupation and went to school together. Gash Kassa and Yilma grew up together, while Asfaw, Tenna, and Ayalew went to school and grew up together, and were relatively free to associate themselves with neighborhood boys, unlike me. Tenagne, my younger sister, stayed with Ma Souer and Emama Tilikwa, detached from us for a while.

I was brought up in an affluent, large family of six brothers and five sisters living in an expansive compound with other relatives, students, and a variety of resident household helpers. Taking someone from rural Ethiopia and giving that person educational opportunities in Addis Ababa, while also helping out with some work at home, came naturally to my father. At a later age, I did realize that he was in fact giving opportunities to young boys to follow in his footsteps, influenced by being taken in and brought up by his grandparent. Interesting to observe, the boys were not selected on ethnic or relationship criteria only. My father held various senior government positions and had close association with the monarchy. He came from a humble background and worked his way up the social ladder in the Imperial Palace, while my mother was from a more affluent background and had some land holdings in the eastern province of Hararghe and Minjar in central Showa.

I now realize that being the youngest of six boys, and having been born at a time when my father was aging and the family was leading a more sedentary lifestyle, gave me an advantage regarding family love and attention in comparison to my older brothers. I was close to my father and was pampered by him. The negative side to that was I could not go play outside the compound with the neighborhood kids, as it was considered inappropriate for my noble upbringing. I also spent most of my weekends with my father or the family in Debre Zeit, a town 47.9 kilometres from Addis Ababa. The restriction imposed on me not to go out of the compound and mingle with neighborhood kids became a shortcoming at a later stage of my life, when I returned to live in the neighborhood, only to realize that I could not relate to the place or its inhabitants beyond my immediate family circle.

My immediate play group of friends in our compound were not my brothers, but my nephews Bekure, Begashaw, Girum, and Dagnatchew, all of whom resided in the compound and had come to stay there from rural Ethiopia for the primary purpose of attending school. All were relatives except Begashaw. He was from Chefebuki, where his father had one day brought him to my father and asked if he could take him in and offer him an education. I knew Begashaw, as he used to help us track guinea fowl when we would go hunting. He was a shepherd who also served the Saint Michael Church as a deacon, at the hill behind our house.

One day, Begashaw's father brought him to our house in Chefebuki, and in front of my father threw his schema (the white cloth that men wear) to the floor and requested that his son be taken to serve Mengesha in Addis Ababa and pursue his studies. My father looked at me and asked if I would look after him as my son. With excitement, I agreed. Thus, Begashaw moved to Addis Ababa with us and shared the bedroom with me and Bekure.

Upon moving in with us, his shorts and tattered shirts were burnt, as they were allegedly full of flees. He was provided with new clothing, and wore shoes for the first time. Begashaw continued his studies, even after I left the country and went on to become an Ethiopian diplomat, serving in neighboring countries.

Other residents in the compound included a group from Gojjam province who came to Addis Ababa when my father finished his governor's term and returned. These included Asalafi

Hailu Kassa—or Ababa Merto, as we called him—Gash Gellaw
Eshete; Aba Degu Woube, the resident priest and teacher; Emahoy
Yeshareg Yimam, the sister of Dejazmatch Abera Yimam; Belay
and Mentwoded Zeleke, children of the well-known patriot
Dejazmatch Zeleke Desta.

Just like myself, my older brothers had their own play groups
residing in the compound, which included Tilahun Wodajo,
Hailemariam Adera, Hailu Kelkile, Mesmia Haile, Mekbib Gonit,
Gizaw Getaneh, Workishet and Kibrete Adelahu, Yehwalashet
Asamenew, and Messele Tilaye.

My father's mother, Desta Tessema, or Emama Tilikwa—the
bigger mother, as we used to fondly call her—resided in a house of
her own within the compound even though she had her own close
relatives and household helpers residing with her. Her house and
compound were given to me by my father when I finished high
school, with the undertaking that I would renovate the old house,
or rebuild a new dwelling, but would not sell or change it for
anything in the world. I have kept my side of the bargain, rebuilt
the house, and I reside there now. My father's brother, Ababa
Metaferia Mengesha, and his family, as well as the children of my
uncle Ababa Tilaye Tessema, also resided in their own dwelling,
but within the compound. Other relatives' residents included the
family of Gash Tadesse and Gashe Yetagesu Beyene, as well as
Gash Adelahu Tsege and his siblings.

Special mention has to be made of Gash Tadesse Beyene, who
also resided with his family on the compound. He was my father's
right-hand man, running errands, paying workers' salaries, settling
electric and telephone bills, and managing various students'
pocket money and the sort. After school and on weekends, he
would invite me to a chess game in the reception room located in
front of the main house. He was surely my favorite mentor, and a
trusted confidant of my father.

Lastly, I would like to recall the story of Girma "Edegelign,"
("grow for me"), who, as a young boy, was brought to our house
by a nun who claimed that he was abandoned by his mother at the
church because he was born blind. The nun handed Girma to my
father and requested that he bring him up. Thus, Girma joined the

family and would play with us. Upon enrollment at the Sebeta School for the blind, he was registered as Girma Kebede, which technically made him my brother.

Girma attended the boarding school at Sebeta, located some thirty-five kilometers west of Addis Ababa. He spent most holidays, weekends, and school breaks at home with us. We would also go to visit him at Sebeta, and bring him home-cooked food. As a gifted student, he was promoted often. When he came home, he would bring his football, which had a bell in it, and would play with us with no inhibitions. He also taught us songs and hymns in English.

Girma completed high school, and while I was abroad, graduated from Haile Selassie University with a law degree. Upon my return to Ethiopia, he had become a judge and was raising his own family.

Hedar Michael

Religious festivals were often interwoven with social activities, which shaped the psychological makeup of children brought up in a similar situation as I was. The breaking of bread following prayers at home, with all assembled on the first day and seventh day of each month on Saint Abo and Saint Trinity Day were occasions to look forward to.

By far, the fondest childhood memories of such religious occasions were how Hedar Michael was celebrated every year. The twelfth day of each Ethiopian month is dedicated by the Ethiopian Orthodox Church to commemorate the Archangel St. Michael. The annual celebration takes place On Hedar 12 (November 21). Saint Michael was the favorite and chosen saint of the family. All boys were baptized, and Saint Michael was named as their god father. I was baptized as Haile Michael, or the "power of Michael."

Upon my father's reassignment from Wellega, a province in the western part of Ethiopia, where he had served as governor back in Addis Ababa, the family threw a big feast on Saint Michael's Day, and ever since, we have celebrated it every year.

A month before Hedar Michael, the rules were relaxed and we all participated in the preparatory work. Preparation work for *tej*, a traditional Ethiopian fermented honey wine, starts about one month in advance, where sacks of honey are mixed in barrels located in the *tej* cellar, or *tej bet*. The brew is checked every other day, where various ingredients, such as *gesho*, banana, and more honey are added. A week before, preparation for *tella* in barrels, and *gembo* resumed. I joined groups of young boys competing in chopping firewood and *gesho* pounding almost daily.

A couple days prior to the feast, preparation of the various sauces to be cooked would start with the chopping of bags of onions. A carnival-like atmosphere would permeate throughout the compound. A flurry of activities in the eve of Saint Michael's Day, with cooking, preparation of *injera*, and mixing of various dough took place. Feasting in the name of tasting the food and the drinks under preparation resumed. Oxen and sheep were slaughtered, and the meat cut up and hung on hooks to be used later in a variety of dishes. There was a designated room for meat, with fresh eucalyptus leaves spread on the floor to ward off ants or any other insects.

Hedar Michel would start with morning prayers, the spraying of holy water, and the feeding of the clergy, primarily drawn from Saint Michael's Church, Batha St. Mary Church, and the Trinity Cathedral. This was followed by a huge lunch party involving family, friends, neighbors and the less fortunate. The presence of English school friends from my class, as well as those from Turuye and Mame's classes, added to the festivities and excitement.

The designated dining structures in the compound would be augmented with additional shades, tents, tables, benches, and chairs brought in from the various *idirs*. Seating arrangements were segregated such that the nobility and close relatives and friends of the family would be seated in the main house. Priests and other clergy would be seated in the big room, built adjacent to the main house (*aderash*), while the rest of the invited guests were seated under the various shades in the compound put up for the occasion.

Moving around and being part of the serving group was a major excitement. The feasting lasted the whole day, with groups of people coming and going. In the evening, we joined the men in ushering the drunks out of the compound.

Cleaning started in the evening and lasted a couple days. Friends, relatives, and neighbors would continue to come and lend a helping hand, while leftover food would be served at mealtimes. The end of the party did not happen in a day, but gradually wound down over a week.

The fond recollections of Hedar Michael enshrined in me the satisfaction one gets by working together and sharing and socializing with different categories of people, some the less privileged than I, as being fruitful and rewarding. Later in life, I reflected on large-scale refugee and internally displaced feeding programs I helped to organize as being Hedar Michael in a different setup, but equally as exciting and fulfilling.

Weekends and Holidays

The original family compound we had in Debre Zeit was located across the street from the Debre Zeit Palace, where the emperor spent a significant portion of his weekends. Visitors to the palace would normally drop in, which became a nuisance for our family, as the unplanned visits disrupted our rest and leisure periods. A new compound was acquired later on, away from the palace, close to Lake Chelekleka. The beautiful house was located next to the mansion of General Abye Abebe.

I cherish fond memories of the new compound, where we spent lovely weekends with my sisters in the orchards and flower-filled gardens. I learned how to swim at our neighbor General Abye's swimming pool. I recall delivering *quanta* (biltong) and *cheko* (spiced barley butter mix) to the general's house and bringing back Greek biscuits in return. I was often offered a sandwich General Abye's wife, Mrs. Nesebu, which tasted great, but I did not know the ingredients. I was simply told not to tell my father that I had a sandwich, and I kept my word. Later in life, I realized the tasty sandwiches were, in fact, ham topped with ketchup and mayonnaise. Eating ham is taboo in the Christian Orthodox culture, which was strictly adhered to in our home. The general's family was more liberal, and accustomed to foreign eating habits.

In Debre Zeit, I befriended an Israeli boy named Ariel Shai.

His father was a training instructor at the air force base. Ariel and I spent time together and also shared a common interest in guns and hunting. We hunted ducks, and I had to provide the rifles and bullets. I also taught Ariel how to dismantle and clean an Israeli Uzi semiautomatic gun. After hunting ducks on the various lakes, we would take the kill to his house for cooking, as eating ducks was also out of the question in my household. I was given the liberty to bicycle to his place and back. Here, I had the freedom to move around as I pleased, unlike in Addis Ababa.

My love of guns, hunting, and war planes was sparked through a relative, Colonel Haile Selassie Dagne, who got me an ID card to go in and out of the air force base, on the grounds that I would make use of the sport facilities. I instead watched aircraft as they took off or landed. I knew of the bombers Canberra, the training T33, the F86, and later the F5A and E fighters and ground bombers. I was made to believe at the time that the Ethiopian Air Force was comparable to that of Iran and Israel, which I later found not factual. However, it was a formidable air force that stood head above shoulders compared to the capabilities of neighboring countries.

I wanted to become a fighter pilot, a dream not supported by my father, or even my air force relative, Colonel Haile Selassie. At the air force base, I watched war films such as *The Longest Day* (1962). Colonel Haile Selassie, who did not have a family of his own, took me out to the Ras Hotel, where I enjoyed ice cream and iced tea. The Debre Zeit and Chefebuki experience, I have no doubt, contributed a great deal to my interest in power politics and international relations.

Upbringing Spanning Two Cultures

My upbringing spanned two cultures with differing values and norms. As member of traditional Ethiopian nobility, I had to learn to be a nobleman by staying clear of the kitchen area and related household work attributed to women. My manhood was to be harnessed through riding horses, farming, shooting, and hunting. Learning to shoot and handle guns at an early age was part of the ritual. I had my own horse, Sinde—meaning *wheat*—brought from the stables of the Imperial Guard into our compound. I attended horse riding lessons at the racing club close to home, and was taught by Sargent Maru Melka. Sinde was purchased by Ababa Wodajo from Chatu Jidda, in Northern Showa province, and was given to Corporal Assefa to be trained in the stables of the cavalries of the Imperial Bodyguard. According to Corporal Assefa Minda, Sinde could not be groomed as a race horse, and thus was returned to our compound.

Most summer breaks, when school closed, I went to our farmhouse with Mother in Chefebuki, situated in a valley on the western slopes of Yarer Mountain, some fifty kilometers south of Addis Ababa. As a daily routine, I hunted dik-dik, wild pigs, and guineafowl. Learning to farm and handle an ox-pulled plough, and related activities, were also part of the daily work. Sinde, my horse, was also relocated to Chefebuki, where I would ride him whenever we went there.

In contrast to my field adventures, my sisters did the cooking and sewing chores at home, as well as weeding on the farm. I cherish fond memories of Gash Debele Shura, who brought us milk every morning, and Gash Chala, whose daughters Meshkele and Beshalu came to reside with us in Addis Ababa.

I am convinced that my father wanted me to experience what it was like to be brought up in his day and age, while also teaching me that I needed to cope with a world that was quickly disappearing, replaced by the so-called modernization of the Ethiopian State. My father had traveled extensively around the world, and had also spent significant time in Jerusalem while in exile during the Ethiopian-Italian War. Therefore, he was no stranger to the new world order, but he still wanted us to experience the local culture and what he had been through.

My parents wanted their offspring to know their past, while being well-prepared for the new world order unfolding. As a result, I was sent to one of the top schools in Addis Ababa at the time, which I will come to later.

My Father

My father, Dejazmatch Kebede Tessema, was born in 1902, in

the Shewa province, in the Menz and Timuga District, to his father, Kegn Azmatch Mengesha Ayanehe, and his mother, Weyzero
Desta Tessema. At the age of two, he was taken by his mother's
father, Tessema, who was an Azajee[1] in the Palace of Emperor
Menelik in Addis Ababa. My father was brought up in the palace,
and took the second name Tessema after his grandfather. I was
named Mengesha after my paternal grandfather.

My father studied at the Amharic school on the palace
grounds. He was first employed at the Ministry of the Pen to gain
work experience in 1912. In 1914, when Lij Eyassu was replaced
by Queen Zewditu Meinelik, my father moved to the palace to
serve the queen, which was a more prestigious undertaking at the
time than the civil service. He attended the Meinelik School on the
palace grounds, but did not continue with his studies, as he was
subsumed by palace chores.

My father, who started as a servant in the palace, was promoted
to head of the Royal Carriage and Automobile Department. In
1930, he was promoted to become Director of Decorations and
Jewellery, and overall head of the palace. In 1935, he took part in
the Maychew Battle against the Italian invading forces, and was
wounded. He was sent as Deputy President of the Jerusalem-based
Ethiopian Refugees Association. In 1939, he led an expeditionary
force with his British advisor, Major Sanford, and entered Gojjam
through the Sudan as head of the advance team to pave the way for
the return of the emperor from exile in the UK. He was supported
by Major Sanford, who headed the British team to assist the
Ethiopian patriotic movement, and was code named *Mission 101*.
The mission took place before the arrival of Colonel Wingate and
elements of the Gideon Force.

In recognition of various successes achieved in battles in
Gojjam, my father was appointed Fitawrari. The restoration of
Ethiopia's independence in 1941 was achieved by the role played
in this Gojjam campaign by the Ethiopian Patriots, who had defied
and obstructed the Italians for five years and became instrumental
in the emperor's return.

In 1939, my father and his army headed to Wellega to get
rid of the Italian forces there. He was appointed as governor of

My Father Dejazmatch Kebede Tessema

Wellega, and in 1942 became the mayor of Addis Ababa and the surrounding area. He was elevated to the rank of *dejazmatch* and appointed Governor of Gojjam in 1945. Further positions he occupied included President of the Senate, *afenegus*, President of the Supreme Court, Governor of Showa, Minister of State Properties and Pension, Deputy President of the Legislative Council Minister of the Territorial Army, Crown Councillor, and in 1966, Minister of the Imperial Palace.

My father grew up with palace mannerisms, management, protocol, and code of conduct up to his last assignment as Crown Councillor at the time of the overthrow of Emperor Haile Selassie in 1974. During the early days of the Derg, he was appointed Minister of the Imperial Court, when Endalkatchew Mekonnen established the last Cabinet after the resignation of Aklilu Habtewold's Cabinet from where he retired. My father also wrote a memoir entitled, *Ye Tarik Mastawasha,* or *Memoirs of History*, covering his upbringing and his recollections of life in the palace, the Italian invasion and the liberation struggle, the liberation and the post-liberation period. He gave the right of use of the book to the YMCA.

As a footnote, my grandfather, Kegn Azmatch Mengesha Ayana, was one of the martyrs of the Yekatit 12 Massacre, carried out by Italian occupation forces following the throwing of grenades by Moges Asgedom and Abraham Deboch. Yekatit 12 is a national holiday on the Ethiopian calendar, which commemorates the massacre and imprisonment of Ethiopians by the Italian occupation forces following an attempted assassination of Marshal Rodolfo Graziani, viceroy of Italian East Africa, in Addis Ababa on February 19, 1937. This has been described as the worst massacre in Ethiopian history. Estimates vary on the number of people killed in the three days that followed the attempt on Graziani's life. Ethiopian sources estimated that 30,000 people were killed by the Italians, while Italian recent sources estimated that 19,200 people were killed, 20 percent of the population of Addis Ababa. My mother and two sisters escaped the massacre, as they were in exile outside of the city.

My Mother

My mother, Weyzero Yetateku Kidane, was born in 1906, in Hararghe province in the Chercher locality, to her mother, Weyzero Turrufat Yergu, and her father, Kidane Benguse, or popularly called "Kidane Kesto" (Kidane the archer). Kidane was a flamboyant character who loved hunting and horse riding and playing *gugse*. He was reportedly close to Lij Eyassu, who contended for the throne with Emperor Haile Selassie and Queen Zewditu Menilik. Because of that, he was reportedly not a favorite of the emperor.

During a court deliberation, Kidane concluded that the emperor was siding with his enemies in passing judgement, which he considered unfair. He reportedly stormed out of said imperial

My Mother Weyzero Yetateku Kidane

court hearing, having told the emperor to get lost because he was always siding with cowards. Kidane reportedly killed those who were sent to arrest him, and went into the bush in the Ogaden area. He was not heard from after that.

Weyzero Turufat was a well-established lady with land holdings in the Hararghe and Shewa regions. She also had property around Addis Ababa. During the Italian occupation of Addis Ababa, she took my mother and her two other daughters to Minjar and Bulga, where they remained in hiding until the return of my father from exile.

My mother was an excellent storyteller, and a poet of a sort. Most of the stories of what my father did in various parts of the country were told to us by my mother, which was significant given the reserved nature of my father. Her recollections of life in exile within Ethiopia at the time of the Italian occupation, and the role she played in support of various patriots fighting occupation in the Shewa province, particularly in the Bulga and Minjar ranges, was graphic. She had to move and hide from place to place to avoid arrest by the Italian occupation authorities and their local stooges. The return of my father, and ultimately the emperor, was a major achievement and a turning point in her life.

Mother spent most of her days managing the house and compound, ensuring that all were fed on time, and that the preparation of work in the kitchens was progressing as usual. She went shopping once a week in the market in a long-wheel Land Rover and bought butter, honey, and spices. When we were young, we would tag along, and she would buy us cookies or candy. She regularly attended church, and for leisure at home, she would sit and enjoy Ethiopian coffee and exchange on current affairs and stories, with friends, visitors, and a few of her relatives who resided inside the compound. She also enjoyed embroidery and sewing of decorative baskets.

Following the passing of my father, and at a later stage of her life, Mother was ordained at the local church as a nun, and was accordingly referred to as "Emahoy Yetateku."

14

Lij Eyassu

My father's career in the Imperial Palace started at a time of transition and power struggle within the palace, which continued to the end of his career. Power struggle and intrigues were no novelty to the palace, nor indeed the country. It is to be recalled that Emperor Menelik II had designated Lij Iyasu Michael, his grandson—Son of Ras (later King) Michael Ali of Wollo and Woizero Shewaregga Menelik—as his designated heir. Upon the death of his grandfather in 1912, Lij Eyassu technically became Emperor Iyasu V, but because he was never publicly proclaimed as such, and was never crowned, he is known to this day as Lij or Abeto Iyasu. Although legally married to Seble Wongel Hailu, Lij Iyasu reportedly had numerous secondary wives, Christian and Muslim women, in violation of the tenants of the Orthodox Church.

Lij Iyasu had ambitions to further expand on the modernization program initiated by his grandfather Emperor Menelik II. However, his approach to reform and modernization took a distinctly different path. He seems to have regarded the Ethiopian Orthodox Church and the aristocracy of the old Kingdom of Shewa as obstacles to his plans, and showed a preference for nobility of the Northern provinces, and a distinct preference for Muslim notables. He was reported to have disdainfully referred to the powerful nobles that had long served Menelik II as "my grandfather's fattened sheep," and preferred to raise his own companions to positions of power and influence.

On the international stage, Lij Iyasu also showed a clear preference toward Germany, Austria, and the Ottoman Empire during World War I, alarming the French and British colonial rulers of Ethiopia's neighbors. In an effort to conciliate Ethiopian Muslims to his regime, Lij Iyasu made a practice of visiting and praying at mosques, taking Muslim women as wives, and wearing clothing of Islamic ethnicities from around the Empire. The Ethiopian conservative establishment could not stomach his trampling of their interests and his controversial behavior. His flirtation with Islam alarmed even progressive elements that might otherwise have been his natural support. These forces, along with the British and French allies concerned with his leaning toward the Central Powers, joined in a conspiracy to remove Lij Iyasu and replace him on the throne with a figure more in line with their interests.

After offending the bulk of the nobility with his irresponsible behavior, his numerous liaisons with prominent and not so prominent women, his support of Germany Austria and Turkey during World War I, and his purported conversion to Islam, Lij Iyasu was deposed by the nobility and excommunicated by the Orthodox Church in 1917, and replaced by his aunt, Menelik II's daughter Zewditu, who became Empress of Ethiopia, and by his cousin Ras Taffari Makonnen, who was named Crown Prince, Heir to the Throne and Regent.

Lij Iyasu died in captivity in 1935. My father stood with the Zewditu block and became her close confident. His position on that subject matter was made clear to all his siblings and other residents in his compound.

On April 1, 1930, Zewditu died, and Tafari was crowned emperor. He was crowned Haile Selassie I ("Power of the Trinity," his baptismal name) on November 2, 1930. Haile Selassie's success was shortly followed by Italy's ruler Benito Mussolini's decision to incorporate Ethiopia into the Italian ambitions in the Horn of Africa. After an Ethiopian patrol clashed with an Italian garrison at the Welwel oasis in the Ogaden, in November–December 1934, Rome began seriously preparing for war. Haile Selassie continued to trust in the collective security promised by the League of Nations. Only on October 2, 1935, upon learning that Italian forces had crossed the frontier, did he order mobilization. During the subsequent seven-month Italo-Ethiopian War, the Italian command used air power and poison gas to separate, flank, and destroy Haile Selassie's poorly equipped armies. The emperor went into exile on May 2, 1936. My father followed, being assigned to Jerusalem.

For five years (1936–41) Ethiopia was, in a way, joined to Eritrea and Italian Somaliland to form Italian East Africa. During this period, resistance to the occupation continued and the independence of the country was vigorously defended. The

Italians dominated the cities, towns, and major caravan routes, while Ethiopian patriots controlled most of the country and harried the occupiers, and sometimes tested the larger garrison towns.

When Italy joined the European War in June 1940, the United Kingdom recognized Haile Selassie as a full ally, and the emperor and his advance team were soon in Khartoum, Sudan, to help the British-trained Ethiopian Army. As mentioned earlier, an advance delegation headed by my father was sent to mobilize patriots to stand with the emperor, and a joint force entered Gojam on January 20, 1941, and encountered an enemy quick to surrender. On May 5th, the emperor triumphantly returned to Addis Ababa. Defying the British occupation authorities, he quickly organized his own government. The return of the emperor, and the consolidation of the monarchy in power, set the tone for what was to come later on.

Return to Power and "Recovery of Eritrea"

Another significant development that impacted the geo-political environment during my upbringing and adolescence was the lingering issue of Eritrea. History recalls that between 1885 and 1890, the Italians occupied the costal territory as part of their participation in the scramble for Africa. Their southward expansion into the Ethiopian Empire was checked by Ethiopian Emperor Menelik in 1896, when he defeated them at the Battle of Adwa. This did not stop the Italians from carving out a colony along the Red Sea from a conglomerate of peoples without the slightest regard for its complex historical makeup. The Italians named this colony Eritrea, from the Roman name for the Red Sea, Mare Erythrium.

Eritrea remained under Italian occupation until 1941. As of 1936, it was administered under the East African colonial administration of Italy, which included the rest of Ethiopia and Italian Somaliland. In 1941, British forces ousted the Italians from the territory and took over the administration. Several movements surfaced in Eritrea in opposition to British rule. The most notable were the Union Party and the Muslim League. The Union Party was set up predominantly by Christian Abyssinians in 1942, and favored unification with Ethiopia. The Muslim League rejected the idea of union.

The British occupation of Eritrea was a bone of contention not only inside Eritrea itself and with Ethiopia, but also between Britain, France, the USA, and the USSR. The four powers failed to agree on the fate of the territory, and presented the case to the UN General Assembly, after signing the peace treaty with Italy in 1947.

The US supported the Eritrean federation with Ethiopia, and that position is said to have been made clear in February 1945, at a meeting with US President Franklin D. Roosevelt and Haile Selassie. It is reported that the emperor had submitted a memorandum stressing the imperativeness for recovering Eritrea and thereby gaining free access to the sea. In 1948, and again in 1949, two commissions established by the wartime Allied Powers, and by the United Nations, reported that Eritrea lacked national consciousness and an economy that could sustain independence. Washington, wishing to secure a communications base in Asmara, and naval facilities in Massawa—and also to counter possible subversion in the region—supported Eritrea's federation with Ethiopia.

The UN General Assembly, after a referendum organized by a special committee, passed the USA-sponsored Resolution 390 in 1950, recommending that Eritrea be federated under the Ethiopian territory in 1952. The union took place in September 1952, and Eritrea attained autonomy in the form of self-government, with a free press, political parties, parliament, elections, and labor organizations.

The federal status of Eritrea was in complete contradiction to the Emperor Haile Selassie's drive for centralized development. The emperor resorted to a policy of the carrot and the stick to bring about complete integration and to undermine its federal status. Highlanders from the plateau, who were mainly Christians, were accorded titles, land, and government positions. The low landers, primarily Muslims, were neglected, and the Arabic language was gradually eliminated from the school system. Disgruntled Eritreans started crossing over into Sudan as refugees, and ultimately formed the Eritrean Liberation Front in 1961.

By 1962, the Unionist-dominated Eritrean parliament was encouraged to dissolve itself, and Eritrea was declared the 14th province of Ethiopia. The local languages were discouraged and Amharic was actively introduced by the state. Eritrea was brought under the firm grip of the Ethiopian state. Labor organizations were banned, and troops were sent in to crush and deter resentment.

During the 1950s, Ethiopia's coffee sold well in world markets. Revenues were used to centralize the government, to improve communications, to develop a national system of education based on the Western model, and to modernize urban centers. In November 1955, the emperor promulgated a revised constitution, which permitted the parliament to authorize finances and taxes, to question ministers, and to disapprove imperial decrees. The constitution also introduced an elected lower house of parliament, a theoretically independent judiciary, separation of powers, a catalog of human rights, and a mandate for bureaucratic responsibility to the people. At the same time, the emperor retained his power of decree and his authority to appoint the government. Among his ministers, he subtly established competing power factions—a stratagem that had the ultimate effect of retarding governmental functioning and bureaucratic modernization. Newly trained and well-educated intellectuals were lumped together with feudalists, aristocrats, and church-trained nobility. The lack of a cohesive executive body that resulted appears to have worked in favor of the emperor's divide and rule architecture, as he remained the final arbiter. However, the inbuilt tension, coupled with the full absorption of Eritrea, was set to explode. It was only a question of time.

Internal Conflicts Leading to the Fall of the Monarchy

In December 1960, while the emperor was abroad, members of the Security and Imperial Bodyguard forces attempted a coup d'état. I recall vividly being rushed into the family Land Rover, with my sisters and mother, and being taken to a relative's residence across town, as our house was said to be in the direct line of fire between the coup leaders sheltered at the Imperial Body-guard headquarters, and the pro-monarchy housed at the Ethiopi-an Army barracks. F-86 fighter jets were flying low over the city, dropping leaflets and conducting mock attacks, apparently to de-moralize the coup leaders and their supporters, and let them know that the Air Force stood with the pro-monarchy camp and could bomb them at ease, as the Imperial Bodyguards were not armed with aircraft weaponry.

We were informed that, should resistance of the coup plotters persist, the Air Force was set to bomb its headquarters, which was close to our home, and thus there was an additional impetus to move out quickly. I recall my mother crying, and her anxious looks were visible as she prayed nonstop for deliverance. We were all scared as we took a few of our personal belongings and headed to a house we had to share with people said to be relatives, but we hardly knew. Soldiers with metal helmets with white crosses painted on top were visible along the route. Both the Army and the Imperial Bodyguard shared the same battle uniform and personal weapons, as they were both supplied by the US government. The Army painted the white cross to separate it from the Bodyguards.

That traumatic development, engulfed in fear of war and the unknown, lasted only a couple days, but felt like weeks. My father stayed behind, and later on I found out that he, as then Minister of Pension and commander of the Territorial Army (the rural militia), was involved in mediation between the coup leader, and commander of the Imperial Bodyguard, General Mengistu Neway, and the head of the Ethiopian Armed Forces, General Merid Mengesha. During the trials of the coup leaders, my father had outlined his role in undertaking a shuttle diplomacy between the two leaders and their respective camps in a failed attempt to bring about reconciliation and avoid bloodshed. My father had refused to bring in the rural militia into Addis Ababa in order not to exasperate the situation, and avoid further bloodshed. His role as a mediator, I assume, is what saved his life, while other officials and ministers in detention at the Bodyguard headquarters and the palace were executed, including the close friend of my father, and older brother of my mother, Afenigus Eshete Geda.

Upon return home from our temporary exodus, the burial and prolonged morning of my uncle Afenigus Eshete Geda dominated the recovery phase of that post-conflict situation at home. My mother never stopped talking of Afenigus Eshete, here favorite brother, 'til her final days.

The attempted coup, which is considered the initiation of the anti-monarchy drive in Ethiopia, was spearheaded by two legendary brothers in Ethiopian recent history, Germame and Mengistu Neway. In 1960, according to the testimony of General Mengistu, it all started after years of witnessing the brutal treatment, torture, and pain of Ethiopians under the emperor's regime. Since many were tired of being exploited for the interest of the few, the brothers thought if they removed the king, the people and the Army would support them.

The brothers first communicated their intention to the third mastermind, Colonel Workneh Gebeyehu, a man who was a Cabinet member and chief security officer of the emperor. Colonel Workneh indeed agreed with the plan. After that, the three met several times to discuss how they would materialize the coup.

In addition, they approached the US Embassy in Addis Ababa for support. The ambassador, Arture Richards, was reportedly keen with the plan and gave them his complete support. He is said to have even suggested that his country would assist financially, and would get them military support from Egypt. According to Mengistu's testimony, that news convinced them that they would succeed. Therefore, they agreed to come up with a detailed plan. Germame took the initiation to write out the steps and procedures.

When the emperor got an invitation to visit West Africa, he thought he was leaving the country and his power in reliable hands. Therefore, he extended his travel from West Africa to Brazil. For the coup schemers, this was an excellent opportunity. Before the king arrived back, they planned to demolish his power. Therefore, the coup was set to commence on December 12, 1960.

When the king got to Brazil, Germame, General Mengistu, and Colonel Workneh started executing their plan. Mengistu seemed to take this part of the military for granted. He did not even explain his plan or inform them of what they were about to be part of. Instead, he deceived them with information that says the military was attempting a coup, so they would be getting orders to defend the power of His Majesty Haile Selassie. Since that was their primary task, they were more than happy to do it.

Meanwhile, they called every top government official, including ministers, Cabinet members and military leaders, and told them the Queen was sick. Most of them bought this story and came to the palace in their own cars. Unfortunately, the Royal Guard was waiting to arrest every one of them.

The coup allies also thought they should get the city police on their side. Therefore, after calling the chief of police, General Tsige Dibu, they forced him to order the police to be part of the coup. Unfortunately, he was able to let his officers know that this was an order, and not voluntary. Therefore, the plan to get the police on their side failed.

One of the terrible mistakes made was Mengistu and his allies failing to arrest the military's commander-in-chief, General Mered Mengesha. Mengistu admitted to the investigative bodies later that if they had arrested him, the whole story might have gone differently. Instead, they hurried to write announcement about the end of the empire rule in Ethiopia, and made Prince Asfaweson read it on radio. Though Mengistu did not mention about forcing the prince to read this announcement, many testified that Mengistu put a gun on the prince's head and made him read it.

The announcement told the Ethiopian people that the three-thousand-year rule of the Solomonic Dynasty had ended. In addition, it promised a salary raise, ownership of land by peasants, and many other improvements for residents of the city. While declaring all of this, the only thing the coup allies had controlled was top officials, the prince, and the radio station. The military, including the Navy and the Air Force were running themselves, and they failed to see the importance of taking measures in that area. Since they did not arrest the commander-in-chief, he started plotting to crash their scheme.

In fact, it took only twenty-four hours before the whole plan went awry. The military and the police took control of most of the city. Though Mengistu ordered the Royal Guard to fight back, they were outnumbered and did not know whom they were defending exactly. In addition, the people, ordered by the church to stick to the divine rule of the emperor, and who believed the Royal Guard had betrayed the king, fought on the side of the police and the military. Emperor Haile Selassie, who traveled back to Asmara as soon as he heard the news, played a big role in crushing the coup by pleading for the people to be on his side.

The dark side of Mengistu, his brother Germame, and their allies came out when they knew they had lost the game big time. In his own words, Mengistu said that he ordered the murder of the top fifteen political and military officials. He said he shot some of them himself to make sure they were dead.

The court informed Mengistu that he had the right to appeal to the emperor's court, known as Yengus Chilot. He refused to stand before Haile Selassie and beg forgiveness. Therefore, on March 28, 1961, General Mengistu Neway was hanged on TekleHaimanot Square. His body was displayed the whole day to the public.

The coup rapidly unraveled, but not before the country's social and economic problems had been described in radical terms. The emperor ignored the coup's significance and did not address most of the issues raised. He continued to depend on the landowning military, aristocracy, and oligarchy for authority. Haile Selassie showed himself unable to implement significant land reform, and as a result, progressive and student opposition became louder by the day. The monarchy was further weakened as it became embroiled in intractable conflicts with Eritrea and Somalia.

Somalia's independence in 1960 stimulated Somali nationalists in Ethiopia's Ogaden to rebel in February 1963. When Somalia joined the fighting, the Ethiopian Army and Air Force crushed its enemy. Somalia's consequent military alliance with the Soviet Union upset the regional balance of power, driving up Ethiopia's arms expenditures and necessitating more US assistance. Meanwhile, an insurrection in Eritrea, which had begun in the early '60s mainly among Muslim pastoralists in the western lowlands, came to attract highland Christians disaffected by the government's dissolution of the federation in 1962. At the same time, an increasingly radical student movement in Addis Ababa identified Haile Selassie as an agent of US imperialism, and his landowning oligarchs as the enemy of the people. Under the motto "Land to the tiller," the students sought to limit property size and rights, and by fostering debate on the issue of ethnicity, they confronted a problem marginalized by Haile Selassie. Some students espoused the Leninist notion that nationalities had the right to secede, and in so doing, gave strength and ideological justification to the Eritrean rebellion.

By the early 1970s, one-third of Ethiopia's forty-five thousand soldiers were in Eritrea, and others were putting down rebellions in Balē, Sīdamo, and Gojam. In January 1974, there began a series of mutinies led by junior officers and senior non-commissioned officers who blamed the imperial elites for their impoverishment, and for the country's economic and social ills. For the government, the situation was greatly worsened by drought and famine in the north, the denial of which became an international scandal that we exploited in Lebanon. In June, representatives of the mutineers constituted themselves as the Coordinating Committee (Derg) of the Armed Forces, Police, and Territorial Army. Major Mengistu Haile Mariam of Harer's 3rd Division was elected chairman. The Derg proceeded to dismantle the monarchy's institutions, and to arrest Haile Selassie's cronies, confidantes, and advisers. It then campaigned against the old and senile emperor, who was deposed on September 12, 1974.

The Provisional Military Administrative Council (PMAC) was established. The PMAC was administered by the Derg, and assumed the functions of government, with Lieutenant-General Aman Andom as chairman and head of state, and Mengistu as the first vice chairman. Tensions within the Derg soon fueled a power struggle and led to Bloody Saturday (November 23, 1974), when as many as sixty leaders, including Andom, were executed. Amam was replaced by Brigadier General Teferi Banti. The new government issued a Declaration of Socialism on December 20, 1974.

Brought Up in Two Worlds

My love for guns and hunting turned me into a collector of firearms. Moreover, the armory at home had a variety of vintage rifles, guns, and machine guns, which had to be cleaned and polished once in a while, an activity I enjoyed and looked forward to. I later learned that all my guns, together with the armory at home, were confiscated by the Derg regime when I was studying in Beirut.

In contrast to the traditional aristocratic and semi-feudal upbringing, I attended the international educational environment offered by Sanford International School in Addis Ababa. I, together with Turuye and Mame, were walked to the school daily by Ababa Merto, the guard from our home, who was given specific instructions to drop us off at school and pick us up for home. He walked us to and from different worlds—from the disciplined and controlled environment at home to the playful and liberal school compound. I, and indeed my sisters, developed the art of living in two worlds on the same day.

The contradictory lifestyles experienced by my sisters Turuye, Tenagne (attended the French school Lycée Guebre-Mariam), Mame, and myself, I assume was the same for most Ethiopians attending the Sanford International School. The great majority of students in each class were non-Ethiopians. All classes, except for Amharic classes, were taught by teachers from the United Kingdom.

Extracurricular activities at Sanford primarily revolved around sports. Students were divided into blue, green, yellow, and red teams and played football, basketball, volleyball, rugby, and baseball. Each school day, a particular team would stay behind after school to practice. The final games and athletic competitions were held during the annual sports day, which lasted a full day, with traditional food and drinks served in a carnival-like atmosphere. I was on the Blue Team, but with negligible contributions, as I only played football, and even then, I was mediocre.

Ethiopian holidays were not observed in any memorable fashion. While in contrast, European Christmas carols and plays would last a month. Bonfires being lit, and a carnival-like situation, remains a memory of how Guy Fawkes Day was celebrated in an annual commemoration observed on November 5th. All students recall the details of how on November 5, 1605, a member of the Gunpowder Plot, Guy Fawkes's plan to blow up Parliament was discovered. We celebrated the fact that King James I had survived an attempt on his life. The school, being primarily a British community school, was visited by Queen Elizabeth II during her state visit to Ethiopia in February 1965. As young students, I recall that after months of preparations, we sang a specially adapted Harambe song for her, and "God Save the Queen," as an expression of our dedication and hope for the long life of the monarchy.

The school was also partially insulated from the student activism taking shape at other schools in Ethiopia, primarily because the majority of students were foreigners who avoided engaging in local politics. A few individual students had attempted, once or twice, to mobilize a significant student population in order to organize a strike or a march in solidarity of the larger Ethiopian student action. Such attempts were not successful.

Ethiopian students had to attend Amharic classes in addition to regular classes. Ethiopians attending the same grade but in different classes, such as Forms I, A, B, and C, were grouped together into one Amharic class. There was not a sufficient number of Ethiopian students for one class at each level. At the secondary school level, such classes were taught by Ato Alemayehu Moges, who also lectured at Haile Selassie University at the time. Amharic grammar was not taught much, as Ato Alemayehu enjoyed telling stories and jokes that kept us entertained and fond of his classes.

His stories of bravery, heroism, and patriotism were intermingled with ethno-chauvinism. Amharic poems, including the "gold and wax"[2] ones, were his favorites. We were influenced by him to be patriotic, and to believe that Ethiopians were a super race, even if some amongst them were more equal than others.

He was pro-Israeli regarding the Middle East conflict. But even then, he insinuated that Israel was lucky not to share a border with Ethiopia, or else the outcome of a war would have been devastating for the Jewish state. To Ato Alemayehu Moges,

Ethiopia was above all. His exaggerations of his adventures hunting as a young man, where he would kill a leopard that, when skinned, became fifteen arms' length. My classmate and close friend, Tassew Molla, who loved challenging Alemayehu, would raise his hand and say, "But sir, fifteen arms' length is over seven meters." Alemayehu would reply by making a point about the difference between a total lie and exaggeration. He would admit his story was exaggerated, and bring down the measurements to ten arms' length, which would get Tassew going with yet another challenge. The exchange would upset Ato Alemayehu, who would order Tassew to kneel, and would simply conclude by rejecting Tassew's point by saying that "he wants to cut off the tail of my kill." It is indeed fascinating how most of the Amharic students in my class also passed the Ethiopian School Leaving Certificate (ESLC) with good grades.

Lunch breaks were yet another memorable event at school. Most students brought lunch in a box which was shared amongst groups of friends. My lunchmates were Tassew Molla, Tadesse Ferede, and Mulugeta Ferede. We all attended the Amharic class together and enjoyed each other's company. Right after lunch, we usually played football, particularly on days when we did not have Amharic classes.

Love of country, flag, and the monarchy were constant themes of stories told to me as a child by all members of my family—relatives and visitors alike. My recollection of the emperor included me and my twin sister being invited to celebrate Christmas in the palace, where at the end of the children's party, we would receive gifts from the emperor. On one occasion, I recall approaching the emperor to receive my Christmas gift when he held it back and asked about my family and what grade I was in. He encouraged me to study hard and to also do some exercise, hinting that I was overweight. On that occasion, I received a camera, which I greatly appreciated.

At the Debre Zeit Palace, we often went to pay our respects to the emperor. I recall winning a double-barreled shotgun with the emperor's insignia on it following a target shooting competition with kids of my age group. At a later stage, while finishing high school and attending first-year university, my recollection of the emperor was limited to primarily driving my father to either the Jubilee or Menelik Palace, either early mornings or late afternoons, when the driver was off duty. I got to know the Imperial bodyguards and palace servants, who, as my father went in to see the emperor, would usher me into a room where I would be served cookies and tea. On occasion, I recall being told to go in and greet the emperor by bowing from a distance, which I did, and recall getting a nod back. The minister of the palace would usually be next to the emperor, and would explain who I was. He had aged and looked smaller and frail.

Endnotes

1   Azajee is the highest-ranking head of services function in the palace.

2   "The wax and gold tradition, where wax is a natural secretion of gold that is produced in the process of purification. It is an element that covers the gold; in order to get the purest gold, it has to undergo the process of melting in fire. This metaphor, therefore, that is applied to a given literary system. *Sem-ena-Werq* (wax and gold). As a literary system, often composed in the form of poetry or prose, the wax and gold method plays with a double-layered meaning. While the apparent meaning, on the surface, is known as *Sem* (wax), the underlying, true meaning is the gold. But it is a serious intellectual exercise that differs from ordinary poetry." Levie, Donald N. *Wax and Gold:Innovation in Ethiopian Culture.* ⌈University of Chicago Press,1995.

CHAPTER TWO

University Days and Militancy

My family celebrated when the 1972 ESLC results were released and I had passed the exam. I received the high school successful completion certificate from Emperor Haile Selassie in a ceremony held at the Grand Palace. I was enrolled at Haile Selassie University (HSU), Addis Ababa campus, in the social science department. Most of my Sanford friends, including Ethiopians who passed the ESLC, went abroad, mainly to the USA. I had to make new acquaintances and mingle with new friends that came from all over the country.

I attended HSU at a time when the revolutionary student movement was taking shape under various spells of radical Marxist thoughts. Gone were the days of looking forward to going to school to enjoy the company of friends who shared the same values and enjoyed similar sports activities. I also found out that trivial things such as the type of socks I wore, or the brand of watch I had on, or even the color of the shoes I wore, would have me labeled as being a stooge of a particular class—a bourgeois or a feudal. What you spoke of, how you walked, and who you hung out with determined the basis upon which you were to be classified. In order to conform with the mob, or the prevailing herd mentality, you had to hide your true feelings and what you enjoyed, and simply comply with expected dressing habits, hair styles, and group affiliations.

Conflict and contradictions raged in my mind, resulting in frustration and bewilderment. Under the prevailing peer pressure, and the urge for conformity with the majority, I started using revolutionary words I did not really understand. The choice was between "Jolly-Jackism"[1] and revolutionary posturing.

The long-term effect of the contradictions created in my mind between national heroes and I was brought up to cherish and admire, such as my own father, patriots, kings, and emperors— Tewodros, Yohannes, Menelik, and Haile Selassie—were suddenly replaced by new heroes such as Che Guevara, Mao Zedong, Ho Chi Minh, Marx, and Lenin. You either followed the new world outlook based on Marxism, or you would be labeled a reactionary with feudal bourgeoisie thoughts. As if by divine intervention, we were all baptized to become soldiers fighting for the rights of the proletariat and peasants.

Chanting songs in public that said we would no more be ruled by the US stooge and the Israeli puppet regime, became our daily mantra. All chanted the slogans, whether they really believed in them or not. The bottom line was that no one was willing to stand contrary to the prevailing direction of the wind . If nothing else, no one wanted to stand out.

Marxism-Leninism was embraced by most as a religion rather than as a system of thought to help interpret the Ethiopian reality. As several scholars have observed, "Slogans came to be mistaken for theory." It is true that some of the principles and issues the student movement was advocating for were just and noble. However, how it was to be achieved, and what was to replace the old order, was not clear, to say the least. A long-term vision of a classless society was presented as being the ultimate goal. The turmoil we were going through was explained as being a necessary precondition for the realization of a bright future.

The glaring contradictions, and the two worlds that simultaneously coexisted at the time, can be illustrated by recalling an incident where the rapid deployment police were deployed on campus to contain a student strike. The rapid deployment police deployed on campus at Sidest Kilo campus included my brother, Captain Tenna Kebede. Avoiding him was an effort, as I did not want to be labeled as a government stooge on campus. At home, in the evenings, we would meet and exchange our experiences of the day and laugh over them while having dinner.

As a footnote, it has to be mentioned that the evolution of the Ethiopian revolution saw family members gradually finding themselves in different camps and endorsing opposing ideologies. My immediate older brother, Ayalew, joined the Ethiopian People's Revolutionary Party (EPRP) and ultimately left for the bush. Tenna remained with the rapid deployment police for a while, before being arrested for allegedly shooting a police officer. While another brother, Asfaw, continued to work at the government printing press, and received various recognitions as a star proletariat. Major Yilma (another brother) served as a soldier in Hararghe, and as a member of the Special Forces in Addis Ababa. He later became an anti-hijacker and was stationed in Rome before returning to Addis and becoming a civil servant in the industrial management sector. Our oldest brother, Kassa, through circumstances linked to the militia training center that was set up in a rehabilitation center he was running, became acquainted, and ended up being close to, Mengistu and the Derg. Kassa served as an administrator of the Tatek Military camp before being appointed as Minister of Labor, and then Ambassador in Geneva. He ultimately became head of the Foreign Department of the Workers Party of Ethiopia until his departure into exile when the government was overthrown by the Ethiopian People's Revolutionary Democratic Front (EPRDF) in 1991.

My oldest sister, Wederyelesh, continued to work with the Ministry of Labour until her retirement and untimely death in 1989. My youngest sister, Asnaketch, worked with the Tourist and Hotels Commission. My nephew Bekure studied law and joined the Foreign Ministry. Turunesh and Mame teamed up in the USA as supporters of the student movement branch that ultimately became the EPRP. Both my father and mother remained pro-old-order to their last day.

My sister Turunesh joined Haile Selassie University and went

31

through the same shock and baptism of fire into the Marxist world. Following a couple incidents, including mass arrests on campus, which included me, and with the revolution unfolding, the family decided that we had to leave the country. Whenever we were consulted about where to pursue our studies, we both indicated that we preferred the US.

Given my young age, Kegn Azmatch Lulseged Beyene, a relative, a patriot, and a close friend of my father, was tasked to run my affairs, including the rental and management of my house, and to act on my behalf in my absence. His sons had attended the English School with me, and their dwelling was close to the school. Gash Lulseged, as I called him, would give me advice on what I should do and not do if I were to travel abroad. He had conservative and strict religious views. His story about how he had been repenting for several years for having wrongfully slept with a Muslim woman as a youngster while out in the bush hunting was repeatedly told to me to ensure I did not make the same mistake. Those stories gave me a hint as to where the family was planning to send me to continue with my studies.

Visit to the Ancestral Domain

Prior to my departure to Lebanon, I visited my father's birthplace in Sekelti, Efreta, with my nephew Bekure Herouy. Father assigned us the family's Land Rover with a relative driver, Yehwalashet Asseminew, under the overall guidance of Gashe Tadesse Beyene. My friends who resided in the family compound, Dagnatchew Wolde and Begashaw Mengesha, completed the mission members. We started early in the morning and drove north of Addis Ababa, with a stopover for lunch at Debre Berhan. After lunch, we proceeded to Karakore, 185 kilometers northeast of Addis Ababa, on the main road to Dessie, before turning west and driving for an additional 15 kilometers on the paved road to Majete town.

Majete is the market and meeting place for inhabitants scattered all over the mountain ranges around it. We were met by a relative who had made all the arrangements for our reception, stay, and onward journey. My uncles, Kemaw and Kefyalew Aydefruhim, acted as our hosts and accompanied us throughout the trip. My great-great-grandfather, at one time, had his farm south of Majete in the valley, which has now been divided amongst relatives and offspring. We spent the night in a hotel, and the following day, went down into the valley, crossed the Jama River, and visited an irrigation scheme managed by the local branch of the Ministry of Labour and Social Affairs.

My oldest sister and mother of Bekure, Etye Wedereyelesh, worked in the Ministry, and some years back had initiated setting up the farm as a rehabilitation center. She was highly spoken of and respected by town dwellers and farmers alike for helping individuals with disabilities achieve and maintain optimum functioning in interaction with their environments. We were offered a variety of fruits and vegetables by the farmers as an expression of their gratitude for what Etye Wederyelesh had done for them, and for us visiting them. I, and indeed most mission members, were honored by the appreciation we received due to my sister's contribution to the community.

Back in Majete, the evening was spent visiting relatives, being hosted for food and drinks, and stopping at the few entertainment centers hosting traditional singers who would include our names in the melancholic lyrics of traditional songs they sang, accompanied by traditional string instruments.

I recall the town had no electricity and was dark in the evenings. I had brought my torchlight with me to help me move around in the dark, and was not aware of the local population's sensitivity about torchlight being directed at them. While walking with the mission members, a passerby loaded and cocked his gun and demanded that we turn off the light and tell him who we were. I turned off the torch, and our guide explained who we were and that we did not mean him any harm. Following the scary incident, we understood that we had to be extra careful in the evenings, as the local populace was more vigilant and feared being attacked by intruders from the lowlands, who allegedly would go out hunting for men for dowry purposes. The lowland dwellers were alleged to be looking for trophy as part of their dowry offering for marriage, where, in addition to offering cattle, a man had to kill at least one enemy, and he had to prove this act by bringing back the enemy's genitals. The highlander was understood to be the enemy. Walking together and being escorted by armed guards became a common feature of the mission after that incident.

We visited Atura Selassie Church, where my father had attended church school, before we proceeded on foot up the mountain range to Tsekelti Village, his birthplace, where he spent his childhood playing with shepherds. We were met by wailing relatives, some dancing and singing while armed men fired volleys up into the air in celebration. We were led into a compound full of scattered mud-thatched roof dwellings where my other uncle, Titche Zik Argachew, and his extended family resided. A feast, with constant visitors coming and going from neighboring villages while we drank *tella* and ate roasted meat, went on endlessly. We spent the night there, and the following day, proceeded on mule to Tsankaber and Seret to visit more relatives.

A memorable incident was the visit to Dagnatchew's father, Welde, who resided close to Dulete Michael Church. We were received by armed relatives lining the dirt entrance to the compound, waving the national flag. The guards fired into the air to welcome us. The customary sheep was slaughtered at the entrance, and we were ushered into the compound, where feasting and singing commenced. A room was prepared for us, where grass was placed under cow hides and covered with cotton cloth. Warm blankets were provided, and with the help of the *tella* we had consumed, we went to sleep without a problem. I was woken up by Bekure, who had noticed movement and a strange noise close to the "mattress" on his side. I looked toward where he was pointing and saw that an ox that had broken loose from the adjacent room and was enjoying the grass that had been put there to serve as our mattress. Our hosts, having heard the commotion, intervened and the ox was taken and tied at an alternative location.

The following morning, we proceeded on mules back to Majete. From Majete, we stopped over at Debre Sena to enjoy the view before proceeding to Addis Ababa. We arrived in the evening, fully satisfied that the mission objectives had been met.

The lingering impact of that visit to the ancestral birthplace of my father lives on in me. The picturesque mountain ranges and the breathtaking valleys remain an attraction. The role of the church was more than religion. Every village had its own church named after a favorite angel, or Saint Mary. The sizes of the church varied in accordance with the size of the population it served. Endless stories told by our hosts revolved around Christian values, love of country and God, as well as the sacrifices made by relatives long gone to have preserved the unity, territorial integrity, and independence of the nation. Their rich cultural and historical heritage, and the value that every individual attaches to it, in a way, made up for the visible material shortfall. The proud relatives we met all had a sense of purpose and were grateful and satisfied with what they had. I remain puzzled to this day as to how they appeared not to have much, but still had everything.

My visit to the ancestral domain also gave me a hint as to what could happen in the future, as the location was placed on an ethnic and religious fault line, which, if not properly managed, could result in conflicts and displacements.

American University of Beirut

With the university closing on and off, and with the revolution becoming louder, I was sent off to Beirut with my twin sister. Since there were no direct flights to Beirut, we were sent to Cairo, where we were picked up by the Ethiopian Ambassador, who accommodated us at the embassy overnight and put us on a flight to Lebanon the following day. Thus, I plunged into unchartered waters to experience university dormitory life, supposedly fleeing from turbulence and revolution to the tranquility of the American University of Beirut (AUB).

Upon arrival in Beirut, we were met by Seble, an Ethiopian lady whose father was a parliamentarian known to our family. Seble took us, by taxi, to the AUB. She introduced us to a senior fellow student in the Education department, Tesfaye Tadesse Woldemedhen, who became our mentor. We also met Mohammed Mahdi, an Ethiopian Somali from Harar studying medicine, who later took Djiboutian nationality.

That relocation put an end to the family environment I had

My twin sister Turunesh Kebed and I

been accustomed to.

Arabic was widely spoken on campus, even though the student population was very much mixed. New arrivals like myself, who did not speak Arabic, had to adjust to an environment where we could not understand what was going on around us most of the time.

During the school acquaintance party, where we were to meet new friends and get to know the student community, Mohammed Mahdi and I ended up seated with two American young ladies who were attending the Junior Year Abroad (JYA) program. With no language barriers between us, we befriended the two young ladies. One of the young ladies, Rosanne, became my close friend in no time. I later realized that we were talking but not communicating.

At the Penrose dormitory, in order to mitigate the language and cultural barriers, I swiftly associated myself with Ethiopians and English-speaking foreigners. The search for English speakers brought me close to American students, who had come in significant numbers to complete the JYA program. I picked Ross to be my roommate, who knew Rosanne. Both were slightly older and more mature than I was.

Spending time at each other's dormitories, and eating out

and going to the movies—even though I enjoyed it and cherish it to-date, I later realized that it had created different expectations between myself and Rosanne. As she had come for a year on an exchange program to end in June, she wanted us to decide on our future there and then. I was not ready for that, to say the least. I was dumbfounded when I found out that Rosanne had befriended my sister, and that the two were planning to travel to Ethiopia during the summer break. I refused to join them, and the two left to Ethiopia without me. I received a strongly worded letter from my father, ordering me to come home. I complied and left for Ethiopia a week later. I was met at the airport by a family delegation, which included Rosanne and my sister. ,

The two weeks spent at home with both of us playing hide and seek, and me going out to spend evenings with my friends until I knew Rosanne was sound asleep in my sister's room, were not at all pleasant. I explained to Rosanne that I could not act freely and do as I pleased in Addis, let alone in my family compound. That was interpreted by her to mean that I was not interested in our relationship, and that I was simply avoiding her. As she finally came to the end of her planned visit, we departed amicably and she flew directly to the USA from Addis, as she had completed her study program in Beirut.

As my sister and I were preparing to depart for Beirut, an announcement was made by the Military Council that all students who had come on vacation were to stay on and take part in the planned national literacy campaign. The only exception to be made was for those students who were studying a subject that was vital for the country's development. I followed a two-pronged strategy by applying and sitting for an entry exam with Ethiopian Airlines to join as a purser. I also applied, together with my sister, claiming that I was studying marine biology, and that the subject was vital for the development of the Red Sea and the various lake resources throughout the country. The respective applications were typed at a public notary stand, where the typist suggested we sign the submission and conclude by stating, "Ethiopia First." We did, and submitted the application to the Fourth Army Division headquarters, as instructed.

A couple days following the submission of our applications, we received news that the first batch of applications received had been processed, and that the names of those authorized to travel had been posted. We rushed to the Fourth Army Division headquarters and found out that both our names appeared on the list of approved submissions. We were literally put on the next available flight to Cairo on our way back to Beirut. Several years later, upon inquiry, I found out that the first batch of applicants that had signed "Ethiopia First" were cleared by the reviewing team, as we were presumed to be supporters of the change headed by the military.

Back in Beirut, I continued my studies at the AUB, as well as my participation in the Ethiopian Student Body activities. The Lebanon branch of the Ethiopian Student Body was affiliated with the student movement in the Middle East and North Africa, which in turn was affiliated with the European Wing Union, which was led and organized by Tesfaye Tadesse.

Tesfaye took time to lecture me and my sister on the Ethiopian Revolution, and I was mesmerized by his explanations and logic. I started my engagement by joining a group set up to publicize the hidden famine in Ethiopia. The Committee on Solidarity with the People of Ethiopia had members from the Lebanese Communist Party and various left-wing Palestinian organizations. Posters printed in English and Arabic depicting starving Ethiopians explained that more than two million had already died, and that more than two thousand were dying daily. The black and white posters with pictures of starving Ethiopian mothers and children were printed by the Lebanese Communist Party. We spent evenings putting up the posters all over Beirut, Sidon, and Tripoli.

I took over from Tesfaye and became the editor of the *Teramed* (progress) newsletter, focusing on recent developments in Ethiopia, and issued in the name of the Ethiopian Student Movement in the Middle East and North Africa, but printed and distributed from Beirut. The majority of student members of the Lebanon Union were predominantly attending the Seventh Day Adventist College in Mt. Lebanon. The few who were in West Beirut were attending

Beirut University College (BUC) or the AUB.

The largest number of Ethiopian students in the Middle East and North Africa were studying in Cairo. As the editor of *Teramed*, I visited Cairo and met students who were mainly attending Al-Azhar University. The majority of the Ethiopian students were Muslim Oromos from either Bale, Sidamo, or Hararghe provinces. Even though we all agreed on the need for change in Ethiopia, the priority in Cairo was the independence of Eritrea and Oromia.

The Cairo group argued that the promotion of the rights of nationalities up to, and including, secession should be the main focus of the *Teramed* newsletter. I agreed that subject was important, but it could not be the only issue, as the favorable outcome of the ongoing class struggle could have a favorable outcome for all Ethiopians. I argued that we needed to focus more on the struggle of the Ethiopian people, including the Oromos, Tigrayans, Amharas, and Eritreans, as we were all fighting an oppressive regime supported by US imperialism. The bottom line was that we all needed to address oppression and meet the number one need of our people—fighting hunger and poverty. I also explained that my views were also the views of the majority of students in Lebanon, and that I was also representing that body. Unable to reach a consensus, the meeting was postponed for the following day.

As the meeting took place during the holy month of Ramadan, I was invited to the Chairman Mohammad Arabi's apartment. He originated from Bale. I fondly cherished the breaking of the daily fast (*Iftar*) at Mohamed's apartment in downtown Cairo. The apartment was located in a low-income congested neighborhood, where I was made to understand that rentals were affordable for foreigners, and that the apartments were built to accommodate the displaced from the Suez War with Israel. For dinner, the traditional Egyptian *fowl* and bread would be pulled up in a basket from a donkey cart peddler standing in the street below. Money would be lowered into the basket, where the peddler would put in the equivalent amount of *fowl* and bread.

I could not take part fully in the evening discussions, as the main languages of communication of the gathering were *Oromiffa* and Arabic. My spoken Arabic was poor then. I could not follow all of the heated debates, which were aggressive at times. The Cairo students were clear on the Eritrean liberation issue, which they understood to be a decolonization process. They argued that their understanding was that Oromia was under Amhara Orthodox Christian occupation and rule, supported by US imperialism and Zionists.

According to the Oromo community in Egypt, General Waqo Gutu, as he was known, was their symbol of Oromo resistance, and the initiator of their right to self-determination. It is understood that an ill-timed attempt by the government to collect unpaid taxes from local peasants fanned the flames in the Bale Province in southern Ethiopia, and at the end of 1966, about three-fifths of the province was reportedly in turmoil. This peasant revolt ran from 1964 to 1970, stemming from issues involving land, taxation, class, and religion.

Waqo Gutu surrendered to the Ethiopian government on March 27, 1970, and he was given a villa in Addis Ababa and treated well by the emperor. With the eruption of the Ethiopian revolution, Waqo returned to Bale, and in 1975, initiated an Oromo revolt against the Derg. He visited several Arab countries, including Egypt, Libya, and Somalia, to raise funds and arms to galvanise the Oromo Liberation struggle.

The Oromo Liberation Front (OLF) program published in 1974, says it was fighting "Abyssinian settler colonialism." This concept was endorsed by the Cairo students. I was handed a copy of a publication issued by the Damascus-based OLF Foreign Relations Office, which made it clear that, regarding "the Struggle of the Oromo People," that "nothing short of political independence will quench the thirst for freedom of the Oromo people." The call by progressive Ethiopians, or any other Arab party, for a joint struggle by all the oppressed peoples to bring an end to injustice collectively fell on deaf ears.

Some of the students would argue that the Oromo state to be realized was going to be Islamic, representing the majority of the Oromo people. What they expected from us was support in that drive. I explained that I could not endorse such a divisive move.

The following day, there was a quarrel amongst the students, and I was asked by the police to leave for Beirut, which I complied with and subsequently reported my findings to the Lebanon group.

Back in Beirut, I had started dating an Ethiopian young lady who was studying nursing and worked as a babysitter for an affluent Lebanese family. As we were getting to know each other and becoming close, she informed me that she was coming under pressure from her sister, a nurse with the Eritrean People's Liberation Front (EPLF), and other friends to end the relationship, as I was an Amhara. Lemlem was an Eritrean, and we could not be seen together in public, as she was allegedly being criticized for dating the enemy. My revolutionary outlook and visible support of the Palestinian cause did not count for much. It was tragic, and a mystery that Lemlem left the country without informing me, and I have never heard of her whereabouts.

A lot has been written about the split in the worldwide Union of Ethiopian Students' two camps—Ethiopian Students Union in North America (ESUNA) and Ethiopian Students Union in Europe (ESUE)—and grey in-betweens. Two leftist political organizations evolved into the Meison, or the All-Ethiopian Socialist Movement and the Ethiopian Peoples Revolutionary Party (EPRP), which will be elaborated later. Working from within, or change through a revolution, was the dividing point. The narrow nationalists focusing exclusively on the national question offered a third option of total liberation of their region only.

The Middle East and North Africa had long been involved in fostering political dissent in Ethiopia. It is worth recalling that by 1967, activists at the different universities in Addis Ababa had come together and formed the University Students Union of Addis Ababa (USUAA). Given the absence of political parties in the country, the USUAA had become the most outspoken opposition to the regime. Demonstrations under the banner of "land to the tiller" had become common, leading to the killing of the president of USUAA, Tilahun Gizaw, in 1969. The harsh step taken by the Imperial Bodyguard during his burial ceremony and its aftermath, pointed to the limitations of the student movement. One segment of the student body advocated immediate armed resistance. Some

41

members of this group, in the summer of 1969, hijacked a plane to Libya. By 1973, one of its members, Berehan Milemeskel, in an interview with the Libyan newspaper *Al-Fajr Al-Jadid*, published in Tripoli on August 17, 1973, had openly admitted, "I do not reveal a secret if I say that there are struggling Ethiopians who get training in the Eritrean Liberation Front (ELF) bases. I can affirm that appropriating an annual budget for us, not exceeding one million dinars, will enable us to overcome many problems and step up our struggle." This tendency won some acceptance amongst the Ethiopian diaspora, mainly in the USA, and was supported by the ELF long before the formation of the EPLF or any other "progressive" Eritrean movements.

The movement, which was advocating armed struggle, formed the EPRP under the name Ethiopian People's Liberation Organization (EPLO) in April 1972 in West Berlin, West Germany, supported by the Democratic Front for the Liberation of Palestine. At this first congress, a central committee was elected, and included Berhane Meskel and Iyasu Alemayehu, who was later elected the organization's secretary general. Some committee members were reportedly suspicious of Tesfaye, and alleged that he could be a CIA spy.

Tesfaye attributed the defamation campaign launched against him to be a personal conflict between himself and Iyasu Alemayehu. According to Tesfaye, the ELF and reactionary Arab forces were using the student movement to derail the Ethiopian revolution for the sole purpose of dismembering the country, focusing on Eritrean independence at any expense. I tended to agree with Tesfaye, as the ELF cadres I met with in Lebanon were predominantly Islamic fundamentalists who were not interested in hearing about the Ethiopian Revolution. They argued that Eritrea was an Arab country, and upon independence will join the Arab League. Later, the ELF went into an internal conflict with the establishment of the relatively progressive, multi-ethnic and multi-religion organization, the EPLF. The ELF, the founding organization of Eritrean Independence, was defeated militarily in the late '70s and early '80s by the EPLF, which managed to forge an alliance with the Tigrayan Peoples Liberation Front (TPLF).

The Middle East became a breeding ground for those advocating liberation and secession, primarily because of the vocal and historical presence of the Eritrean liberation movements. Various Oromo organizations and individuals were visiting Lebanon and Syria, asking for support and recognition to set up their own liberation movements. Supporting any movement that would weaken the Ethiopian state was seen as either a strategic objective, or a requirement for the secession of Eritrea and Arab dominance along the Red Sea coast. Various Arab nationalist and Arab revolution movements saw a strategic geopolitical advantage and openly expressed support to the Eritrean movements. The increase in liberation movements emanating from Ethiopia drowned out the call for a nationwide focus to build a united free and democratic state. The Eritrean Liberation Front (ELF), Eritrean People's Liberation Front (EPLF), Eritrean People's Liberation Front Revolutionary Council (ELF-RC), Tigray People's Liberation Front (TPLF), Oromo Liberation Front (OLF), Western Somali Liberation Front (WSLF), Islamic Front for the Liberation of Oromia (IFLO), and several other acronyms I cannot recall, flourished.

Tesfaye had become controversial ever since his membership request at the 1972 Berlin meeting to establish a worldwide union of Ethiopian students as the membership of the Middle East Branch of the Ethiopian student movement was put into question. Tesfaye was portrayed as an agent of the CIA by some. Moreover, his departure to Addis was presented as being a capitulation to the Derg. The ESUNA branch of the worldwide movement had also opened an office in Algeria, which became vocal toward the Student Union in the Middle East and Africa, which it perceived as part of the genesis of the Meison.

The return of Meison leaders from Europe, and Tesfaye from Beirut, led to suspicion that part of the opposition was going to join the military regime and undermine the revolution. Their return triggered intense internal debates. On February 3, 1975, the Derg issued its far-reaching Land Reform Proclamation No. 31. The resultant transformation of entrenched power and property relations made the case for viewing the Derg as a revolutionary tenable force. Meison leaders had already been involved in talks with the Derg in January 1975. The road toward such talks had been paved by the regime's ambitious *Zemecha* (Campaign) for Development through Cooperation, in which sixty thousand university and secondary school students were sent across the country on a literacy and education campaign.

The Derg's celebrated land reform of February 1975 was largely based on a proposal submitted by Meison members. The land reform proved the most popular measure adopted by the government, especially in the south of the country. It made the Derg look good in the eyes of progressive forces in the Middle East.

Between 1976 and 1978, urban Ethiopia became a site of collective violence. Rival campaigns of revolutionary terror were fought out, most notably in the capital city of Addis Ababa. Opposition forces launched targeted assassinations against the military regime and its collaborators, prompting the latter to widen early campaigns of repression into one of the most brutal reigns of state terror in modern Africa. Tens of thousands of Ethiopians, most of them young, and many educated, lost their lives. Thousands more were systematically tortured or otherwise abused. Many escaped to the countryside or fled abroad, invigorating rural insurgencies and strengthening the various liberation incarnations in the Sudan and throughout the Middle East.

As a non-Oromo, Tigrayan, or Eritrean, it was becoming more and more difficult for me to find friends amongst the Ethiopian community in the Middle East. With the civil war unfolding in Lebanon, the few Ethiopian students in the country gradually left the country. A significant number of Eritreans affiliated with either the ELF or EPLF were coming in for either training or medical treatment. Even though officially we shared the same ideology, we simply could not develop relationships that would go beyond the surface exchange of smiles and nods. That is the time I realized that the Ethiopia-Eritrea divide was more deep-rooted in the psychic of Eritreans of my generation than I had anticipated.

Various Ethiopian "comrades" that were reportedly brought

for military training by one or another Eritrean organization would be introduced to me by the Democratic Front for the Liberation of Palestine, or other left-wing Palestinian or Lebanese friends. The trainings were provided in South Lebanon, Syria, or Iraq based on the affiliation of the sponsoring organization. Moreover, my comrade and friend Tesfaye, who had left for Ethiopia, became a prominent personality in the Foreign Ministry. The Red Terror was unfolding, and disillusionment and isolation became my fate.

Part of the challenge in explaining the Ethiopia situation to the comrades from my perspective was the groundwork that had been laid by the various Eritrean liberation organizations that have sold the struggle to be against Zionist-Amhara national occupation, akin to colonialism. The class struggle of all the Ethiopian people against feudalism and oppression was becoming a nonstarter for some Arab socialist parties and movements. The Baath Parties of Syria and Iraq helped organize discussions on the subject in Damascus and Baghdad, but they were obsessed with Eritrean independence. Ousting the Israeli, Zionist imperialism influence from the Red Sea region was more important. Damage to Ethiopia was viewed as simply being collateral and affordable.

A year or so following Tesfaye's return to Addis, news started filtering out of his involvement with Cuban, USSR, and South Yemen embassies in efforts at reconciling Negede Gobeze with Mengistu, and advocating for the establishment of a civilian Marxist party. That initiative did not go well, and it was reported that Tesfaye was killed by the Derg for his involvement in what was interpreted to be a plot to overthrow the military government.

I developed friendships with international students at the AUB, who found themselves in a similar situation. We rented a small flat next to the AUB, with an Iranian, Hossain Shehedi; an Afghan, Seief Tora; and a Yemeni, Mohammed Medari. Two Americans dating a Shia Lebanese and a Palestinian were also part of our group. At the Palestian Liberation Organisation (PLO) Foreign Information Section, David Butter from the UK, and the editor of the Palestine Magazine, George Phillip from Germany, were friends. The PLO reasoning that one option for the resolution of the Middle East conflict could be the creation of a democratic state in Palestine, where Jews, Christians, and Muslims could reside and coexist in one state, appeared plausible but was rejected by Israel. The alternative would be the creation of two states— Israel and Palestine—that would coexist as neighbors. The latter option appeared to be the most attainable, and was to my liking.

At the Middle East Research Institute, I met Ms. Van Kraken from Sweden, who introduced me to her husband, Pieter Van Kraken. Pieter and I became friends and exchanged information on developments in and around the Horn of Africa. Pieter worked at the UNHCR Regional Office in the Middle East, which was then based in West Beirut. At the time, UNHCR was providing scholarships to Eritrean and Tigrayan students to study mainly in Syria, and some in Iraq. I was informed that Oromo students were being sponsored by the same UN agency in Egypt, and elsewhere in North Africa. The only ones not supported or recognized as asylum-seekers were those claiming to be Ethiopian. Prior to the Red Terror, the assumption was, for one to be fleeing persecution, you had to belong to an ethnic or religious grouping, including Eritrea. This understanding gradually changed after the Red Terror, and the fleeing of Ethiopians for asylum purposes was recognized. Even then, Ethiopians were considered for resettlement out of the region, or were supported in their first country of asylum, understood to be the neighboring countries of the Sudan and Kenya. This limited the number of Ethiopians coming into Lebanon, Syria, and Iraq.

It was interesting to observe that all the ethnic-based Ethiopian liberation movements and their local officials referred to domestic workers in Lebanon and Syria, estimated to be in the thousands at the time, as Ethiopians or *Habesha*. There were allegedly no Eritrean, Tigrayan, or Oromo domestic workers. This type of ethnic stratification and labeling only applied to students and liberation movement employees, and not to household helpers employed by affluent Lebanese and Syrians. All my acquaintances in the various Ethiopian-based ethnic liberation movements would argue that all women from their locations were out in the field fighting. The Eritreans I saw in Beirut were described to be either from Addis Ababa, Gondar Province, or were in fact Tigrayans posing as Eritreans. The Eritrean Liberation leaders somehow considered earning a living as a domestic worker in the Middle East not to merit condescension.

My safety net revolved around the English-speaking groups working with various Palestinian organizations primarily affiliated with *Fatah*. I got my Fatah (Palestinian National Liberation Movement) ID card, which helped me move around in relative freedom throughout Western Beirut and Southern Lebanon.

Mengistu and the Kebede Family Narrative

In Beirut in 1975, I heard of the story of Mengistu's relationship with my father. The first I heard of it was when Dr. Bereket Habte Selassie, having arrived from Addis with the latest news, addressed a gathering of progressive youth in Beirut. In English, he "enlightened" all gathered that the Provisional Military Administrative Council (PMAC) regime, headed by Colonel Mengistu, was in reality not a progressive movement but a continuation of the Amhara Empire under a new dressing. He eloquently explained how the upbringing and psycho-social makeup and thinking of Mengistu was shaped by the upbringing he had in the house of Duke Kebede, a feudal Amhara nobleman whose house was akin to the Menelik Palace. The norms and values installed in Mengistu as a child gave him his Amhara identity. It took me a while to realize that he was, in fact, talking about my father. I confronted the speaker, who simply pushed aside my interjection, and even told me off stage that he had checked with my father in person, and that my father would neither deny or confirm anything.

Dr. Bereket Habte Selassie had held several high-level positions within the Ethiopian government, including Federal Supreme Court Judge, Vice Minister of the Interior, and the Mayor of Harar during the reign of Emperor Haile Selassie. He is mostly remembered for his role as Co-Chairman of the Inquiry Commission established by the Derg regime. The commission was to investigate alleged corruption and breaches of responsibilities by officials in Emperor Haile Selassie's regime in the aftermath of the Ethiopian famines.

While the record shows that Dr. Bereket Habte Selassie was appointed by the Parliament of Ethiopia and the Derg to serve in the newly established Inquiry Commission, he now claimed that the late General Aman Andom prodded him to return to Ethiopia and serve the revolution headed by the Derg regime. His departure from Ethiopia was thus linked to the killing of the Head of State, General Aman, who was a distinguished military officer of Eritrean descent. Dr. Bereket also "informed" the gathering that Aman was killed because he refused to send additional forces into Eritrea.

Upon further research, I found that these claims are even documented on Wikipedia, according to the page on Mengistu, who father, Haile Mariam Wilde Ayanan, was Oromo. According to Wikipedia, "Mengistu was in the service of the Shewan landowner Afenegus Eshete Geda, who had encountered him while he was on a hunting expedition in the administrative district of Gimira and Maji, then under the governorship of Dejazmatch Taye Gulilat. He later became an enlisted man in the Ethiopian Army. Afenegus Eshete Geda was the half-brother of Dejazmatch Kebede Tessema's wife, Woizero Yitateku Kidane, and it was through this connection that Mengistu's parents are alleged to have met. Unsubstantiated accounts allege that Mengistu's mother was the illegitimate daughter of Dejazmach Kebede Tessema, a high-ranking nobleman and Crown Councillor to Emperor Haile Selassie, and he himself suspected of being the illegitimate son of Emperor Menelik II. These rumors of Mengistu being the grandson of Dejazmach Kebede are widely believed but have never been confirmed by either Mengistu himself nor by the late nobleman's family."

Various members of the Kebede family, and indeed Mengistu himself, have denied the claim. But the politically orchestrated and politically driven rumor lingers on.

The Ethiopian Democratic Union, a right-wing opposition to the Derg, issued a publication explaining the sparing of my father from the killing of officials by the Derg to be based on his relationship with Mengistu. Different concoctions of the story were released to simply make the point and argue that the leadership of the Derg was driven by the Amhara feudal imperialist school of thought. The secession-focused politicians, excluding the EDU, would argue that recognizing the rights of nationalities up to secession was problematic to such thinkers as Mengistu. They would conclude by affirming that "their social and economic upbringing preconditioned them to consciously or unconsciously lean toward the preservation and maintenance of the Empire at all costs." Thus the alleged and fabricated relationships and upbringing of Mengistu offered many an ideological justification in their assertion of a continuation of Amhara domination in the guise of a revolution. The real revolution, they argued, can only be realized with the overthrow of the Derg and the establishment of ethnic-based federalism.

These false stories started affecting my sister Turuye, who was in London at the time, where I had gone to see her, and to also renew my passport. Close relatives who knew the family, but had lost relatives through executions by the Derg, were falling into the trap of believing the rumors. Some were calling Turuye the sister of Mengistu, which significantly impacted her. As the Ethiopian Democratic Union (EDU) members and relatives were in London in large numbers, Turuye moving to the USA to join our sister Mame was the preferred option, and I returned to Lebanon.

Neither the alleged relationship with Mengistu, or the Amhara label, affected my relationship with my Lebanese and Palestinian comrades, who remained objective in their outlooks. Class struggle was viewed as the objective to be achieved through a revolution and not an ethnic division of territory, or the loot. At the Palestine news agency, I helped draft English news articles under the supervision of Rashid Khalid of Wafa, the Palestine News Agency. I wrote articles for the bimonthly published *Palestine Issue Magazine,* in English, focusing primarily on the Camp David Peace process, which was not going far. I remember an article which was much appreciated, as I depicted the peace process as passengers boarding a train which was going nowhere, as it had no wheels. Mahmoud Labadie was responsible for the *Palestine Issue Magazine* and the Foreign Information Section of the PLO.

At a later stage, upon my return to Ethiopia, I did check with my father about the authenticity of the alleged relationship he had with Mengistu, and the story I had heard from Dr. Bereket. My father was clear that there was no relationship at all, and that he had never met Mengistu in person. Regarding Dr. Bereket, he also confirmed that he had not seen him prior to his departure, nor had they ever discussed Mengistu's relationships with anyone. In short, he said he was a "ketafi," a downright liar.

I have long concluded, after examining all the facts and allegations, that the fabricated story was nothing more than a decoy to push down peoples throat the wrongful assertion that Colonel Mengistu led the Derg was in fact a continuation of the Amhara rule. The Derg was nothing more than a continuation of Imperial Ethiopian rule, under a new label of socialism. Such an assertion has been allowed to flourish by the likes of the TPLF and OLF in order to legitimize their call to arms. Their struggle brought the Derg down and paved the way for the 1991 conference which ultimately resulted in the adoption of the Transitional Period Charter of Ethiopia, and the establishment of a transitional government led by the TPF. The Transitional Period Charter, under its first two paragraphs, noted that "the military dictatorship was, in essence, a continuation of the previous regimes (Emperor) and its demise marks the end of an era of subjugation and oppression."

In Vogue: Leninism Distinct from Marxism

Between Haile Selassie University and the AUB, within a couple years, like most youth of my generation, I was indoctrinated to become a Marxist-Leninist. In hindsight, I realized that conforming to the prevailing school of thought and world outlook was misplaced. I tried to sum up my thoughts in an article that appeared in *Fortune* magazine on April 8, 2018. I argued that it would be significant that we all realize that many Ethiopian politicians and intellectuals, within and outside the country, continue to suffer from the hangover of that period of the Marxist-Leninist outlook on the world defining, in a simplistic way, concepts such as the rights of nationalities to self-determinate, and the perils of feudalism.

My generation of Ethiopian students have all engaged in that fashionable debate and diatribe that has contributed to the current impasse and political stalemate in Ethiopia. The fallacy of the so-called politically correct and revolutionary notion of equating feudalism to one language group continues to hinder dialogue and progress based on facts and realities on the ground.

These superficial Marxist-Leninist slogans and concepts, which were never adapted to the prevailing Ethiopian reality in a sober manner, have been used to sow discourse and distrust, draw national state boundaries, as well as set up regional state governance structures that have resulted in territorial disputes, conflict, and forced displacements. Given the leadership role played by the TPLF in the establishment of the EPRDF, and the overthrow of the Derg, it is widely perceived that all had been orchestrated for the benefit of its party, and its core membership, in order to retain power through a divide-and-rule system.

The fallacy of the existence of a territorially defined national region with demarcated boundaries, such as the Amhara, Somali, Afar, and Oromia regions, not only negates facts on the ground, but continues to fuel conflicts based on ethnic territorial claims and disputes. State land ownership and the role of regional or federal authorities, in its dispensation only, adds fuel to the fire.

The Gondar, Gojjam, Wello, and Shewa kingdoms and provinces have had a different administrative and historical evolution, and different ethnic configurations. Lumping all together as one Amhara state because of linguistic similarities is but an oversimplification that is bound to have grave consequences. The same is true for the Oromo grouping as one state of varying religious and administrative provinces, which had never been ruled, nor had it existed, as one entity or a single state.

Shortcomings in the national states or regions, conception and design, were further amplified by negating that feudalism in Ethiopia was fundamentally an economic exploitative governance system that safeguarded the interest of the landlords, who were of various ethnic origin, including the Amhara, Oromo, and Gurage, among others.

The Ethiopian feudal system, like its counterparts in Europe and Asia, was nothing more than a powerful landlord-centered exploitative system over the peasantry. No *one* ethnic group was spared from exploitation under that system, and no *one* linguistic group was the sole beneficiary either.

Moreover, the land nationalization by the Derg had brought that system to an end long before the ascent to power of the EPRDF. Therefore, there was no validity in the claim by some that the current government setup was primarily actualized to address the alleged evils of one ethnic group's vested feudalism.

I would argue that examining solutions not boxed in by flaws enshrined in the national debate of past years, or by the Amhara feudal rule dogma, is long overdue. By the same token, equating the Tigrayan people with any perceived or actual wrongdoing of the TPLF or EPRDF would be neither factual nor productive in the search for lasting solutions.

We all need to realize that there is no political alternative to an all-inclusive democratic Ethiopia owned by all its citizens, as being the only way out of the current impasse. Ethiopia designed on the basis of free movement and residency of all its citizens, enjoying the same political and economic rights and privileges throughout the country, is the future.

The Ethiopian state has to ensure respect for all fundamental human rights of its citizens, irrespective of their ethnicity, race, beliefs, creed, gender, or political thought. Accountability and the supremacy of the rule of law have to be ensured. Citizens should enjoy the same rights and privileges as citizens, and not as members of a specific national, ethnic, or linguistic grouping. Political parties should have a national focus, encouraging citizens to engage and participate in order to prosper as citizens of Ethiopia. Political discussions should be steered away from the language of ethnic identity and ethnic group benefits.

The right of each language group and nationality to develop and practice every aspect of their cultural heritage within a democratic state has to be ensured. A dogmatic and irrational application of ethnic boundaries in the drawing of administrative units should be avoided. A more rational federal administrative structure should not be ruled out in the redesigns of the new Ethiopia.

A Homeless Student

The political turmoil in Ethiopia, together with the unfolding of the civil war in Lebanon, was further capped by the ruling of the non-transfer of money from Ethiopia abroad. I was left jobless, with no money. I was asked to leave the university and the dormitory. I kept my comb and toothbrush and a few personal belongings in an Ethiopian Airlines bag, and wandered from one dormitory to another, spending nights in basements where students used as gym and studies. As a homeless person, I slept on sofas and took showers whenever I could in the basement of either dormitory. I recall going to the port area and buying secondhand clothing. I accepted invitations in the cafeteria. As if sent to be my guardian angel Nedira Saquaff ,a half-Yemeni half-Ethiopian, would buy tickets to the movies and ask that I escort her, as she was afraid to go on her own. At her dormitory, she would prepare food and spiced tea, which we enjoyed.

I applied for work in the library and simultaneously worked at the PLO Foreign Information Office. I registered with departments at the university but avoided the Registrar. The only computer available was in the basement of the Registrar's Office in the main administrative building. I studied without paying. Upon completion of 122 credit hours, I addressed a letter to the University Board and was authorized graduation on condition that I pay when I could. However, I was also granted a half-scholarship to pursue graduate school.

The Civil War created a supportive relationship amongst students attending the AUB. The school, being on the East, or Muslim, side of the divide, was dominated by leftist and pro-Palestinian students. Ethiopians, Palestinians, Lebanese, Cypriots, US citizens, Afghans, Iranians, British Maldivians, Yemenis, South Sudanese, and Omani students stood up for one another and shared what they had, as all became one family. The support extended by one to another remains engraved in my memories, which I cherish to date.

In those days, communication between Addis Ababa and Lebanon was weak on good days, with no direct flights, no mail, and poor telephone connection. What we had was disrupted by the war. A visitor coming was the only reliable communication to bring news and goodies from home. In that regard, a former Navy officer, Wondimu, upon retirement, got the right to import films to Ethiopia. After buying a cinema in Asmara, from a departing Italian owner, he came to the AUB campus looking for Ethiopians, and introduced himself to me. During our introductory exchanges, I found out that he knew my family back home. He became my link with Addis Ababa, and the courier of all sorts of goodies from home.

At the time, American film distributors for Africa were based in Beirut. I would accompany Wondimu to the various meetings he had with suppliers, mainly to help translate, as his spoken English was poor. The film importer would be invited to high-class hotels up in the mountains for lavish business dinner parties. He also had money and spent a lot from my perspective. He explained that, with the escalation of the war in Eritrea, he was allowed to take out some hard currency in order to bring back films that would help maintain the morale of troops and civilians in all major cities such as Asmara, Dire Dawa, and Addis Ababa. He shared his films for free with the troops. I recall that Indian and Western movies were his favorite.

Wondimu, my link with home, was liked by my friends in Beirut from the time he accompanied me to a school party and mesmerized all with his Arab dancing talent, which he claimed to have picked up while serving in the Ethiopian Navy and frequenting Egyptian night clubs.

Endnote

1   If you are not a revolutionary in the university, then you are considered reactionary. If you are reactionary and perceived to be well-dressed, then you were labeled as being a Jolly Jack.

CHAPTER THREE

Life Under the Lebanese Civil War

I t was indeed a tragic development that I, having come to peaceful Lebanon because of conflict and turmoil in my own country, suddenly faced a civil war much more intense and devastating than the situation back home. It became even more tragic when the airport and the ports closed, and the only way out was on land through Syria. The Syrian authorities made it clear that no one carrying an Ethiopian passport was allowed in. That land exit option was also not available. Thus, I stayed put and observed the war unfold.

The population of Lebanon comprises Christians and Muslims. No official census has been taken since 1932, reflecting the political sensitivity in Lebanon over confessional (religious) balance. It was estimated that more than half of the population was Muslim (Shi'a, Sunni, and Druze), and the rest was Christian (predominantly Maronite, Greek Orthodox, Greek Catholic, and Armenian). Shi'a Muslims make up the single largest sect. Claims since the early 1970s, by Muslims, that they were in the majority, contributed to tensions preceding the 1975–76 civil strife, and have been the basis of demands for a more powerful Muslim voice in the government. There were over four hundred thousand

Picture of me with PLO leader Yasssir Arafat

Palestinian refugees in Lebanon registered with the United Nations Relief and Works Agency (UNRWA).

Upon my arrival in Lebanon in 1974, the time was marked by periods of political turmoil interspersed with prosperity built on Beirut's position as a regional center for finance and trade. On campus at the AUB, speakers' corners were a regular feature, focusing on support for or against the presence of Palestinian refugees, many of whom arrived after the 1967 Arab-Israeli War, and the Black September 1970 hostilities in Jordan. Among the latter were Yasser Arafat and the PLO. Coupled with the Palestinian problem, Muslim and Christian differences grew more intense. The pro-Palestinian groups also supported the Ethiopian Left and denounced the imperialist Zionist regime of Emperor Haile Selassie.

The Civil War started with an incident that occurred in Beirut on April 13, 1975, when gunmen killed four Phalangists during a reported attempt on Pierre Gemayelal's life. Perhaps believing the assassins to have been Palestinian, the Phalangists retaliated later that day by attacking a bus carrying Palestinian passengers across a Christian neighborhood, killing about twenty-six of the occupants. The next day, fighting erupted in earnest, with Phalangists pitted against Palestinian militiamen.

The confessional layout of Beirut's various quarters facilitated random killing. Like most of Beirut's students at AUB, I stayed inside the dorms area during these early days of battle, which we all assumed would be over in a couple days. As foreign students, we were convinced that none of the sectarian parties would harm us, and that we would not be abducted for ransom or retaliation. None at AUB imagined that the street fighting they were witnessing was the beginning of a war that would devastate their city and divide the country.

The government could not act effectively because leaders were unable to agree on whether or not to use the Army to stop the bloodletting. As various groups took sides, the fighting spread to other areas of the country, forcing residents in towns with mixed sectarian populations to seek safety in regions where their sect was dominant. Even so, the militias became embroiled in a pattern of attack followed by retaliation, including acts against uninvolved civilians. Students from Christian areas could not come to the AUB.

Although the two warring factions were often characterized as Christian versus Muslim, their individual composition was far more complex. Those in favor of maintaining the status quo came to be known as the Lebanese Front. These groups included primarily the Maronite militias and various militias of Maronite religious orders. The side seeking change, usually referred to as the Lebanese National Movement, was far less cohesive and organized. For the most part, it was led by Kamal Jumblatt, a former AUB student, and included a variety of militias from leftist organizations, and guerrillas from rejectionist Palestinian (non-mainstream PLO) organizations.

By the end of 1975, no side held a decisive military advantage, but it was generally acknowledged that the Lebanese Front had done worse than expected against the disorganized Lebanese National Movement. The political hierarchy, composed of the old politicians, was still incapable of maintaining peace, except for occasional, short-lived ceasefires. Schools adapted to the intermittent ceasefires and would open, then close when fighting resumed.

Syrian diplomatic involvement grew during 1976, but it had little success in restoring order in the first half of the year. In January, it organized a ceasefire and set up the High Military Committee, through which it negotiated with all sides. These negotiations, however, were complicated by other events, especially Lebanese Front-Palestinian confrontations. That month, the Lebanese Front began a siege of Tel al-Zaatar, a densely populated Palestinian refugee camp in East Beirut. The Lebanese Front also overran and leveled Karantina, a Muslim quarter in East Beirut. These actions finally brought the main forces of the PLO, the Palestine Liberation Army (PLA), into the battle. Together, the PLA and the Lebanese National Movement took the town of Ad Damur, a stronghold of the Lebanese Front, formed by the former president, Camile Chamoun, as a coalition of Christian parties and forces located about seventeen kilometers south of Beirut.

In spite of these setbacks, through Syria's good offices, compromises were achieved. On February 14, 1976, in what was considered a political breakthrough, Syria helped negotiate a seventeen-point reform program known as the Constitutional Document. Yet, by March of the same year, this progress was derailed by the disintegration of the Lebanese Army. In that month, dissident Muslim troops, led by Lieutenant Ahmad Khatib, mutinied, creating the Lebanese Arab Army. Joining the Lebanese National Movement, they made significant penetrations into Christian-held Beirut neighborhoods and launched an attack on the presidential palace, forcing Franjiyah to flee to Mount Lebanon. Continuing its search for a domestic political settlement to the war, in May, the Chamber of Deputies elected Ilyas Sarkis to take over as president when Franjiyah's term expired in September. But Sarkis had strong backing from Syria, and as a consequence, was unacceptable to Jumblatt, who was known to be antipathetic to Syrian President Hafiz al-Assad, and who insisted on a "military solution."

Accordingly, the Lebanese National Movement successfully pressed assaults on Mount Lebanon and other Christian-controlled areas.

As Lebanese Front fortunes declined, two outcomes seemed likely: The establishment in Mount Lebanon of an independent Christian state, viewed as a "second Israel" by some. Or, if the Lebanese National Movement won the war, the creation of a radical, hostile state on Syria's western border. Neither of these possibilities was viewed as acceptable to al-Assad.

To prevent either scenario, at the end of May 1976, Syria intervened militarily against the Lebanese National Movement, hoping to end the fighting swiftly. This decision, however, proved ill-conceived, as Syrian forces met heavy resistance and suffered many casualties. Moreover, by entering the conflict on the Christian side, Syria provoked outrage from much of the Arab world. Despite, or perhaps as a result of, these military and diplomatic failures, in late July, Syria decided to quell the resistance. A drive was launched against Lebanese National Movement strongholds that was far more successful than earlier battles. Within two weeks, the opposition was weakened. The Syrians took advantage of the National Movement's weakness and agreed to participate in an Arab peace conference held in Riyadh, Saudi Arabia, on October 16, 1976.

The Riyadh Conference, followed by an Arab League meeting in Cairo, also in October 1976, formally ended the Lebanese Civil War. Although the underlying causes were in no way eliminated, the full-scale warfare stopped. Syria's presence in Lebanon was legitimized by the establishment of the Arab Deterrent Force (ADF) by the Arab League in October 1976. Thus, after more than a year and a half of devastation, relative calm returned to Lebanon. Much of the once magnificent city of Beirut was reduced to rubble, and the town divided into Muslim and Christian sectors, separated by the so-called Green Line. School resumed in earnest at the AUB, and I continued with my studies.

Following my departure from Lebanon in 1981, in June 1982, Israeli troops carried out a ground attack into Lebanon to remove PLO forces. Operation Peace for Galilee aimed at establishing a deeper security zone and pushing Syrian troops out of Lebanon, with a view toward paving the way for an Israeli-Lebanese peace agreement. With these aims in mind, Israeli forces drove twenty-five miles into Lebanon, moving into East Beirut with the support of Maronite Christian leaders and militia. In August 1982, US mediation resulted in the evacuation of Syrian troops and PLO fighters from Beirut. I have to mention that I met some of them in Addis, as they were being deployed to reinforce the PLO and DFLP offices in Addis Ababa.

As a footnote to the Civil War, it has to be noted that over and above the frontline conventional war that raged between the opposing factions along the Green Line that divided the city of Beirut into two, the population on either side of the divide suffered from extortionists asking for protection money. This aspect of the Civil War period did not attract much media attention. The constant blowing up of businesses and residents of those who did not comply with the demands of militias was more terrifying to residents living away from the frontline, than the actual war.

Moreover, various armed political parties on either side of the divide would also exchange fire within their respective territories as turf wars raged in parallel to the official conflict. The official warfronts were known and could be avoided. However, it was difficult to predict when and where the next explosion or turf war would take place. That was terrifying indeed. The trauma suffered by residents of this type of extortion-led violence continued well after the ceasefire agreement.

Charismatic Leaders vs. Intellectuals

The Palestinian movement in Lebanon was the first time I was able to observe the fact that an intellectually sound narrative spoken by a well-educated person did not have the same impact on crowds of people who seem to appreciate and react more positively to simple slogans and gestures.

The heads of the Popular Front for the Liberation of Palestine, Dr. George Habash, and the head of the Democratic Front for the Liberation of Palestine, Nayef Hawatmeh, were articulate, and delivered excellent analyses of events and developments on the ground. The head of the PLO, Yasser Arafat, in contrast, would stand in front of his audience and utter short bursts of slogans and vague statements, as to how one day a young Palestinian boy would raise the flag over the Al-Aqsa Mosque in occupied Palestine. That would get the crowd roaring. It made me realize that what generates political impact on a population is not necessarily the substantive nature of the discourse, but the vague promises of a futuristic situation to be arrived at all costs. A speech that gave hope or created a vision of freedom in some form of a utopia had more impact on winning the hearts and minds of people than a rational presentation of facts.

At a later stage, I observed the same phenomenon unfold in South Africa, where Thabo Mbeki would deliver, in Shakespearean English, a well-researched speech, but would not get half the uproar of appreciation to that of Nelson Mandela walking on to the same stage and uttering a few slogans and simply dancing. During the initial days of the Ethiopian revolution, Colonel

Mengistu would get the same reaction from crowds by breaking a bottle with liquid resembling blood, and chanting anti-imperialist slogans. I could go on and on to even mention the current situation in Ethiopia, which would take me off script.

Developments in the Horn of Africa were unfolding rapidly, and the USSR-US-NATO push for influence was reaching its peak. Naturally, I got sucked into discussing events in the Horn, at school with friends, and with the Palestine Research Institute and the Ethiopian Student Movement. I started doing research and following up on developments on the ground, which I ultimately put together for my thesis submission in partial fulfillment of the requirement for the master's degree of arts in Political Studies and Public Administration at the AUB, in June 1980. The thesis was entitled, "USSR's Involvement in a Revolutionary Situation: The Ethiopian Case 1974–1979."

Following the lull in the Lebanese Civil War, from 1977 to 1979, while still working at the PLO Foreign Information Office and the Middle East Research Center, I also ventured into freelance journalism under the pen name Mohammed Mahdi, my dormitory friend from Djibouti. Stories would be sent by telex from the Royal Hotel in West Beirut, and any newspaper that picked up and printed the story would pay.

Improvement in the Quality of my Life

My income improved along with my quality of life. I was able to afford new clothing and to pay for food. I had joined two students from AUB, an Iranian and an Afghani, and together we rented a flat close to the AUB campus. We cooked in turns and enjoyed each other's traditional foods.

A regular visitor to our flat, Jim Reilly (Jimmy boy), introduced me to Joseph Samaha (Joe boy), who happened to be attending most graduate classes with me. Joe, who had become nervous after having been kidnapped, was looking for a roommate to share a two-story flat in the Mishaalani Building he had identified in the Hamra area near Beirut Express off Souraty Street. Since the place was spacious with more amenities, I moved in with Joe, where I stayed until my departure from Lebanon.

Our landlady, Vivian Mishaalany, an American-Lebanese from San Diego, was sharing the two-floor apartment with us but had a separate entrance. She was nosey and would come once in a while, asking if we could spare sugar or something she had suddenly "run out of" and did not want to go to the shop for this or another reason. These unexpected visits happened when female students would come to our flat.

We became more social and started organizing memorable parties. Many students from the AUB would come to our flat, and many political and economic discussions would take place. Memorable night's playing cards, drinking whiskey, and eating *kitfo* or *doro wotte* prepared by me became the talk of AUB students, and formed the bulk of the exchanges I continued to have with Joe whenever we met to commiserate with nostalgia about the good old days in Beirut. When there would be an occasional bomb blast, we would all pause, make sure we were okay and that the windows were intact, and then continue to play. I met and became close to Sose Karoglanian, a Lebanese-Armenian, who unfortunately was not allowed to travel with us in-country or abroad. Her family was not supportive that their daughter was going out with a non-Armenian, and even worse, an African. Joe had the exact opposite problem, as families of female Lebanese students wanted him to meet their daughters, and I would be invited for lunch or to their respective villages, as it was the wish of many that he would befriend one of them and take them to the USA or make them an American citizen. Unfortunately, none felt remotely the same about the prospect of becoming Ethiopian.

We took memorable leisurely trips in Joe's new Renault 12 throughout Lebanon, mostly with Jim Reilly, Seif Tora, and Hossein Shehidi. Getting stopped at checkpoints was always intriguing, when the army or militia would ask for our IDs. Handing over passports from various countries would always instigate confused looks, turning passports upside down, or opening from back to front. I always felt that we could pass as members of the UN. Not knowing what to make of us, they would always just let us move on.

A couple weekends spent at Joe's family village of Khenchara, "camping" at his grandfather's house with Jim, Nabila Karam, Nathira, and Hossein, were peaceful and extremely memorable. As a group, we visited places in Europe and the USA—spending nights at Hyde Park in London, visiting the grave of Karl Marx, or explaining that we were not American, even though we spoke English in Turkey and Germany. In Paris, meeting with Iranian and Ethiopian students discussing revolutions in both countries was an eventful affair. My Lebanese-Armenian girlfriend unfortunately could not join us in our international travels, as she was also not allowed to spend the night out.

In Paris, I also met my childhood English School friend, Wondwessen Shifferaw, who had become a supporter of the EPRP. I soon realized that we had grown apart. Following an argument, he praised the Lord that we were not in our home country, as we would now be facing each other with the barrel of the gun. In contrast, Mekonnen and Amaha Abye, friends from the Debre Zeit days, and sons of General Abye Abebe, were more accommodating of my views. They were supporters of Meison. It was unfortunate that opposing camps were established, both professing the same ideology and outlook on the world, but out to destroy one another over trivial differences, which none of us recall today. Equally sad in those days, Ethiopians in the diaspora were also divided along party lines, eroding a common identity, friendship, and solidarity. Many, like myself, found safety and security among non-Ethiopians, where one could discuss politics or economics at ease without being labeled as this or that.

I must note that visits to Europe and the US in those days were primarily for tourism. I got the chance to visit most of the historical monuments, museums, and cultural attractions that London, Paris, Washington, New York, and Los Angeles had to offer at the time. It is a sad reality that at the later stage of visits to such locations, given the significant number of relatives and friends that have settled there, my interactions are primarily restricted to visits to Ethiopian restaurants, bars, and similar cultural centers. In particular, the US has become an alternative

Ethiopian destination. Any interaction with the outside world will not go beyond the nearest shopping mall.

I do believe that most Ethiopians residing in Europe, America, and the Middle East have not melted into the host community, but have found safety within their own groups and bubbles. Little Ethiopia and Little Addis Ababa have been created all over because of the sense of security created by such communities. This reality, in turn, appears to have limited the social and political upward mobility of migrants from Ethiopia in significant numbers.

CHAPTER FOUR
Back to Addis Ababa

I returned to Addis in 1981, and things had significantly changed. The compound I had been brought up in, had been divided into small individual family members' dwellings, and even smaller fragmented dwellings. The various workers' and family quarters had been subdivided, with the occupants kept as residents. Open space, such as the playing field, had been confiscated by the Derg and taken over by the Urban Dwellers Association for a settlement project of displaced people from elsewhere in Addis Ababa. That compound resembled a shanty town with some solid buildings scattered, and decapitated housing remnants of the Kebede household.

My father had aged and was visibly upset with developments around him, even though he remained reserved, as usual, in expressing his feelings openly. My mother, in contrast, was strongly outspoken against the military rule and the nationalization of land and property. The family income had shrunk significantly, and they were having a rough time in running a decent life compared to what they had been accustomed to by depending on the pension income of my father. Rental income and free cereal supplies from farms had ended. However, both were grateful and thanked the Creator for keeping them alive and for the life they had, which was much better than their contemporaries and peers. The social transformation that had taken place during the revolution and in my absence was clear. The loss of the monarchy, and the destitution of the nobility, was clearly observed. However, it was difficult to determine which segment of society had gained.

As I had already arranged in Beirut to continue working with the PLO in Addis Ababa, I approached the office headed by Abu Nae, and was appointed as an administrative officer in the Addis office. I worked closely with the Organisation of African Unity (OAU) and the Ethiopian Peace and Solidarity Committee. I helped the office draft news releases, submissions to the Foreign Ministry or other entities, as needed. I enjoyed promoting the cause of the Palestinian people with the OAU Liberation Committee.

The other Palestinian Office was that of the Democratic Front for the Liberation of Palestine headed by Salah Nassir. Salah was more social, and since he was not with his family, enjoyed throwing parties well-attended by embassy staff from Socialist countries, particularly Cuba and the USSR. Between the two Palestinian offices, I got all the reintegration support, as well as strange looks and cynical remarks from people whenever I told them I was working with the PLO. Most found that strange and wanted to know if I had changed my religion. Given years of exposure to the Arab threat posed on the Ethiopia narrative, and the confusion that exists regarding the differentiation between Islam and Arabs, built-in stereotypes would spring up. Standard queries from those who knew my family were, *Does your Israel-educated brother know? How does your father, who lived in exile in Israel, feel?* Ironically, Palestinians and Arabs I used to meet in Beirut, and even now in Addis, would ask if I was an Eritrean, Sudanese or a Muslim, particularly because I spoke in Arabic.

Life in Addis for a returnee like myself was challenging. The old Ethiopia and Addis Ababa I knew as a child were gone and had been replaced, but I was not clear by what. The new norms and values were neither here nor there. Luckily, old English School friends, particularly Tassew Molla and Petros Teklu, were back in Addis from the USA, and they indeed offered me a soft-landing cushion in my reintegration process. Both were running their fathers' businesses. Petros was heading the Teklu Desta goldsmith in Piassa, while Tassew headed the Molla Maru Brewery. It was through Tassew that I was able to make new friends. Teklu Desta remains, 'til this day, the meeting point for former English School friends returning to or visiting Addis.

Returnees like me, who did not take part in the National Literacy Campaign in rural Ethiopia, or had not been in Addis during the execution of the Red[1] and White Terror,[2] found it difficult to engage in discussions which tend to draw on either of the two experiences. At times, you are made to feel as if you were a traitor for having avoided the mass excitement or trauma my generation and social class had gone through.

On the family front, Asfaw Kebede, my older brother, took me around in the evenings for dinner and drinks. Like me, he enjoyed local Azmari music. My nephew Bekure, who was working at the Foreign Ministry, would also join us in the evenings.

During a social event, I met an Australian, Colin Mitchell, working for UNHCR, who invited me for lunch and asked if I was interested in working with his organization in Hararghe. He was talking of exotic places I had heard of but never visited. I decided to try it out, and took a sabbatical from the PLO office.

Joining UNHCR in Hararghe Province

I joined UNHCR in March 1983, under the Dire Dawa suboffice. The first challenge I faced was understanding that my role as a field assistant was monitoring the return and reintegration of Ethiopian refugees from Djibouti and Somalia. I, and the other colleague recruited for the same purpose, Kefellegn Asrat, were to monitor and report on that program's implementation. However, our supervisor and head of the suboffice, Colin Mitchel, was not on good terms with the RRC and other local officials. Those officials, in turn, denied UNHCR access to almost all aspects of the implementation of the program by usually citing security and safety concerns. We were told to wait for RRC reports, which we could then translate and share with the office.

The role of UNHCR in monitoring the 1973 Ethiopian refugee return and reintegration program from Djibouti was defined partially during a train ride that Mr. Nicolas Bwakira, the UNHCR Ethiopian representative, undertook with Ethiopian officials returning from a tripartite meeting, to examine returnee routes and reception facilities between Djibouti and Dire Dawa. I and Kefelegn joined the train at the border crossing point at Dewelle. The special two-wagon train—formerly the emperor's train—had seated, in the first, royal carriage, Major Dawit Wolde Giorgis, head of the Relief and Rehabilitation Commission (RRC), his deputy, Taye Gurmu, and Mr. Bwakira. The rest of us were in the second wagon, which included, amongst others, Colin Mitchell, Tamerat Kebede, Kefelegn Asrat, and me. At the midway stopover at Adigala, both Major Dawit and Mr. Bwakira clearly spelled out the role of UNHCR, and reaffirmed the rights of UNHCR to access everything included in that operation, on par with those of the RRC colleagues. That closed that chapter. The head of the RRC regional office, Gebre Tsadic, was I later removed from his position and replaced by Asfaha Bemnet, who also later joined UNHCR.

The well-publicized Djibouti return and reintegration program involved some 35,000 returnees, mainly from the Dikhil and Ali Sabeh camps, returning primarily to Issa-inhabited locations along the railway. I was stationed at Adigala, which was roughly halfway between the border and Dire Dawa. The only visible connection to either destination was the train. We made extensive use of the various trains that operated on that route for travel and monitoring purposes. Each train had been given a name either customized from a French term or a local name. The trains that delivered water from one site to another were called the *beyole* to cargo trains, such as the Faltu, Hassan Jog, and the fast Autoria. These were used extensively. I also traveled to Addis by the Autoria, or the Kusshet, stopping at each station for an oncoming train to pass. *Kurasma* stops could last hours, which, in the smothering heat, became unbearable.

At the Adigala site, we built a transit shelter facility for returnees, where they spent the night and received their food and non-food items before proceeding to their final destinations. RRC and UNHCR staff slept in the open football field of the Adigala School, with troops assigned to each goal to look after us. We enjoyed the clear skies and the stars at night, with melancholic Ethiopian music by Aster Awoke playing most evenings.

I recall memorable and adventurous weekend trips to Addis Ababa from Adigala by arranging with train drivers to use their bed in the front cabin until I transferred to a passenger train in Dire Dawa. From there, I boarded the train to Addis, with a stopover in Awash for dinner, and arrived in the morning. I proceeded home from the train station and met the family. I would then shower, borrow my sister-in-law's car, and go out to the city to have fun. I would rest on Sunday and board the train to Dire Dawa in the evening. I would arrive in Dire Dawa in the early morning and then take the next available train to Adigala. Upon arrival, I would turn on the communication radio and call Dire Dawa to start the week. Some weekends were spent in Dire Dawa enjoying the vibrant night life the city offered to bachelors during those days.

Following a year of intensive repatriation by train movement of returnees, the irony was that the residual camp population in Djibouti was not dropping as expected. The to and fro by Issa nomads and traders, the sale of refugee ID cards by corrupt officials, and the willingness of UNHCR Djibouti office to claim a higher number of residual refugees still left behind was making the operation a joke. The so-called refugees were moving to acquire documentation and to benefit from assistance packages as either refugees or returnees on both sides of the border. I recall raising my concerns of double-dipping and double-counting with the UNHCR.

The UNHCR program officer in Djibouti, Mr. John Horekens, used to accompany returnee trains. Even though he agreed with me that double-counting could in fact be the case, he was either not willing, or did not have the authority, to decide. The strong and influential government counterpart, Office National d'Assistance aux Réfugiés et Sinistrés (ONARS), was feared and not challenged by UNHCR staff.

A similar discrepancy in numbers was being observed in the Ethiopian refugee return and reintegration operation from Somalia to Hararghe province. Over four hundred thousand returnees were registered by the RRC, working closely with the League of Red Cross Societies (LRCS) and the Lutheran World Federation (LWF). UNHCR had a separate tripartite agreement with the RRC-LRCS and LWF-RRC working throughout the province. The LWF and LRCS were UNHCR's partners for the returnee program in the country, which also included the returnee program in the Province of Eritrean that was managed separately under the suboffice of Asmara, which was on par with suboffice Dire Dawa, covering the Hararghe province. The Ali Ghider returnee settlement in Eritrea was managed on par with the Kelafo and Mustahil returnee projects in Hararghe. LWF also managed the Massawa fishery project for returnees. Both LWF and LRCS brought their own significant resources to the program over and above what they received from UNHCR.

Various field monitoring missions I undertook with the Red Cross, LWF, and RRC staff to spontaneous return areas confirmed new arrivals with their personal belongings, trying to establish themselves. Interviews confirmed where they came from in Somalia, among other things. However, the number of Ethiopian refugees in Somalia did not decrease to take account of the returnees. In fact, new birth figures would be included to increase the numbers to over seven hundred thousand refugees. The two offices submitted their respective refugee and returnee figures to headquarters, which was clearly not in a position to resolve the discrepancy.

The figures issue got entangled in the overall Cold War rhetoric, which somehow had its own partial supporters or sympathizers with one figure or another, depending on their position vis-à-vis the respective governments. The highly charged and politically sensitive figures game underlined UNHCR's inability to pronounce itself one way or another. It is my understanding that the discrepancy over figures was only resolved with the collapse of the Berlin Wall in 1989, and the collapse of the Somali regime in 1991. The refugee and returnee programme came to an end in both countries.

Following what I saw regarding the discrepancy in refugee and returnee figures, I was convinced that the only way to address the challenge was by putting in place a clear coordination mechanism, and the appointment of a manager to oversee the program and have direct line management responsibilities over the local UNHCR representative functions in both the country of origin and countries of asylum. I argued these points at a later stage, when the Delphi Initiative gave me the opportunity. I was long convinced that the "situation management" approach was the only answer.

In the areas of return in the Hararghe Province, in collaboration with our partners and the involvement of the community, we were able to do a lot in terms of construction of community infrastructures, including road repairs, water points, and rehabilitation of health clinics and similar facilities. We did not call these activities Quick Impact Projects (QUIPs) at the time, as the term was not commonly used by humanitarian workers. The term was widely used in the mid-1980s and beyond, as if it were invented or discovered then.

The program in Hararghe had also increased its staffing component, with Ato Solomon Abebe and Abdul Khadir Jamma having joined as additional field Assistant. The international staff now included Tahir Ali, an American of Pakistani origin. The former head of suboffice, Colin Mitchell, had moved to Addis as deputy representative, and had been replaced by Roger Doan-Hay, a French national of Vietnamese origin. Roger will be remembered for hiring the best cook in town ,and for the various imported fish dishes he served visitors.

The Djibouti repatriation program will also be remembered for the number of generals it offered employment opportunities to. Major Dawit Wolde Giorgis, head of the RRC, had offered generals who were retired by the Derg, employment under the project. General Merid Gizaw, a US-educated military officer, was deployed as program coordinator under the RRC regional office. General Seyoum, former police commander of Hararghe, and General Tadesse Melke, former commander of the 4th Army Division, were assigned to the livestock procurement and distribution section. Returnee nomads received a start-up supply of goats and sheep. Other discharged generals, like General Mulatu, joined LWF, and General Bereketeab, a former head of military intelligence, was retained as an advisor and expert on Somali issues. All stayed at the Karamara Hotel and would share stories that were entertaining and educational. The gatherings were so much appreciated that we would all rush not to miss the biggest attraction in town. I became their friend, and family visitors that came to Dire Dawa talk about it to this day. At the time, my friends at the hotel were all old enough to be my father, but we treated each other as equals.

One of the lingering shortcomings observed during my Hararge assignment days was the limited interaction I and the humanitarian team had with the Somali local population. Language and other cultural barriers were cited to rationalize our socialization and other restrictive recruitment justifications at the expense of the local population. Most local workers, like myself, were recruited in Addis or elsewhere in the country. A similar approach was used in the West Ethiopia refugee program.

By early 1984, I applied and got accepted to transfer to Addis, and I became the program assistant for South Sudan. I had followed developments in South Sudan since my university days and was interested in its current events.

The Sudan Conflict and the Resulting Displacement

The most recent conflict in the Sudan has its genesis in the First Sudanese Civil War, a conflict that lasted from 1955 to 1972, between northern Sudan and southern Sudan regions that demanded representation and more regional autonomy. It was also known as the Anyanya Rebellion, or Anyanya I, after the name of the rebels—a term in the local language which means *snake venom*. Half a million people died over the seventeen years, and the war was divided into four major stages: initial guerrilla warfare, the creation of the Anyanya insurgency, political strife within the gov-

74

ernment, and establishment of the South Sudan Liberation Movement (SSLM).

The protracted war was resolved with the Agreement of Addis Ababa, signed between the SSLM and the Nimeiryi regime of the Sudan in 1972. While the agreement ended the First Sudanese Civil War, it failed to completely dispel the tensions and addressed only some of the issues stated by Southern Sudan. The breakdown of the initial appeasement later led to a reigniting of the north-south conflict during the Second Sudanese Civil War, which lasted from 1983 to 2005.

The residual South Sudanese refugees from the 1970s, who had stayed behind in Ethiopia, had locally integrated and married Ethiopian Nuers. It has to be recalled that Anyanya II, or the South Sudan Liberation Movement, established a military presence in Bilpham, Ethiopia, after the 1975 Akobo Mutiny led by Samuel Gaitut. Gaitut was known to be staying at times with his relatives, who remained in Gambella town. The locally integrated residual refugees from South Sudan in Gambella became the local contacts for new arrivals from South Sudan in 1983, which included Dr. John Garang and Salva Kiir. The new arrivals reportedly met Gaitut in Gambella.

The presence of the SSLM, and a significant number of new arrivals in Gambella, created all sorts of commotions that resulted in rioting outside the compound of the Sudanese consulate, which had to be closed for the "protection of the Councillor," who relocated to Addis.

The increase in the number of new arrivals from South Sudan created the need for international support to feed and sustain new refugee arrivals, while also offering the Government of Ethiopia the opportunity to help organize a movement to change the situation within the Sudan.

UNHCR was called upon to assist the new arrivals, while simultaneously the Government of Ethiopia started to facilitate the creation of a strong movement against the government in the Sudan, which it perceived as supporting Ethiopian rebel movements.

The new arrival leaders courted by the government were

taken to Nazareth with SSLM, and agreed to focus not only on South Sudan, but the whole of the Sudan. The focus on the whole of the Sudan was encouraged, as mutineers joining the movement, as well as the large part of the Sudanese armed rank and file, were either Nubians or from Darfur. The SSLM agreed to broaden its scope to include the whole of the Sudan and join in the formation of a new movement, the Sudan People's Liberation Movement (SPLM).

Initial support for the SPLM to establish an armed wing known as the Sudan People's Liberation Army (SPLA) came from Libya, which was opposed to the Nimeiryi regime at the time. During my initial visits to the Gambella region, I recall seeing a group of foreigners who were camping at Bonga and being informed that they were Cubans who had come to help design the new airbase in the region. I did not buy that story, as the "Cubans" spoke Arabic with a North African accent. Upon further enquiry, I found out that they were in fact Libyan military and explosive experts who were training the SPLA. The SPLA was further strengthened with the mutiny of Karobino Kuanya Bol, battalion commander of the 105 Battalion, and William Nyuon Bany, commander of the 104 Battalion, joining the SPLM.

The SPLM, encouraged by the Derg, also adopted Marxism and Leninism as its ideology—at least on paper—to get recognition from the socialist camp. The SPLA did receive significant training and military support from Cuba and the USSR over and above the support it received from the Ethiopian Government.

The formation of the SPLM and SPLA at a time of refugee influx created a challenging environment which was further compounded by the lack of a clearly designated government body to provide material assistance to refugees.

Implementing Partners

Dealing with implementing partners, particularly government partners involved directly in the delivery of material assistance, is difficult all over Africa. In this regard, I consider the confusion that prevailed in Ethiopia at the time worth recounting. Relationships with nongovernmental partners were relatively straightforward and manageable.

The LWF had responsibility for the planned agricultural settlement and self-sufficiency project. The project initially focused on a socio-economic survey that was conducted by the Social Science Department of Addis Ababa University. Extensive soil and underground water yield surveys were undertaken. Based on the findings, an agricultural settlement scheme was initiated some five kilometers from the Itang refugee camp. The Itang project was headed at field level by Ato Haddish, while Mr. Niels Nicolaisen and Mr. Pablo Piet-Cannon headed the Office in Addis. Reports, as per the agreement, were regularly provided, and LWF made tangible financial and material contributions.

The Ethiopian Red Cross Society (ERCS), supported by the Federation, coordinated the ERCS-UNHCR joint health and supplementary feeding project. The operational responsibility of managing and coordinating the implementation of the project was assumed by Ato Getachew Mahateme Selassie. He was a hardworking slave driver—a site planner by profession, who did most of the construction work himself, while also managing the health program. He was supported by the competent public health officer, Ato Mulugeta. Putting aside his non-existent people's skills, Getachew is one of the most impressive and dedicated workers I have ever met.

As per the Ethiopian Constitution, the responsible government ministry dealing with refugee affairs was the Ministry of Interior. Within the Ministry, the department dealing with Borders and Refugee Affairs, headed by Colonel Solomon, was in charge of refugee status determination and protection-related matters. In Gambella district, Annimut Kinde, the provincial administrator for Illubabor, in coordination with the ruling party representative based in Keffa province, Begashaw Atalay, represented the Ministry. The Secretary of the Workers Party of Ethiopia (WPE) western region representative, Simon Galore, involved himself intermittently.

The RRC, primarily working with UNHCR on returnee programs throughout the country, got involved in the distribution of food and non-food items to refugees. Being in charge of the assistance program placed a lot of resources at the disposal of the RRC without necessarily having the authority or mandate to deal with refugee protection matters. For example, the RRC understood registration to be simply for food distribution purposes, while the UNHCR also understood it to be a protection tool that should screen out non-refugees. SPLA fighters were not to benefit from the UNHCR program.

The problem was further complicated when the RRC commissioner, Major Dawit Wolde Giorgis, appointed his friend from the Foreign Ministry, Ato Mismaku Asrat, to head the RRC program. The well-dressed diplomat had neither expertise in the area of refugee protection nor humanitarian work, and he hated fieldwork. He thought highly of himself, refusing to deal with those he understood as being too young or junior. He assigned the field coordination work to the social worker Mintewab. Ato Asrat appeared to have been more interested in the workings of the SPLA and relations with the Sudan, which needless to point out, went beyond the mandate of the UNHCR, and indeed the RRC.

The relationship between the UNHCR and the RRC deteriorated further with regularly reported allegations of diversion of food and other materials from the refugee program. The RRC became open about its desire to expel the UNHCR representative from the country. The RRC was known for its diversion of food intended for drought victims to feed the Army and militias. Being scrutinized for the diversion of food from refugees to feed SPLA fighters was no big deal from its perspective, and the RRC could not understand the fuss.

The RRC and UNHCR's friends of Dawit and Bwakira, including the Ethiopian ambassador in Geneva, and my older brother Kassa Kebede, intervened to resolve the problem. It was agreed to set up a dedicated office within the RRC to solely focus on UNHCR programs to be funded by UNHCR.

The RRC and UNHCR agreed on a joint working group to draw up the management structure of the new office and define its core functions. I was tasked to do this by UNHCR, and worked with my RRC designated counterpart, Tamerat Kebede. Relying on the basic UNHCR management structure of Protection, Program

Management, Finance, and Administration sections, we drew up a management structure. Standard job descriptions for the various functions were taken from the UNHCR and adapted to the local government system. The Protection Unit was headed by a staff member seconded by the Ministry of Home Affairs that had the refuge mandate within the government.

The RRC-UNHCR Coordination Unit was established as an autonomous unit within the RRC but fully funded by UNHCR. The creation of the RRC-UNHCR Coordination Unit brought about its own internal squabbling and jealousy within the RRC. The salary of the coordinator, as well as the UN-plated car at his disposal, not to mention the lucrative fuel allowance, made the post attractive. Major Dawit, with the endorsement of UNHCR, had appointed the Hararghe province RRC representative, Asfaha Bemnet. I was with Asfaha in Gambella when he received a radio message from the RRC deputy commissioner, Taye Gurumu, to return to Addis immediately. I found out later that he was dismissed from the job upon arrival, and was alleged to be a supporter of the Eritrean Liberation Movement. He was immediately replaced by Tesfaye Desta, a close friend and associate of Deputy Commissioner Taye Gurumu. Asfaha was released apparently for lack of evidence. He was later recruited locally by UNHCR. I would like to note that many Ethiopians of Eritrean origin were forced take sides and support the EPLF due to false labelling. The general atmosphere of labelling a specific ethnic group of being a supporter a rebel movement without proof actually results in the effected persons identifying with that entity. Beside Eritrea similar challenges linger with regard to Tigrayan and Oromo people.

Following the departure of Major Dawit from Ethiopia, I and Tamerat were invited to brief the newly appointed commissioner, Berhanu Jembere. We explained the rationale for the office and shared with him the organigram of the management structure. The only question the new commissioner asked was, "Where is Alganesh to sit?" Tamerat looked straight into my eyes and whispered, "Mote," translated *it died*, or *our effort has been killed*. I later found out that Alganesh was the spouse of Colonel Berhanu Bayeh, a senior member of the Derg, who apparently had lobbied with Mengistu for Berhanu to be appointed commissioner of the RRC. The commissioner was looking for a position for Alganesh to pay back the favor. We politely explained to the commissioner that our submission focused on management structures and functions, and not on personalities, to perform those functions. It was up to the government and UNHCR to decide on incumbents.

In hindsight, just like in the Sudan, Djibouti, and elsewhere, in an effort to smoothen the UNHCR-government working relationship, the new Frankenstein was delivered as the RRC UNHCR Coordination Office, which later metamorphosed into the Administration for Refugee and Returnee Affairs (ARRA) by January 1989.

South Sudanese Refugees

My first trip to the Gambella region was by car to Gambella, and then by barge to Itang. New arrivals were being interviewed, with thousands arriving daily. The logistical nightmare of transporting food and Non Food Items (NFIs) to Gambella was significant. Delivery to Itang was a nightmare, as there was no road. The 1974 abandoned health facility from the Anyanya Movement days, where Sudanese refugees were assisted in the early 1970s, was being rehabilitated and served as the nucleus for the development of the camp. The Red Cross ran the health program and construction of the health center, as well as the UNHCR guest rooms. The RRC was responsible for food distribution and related support.

The Ethiopian head of state, Mengistu Hailemariam, had visited the camp by helicopter when returning from an SPLA training camp, and was briefed by the RRC team, of the logistics challenges facing the assistance program because of road inaccessibility. The dirt road linking Gambella with Itang could not be used at all when it rained. When dry, the dirt road was difficult for light four-wheel vehicles, and long-haul trucks had to offload in Gambella. Colonel Mengistu had given instructions for the road to be constructed as soon as possible.

Upon my visit to Itang in late 1984, I was mesmerized by the sight of so many graders and bulldozers working until late in the evenings at different spots of the road simultaneously. In the evening, floodlights from several generators, with the headlights of earth-moving equipment, were impressive to see from a distance, and resembled a freeway during a traffic jam in Europe. Several teams were also working on the construction of bridges and culverts. In a couple of weeks, an all-weather road was completed, which impressed local and international observers. The BBC did a documentary film on Sudanese refugees in Itang in 1985, and called it *The Road to Itang*, as it recognized the achievement on access and capturing the flocking of refugees into the camp.

My friend and colleague, Girmai Wondimu, was brought in from the Asmara suboffice and became the resident UNHCR field assistant in Itang. We maintained contact over the radio with Girmai on a regular basis, and his reports were informative. Ato Solomon Abebe joined the Gambella team as the second field assistant, and he had excellent knowledge of the region, having served as administrator of the Gambella District in the mid-1970s.

Solomon was arrested for allegedly having crossed into South Sudan using a UN vehicle without government permission. I inquired about what had brought about his arrest, and learned that it was a simple misunderstanding with a local security officer who was upset that Solomon had given a pair of sunglasses the security officer had brought for him from Addis to a lady Solomon met in town.

The discussion for Solomon's release involved UNHCR Geneva and was spearheaded by the representative directly with the Ministry of Interior and the Foreign Ministry. The latter was handling issues related to the immunity of international civil servants. I recall hand-carrying a letter calling for Solomon's release, and handing it over to the deputy minister, Mersha Ketsella. He read the letter immediately and smiled cynically, saying that Solomon was his dear friend also. The UNHCR letter, following UN rules of procedure, was requesting the government to either bring charges against Solomon if he had committed any wrongdoing, or to release him immediately.

Deputy Minister Mersha told me to sit down and bluntly asked if I wanted Solomon released or not? I responded that I wanted him released. He then yelled, "My son, how can you guys ask a government like ours to bring charges against Solomon, or to admit wrongdoing and release him? What if we were to inform you that we will press charges against Solomon for having met with the OLF and for carrying illegal arms in the UN car? We can produce the physical evidence and bring eyewitnesses to testify in court. Do you have an idea as to what the outcome could be?"

Mersha composed himself and suggested that I tear the paper up and inform my boss to instead ask for the government's leniency, and to plead for his release. Solomon was pardoned and released in Addis on condition that he will not return to Gambella. He was ultimately reassigned to Aisha in Harar.

The above incident was an eye opener, and I learned a great deal from Deputy Minister Mersha. I realized that dogmatic adherence to principles, rules, regulations, and legality in dealings with the likes of the Ethiopian government at the time could result in undesired outcomes. The absence of a level playing field governed by the lack of predictable, just, and transparent rules and procedures has to be carefully navigated to avoid undesirable outcomes.

Arrogance of Senior Colleagues Visiting the Field

On the South Sudanese refugees front from 1984 to 1985, the first demonstration of Mr. Bwakira's skills was during the mission of the director of assistance, Mr. Zollner, accompanied by the then director of the bureau, Mr. Antoine Noel. At a heated meeting in Gambella involving the regional governor, Annemut Kinde and the Deputy Minister of the Interior, Mersha Ketsella, infiltration of camps by the SPLA, food diversion, and recruitment- and detention-related issues were on the table. The heated meeting nearly broke up as Mr. Noel, who had earlier been disappointed, as he was not recognized as being an Ethiopian by Annemut Kinde, was addressing the meeting in an aggressive tone. Noel's action drew a counterattack by Mersha. Zollner, having consulted Bwakira, requested a break. During the tea break, Bwakira consulted with his government counterparts on all the contentious issues. When the meeting reconvened, it was all smiles once again, and agreements were reached on the need for the government to stop SPLA infiltration into Itang, monitor food diversion, and coordinate on all protection-related issues.

Noel asked whose side I was on. He wanted to know if I was part of the Ethiopian delegation. Following exchanges between Bwakira and Noel, Bwakira suggested that I stay on in Gambella and follow up on the mission. I actually drove a Land Cruiser to Jimma, where I spent the night before getting up early and proceeding to Addis Ababa. I made it to the scheduled meeting in Addis at the Ministry of Interior. I still recall the surprised looks of Noel, when he saw me at the meeting, which made me feel happy.

Arrogance of International Colleagues Assigned to the Field

Another encounter worth mentioning was a PTSS mission from headquarters, including Michel Gabaudan, Rene Thiadens, and Daniel Mora Castro. I flew with the team from Addis to Gambella, where we were met by the head of suboffice, Robin Macalpine. We were taken to the Ethiopia Hotel, where Robin informed us that he had not yet secured the travel permit to go to Itang.

Robin went to the security office and returned fuming, as he claimed that the mission was being denied access to the Itang refugee camp. I called Girmai Wondimu over the radio in Itang, who confirmed that everyone was waiting for the mission's arrival. I also called Addis and informed Raymond "Ray" Fell, UNHCR deputy representative, of the situation. Ray suggested that I help the suboffice secure the pass. My offer to assist was abruptly turned down by Robin.

At lunch time, the head of regional security, Thowath Pal Chay, came for lunch at the hotel and greeted all of us before sitting down to eat his plate of pasta at a corner table. Robin rushed into the hotel and went straight to Thowath and informed him that the mission was canceled and that the team was returning to Addis. He was actually drafting a protest memo to the RLO, informing Mr. Bwakira that the high commissioner's delegation was being denied access to refugees, even though Ethiopia had acceded to the

1951 Refugee Convention. Robin kept on referring to the mandate and the high commissioner several times. Thowath, who remained composed and focused most of the time on enjoying his spaghetti, put down his spoon and fork, cleaned his mouth, and simply told Robin, "Come to my office to discuss such matters." Enraged, Robin said he wanted his response immediately. Thowath got up and paid his bill, then turned to Robin. "You are a racist and chauvinist pig. If that is how you want to play, then fuck your convention, fuck your HC, and more importantly, fuck you." Thowath left for his office, suggesting that we could still come, should we wish to discuss permit issues.

The three PTSS colleagues all expressed their admiration and support for Thowath. I sent a radio message to Addis informing them of the situation unfolding. Ray Fell got back to me and confirmed that he had consulted with Mr. Bwakira, who wanted me to do whatever I could to resolve the issue. I promptly called Gorfeneh, the driver, and requested he bring a Land Cruiser full of petrol and leave the key in the car. We all put our bags in the car and I drove the team to the security office, where we collected the permits and drove to Itang. Robin was busy with his memo. He called me later over the radio and was upset, to say the least. The mission stayed a couple days in Itang, before returning to Addis.

Sometime later, Robin aggressed the deputy commissioner of the RRC, and he was asked to leave the country. And later, he left the organization to join an NGO.

The above was not an isolated incident, inasmuch as I had earlier experienced the difficult relationship we had with an international colleague, Rodrigues, in Dire Dawa. Rodrigues, who was a field officer, and like me, reported to the head of suboffice, had taken for granted that since he was an international staff member, he was to be my supervisor. He came to Adigala and rudely asked me to address him as *Sir* in the presence of the local military commander, Colonel Girma. I refused and had nasty exchanges prior to his departure by train. He brought up insubordination and use of abusive language charges against me. As the head of suboffice was unable to resolve the conflict locally, it was referred to Addis, where I was summoned to explain myself to a committee headed by the deputy, Kwame Afriye, and Colin Mitchell. As the consultation resumed with both of us in attendance, Rodrigues started by referring to me as "This boy." I immediately objected to the use of the term, which I considered derogatory. Mr. Afriye agreed, and a debate between him and Rodrigues started. I was asked to leave, and that was that.

Upon return to Dire Dawa, Rodrigues went to his hotel, and that same evening claimed to have fallen in the bathtub while taking a shower, and had hit his head. The local physician could not verify what was wrong with him. Addis was contacted, and a medical evacuation was immediately undertaken by air to Geneva through Nairobi. Later, we heard that the Geneva doctors could not find anything wrong with him, and the organization had decided not to extend his contract.

The above incidents illustrate that some of our international staff, like Robin, ex-British military, or Rodrigues, would come to Africa and pretend to be the champions of the Mandate without showing any respect or understanding of the prevailing local situation or culture. Racist and condescending attitudes were demonstrated consciously or otherwise. A few of the Western international staff in the UNHCR had what I would call a "we are the donors" mentality, which I have observed in various African countries, Asia, and even at headquarters in Geneva. After all, it will be a long time before a fundraising organization like the UNHCR will have an African high commissioner.

In sharp contrast to the arrogant behavior demonstrated by some international colleagues, there are also those that adopt the refugees as their children, like the replacement of Robin, Ms. Candida Toscani. She would bring refugee children gifts from Italy, and invite local officials and refugee leaders to her house for drinks and dinner. She took a special liking to young, tall Dinka men, and had adopted as her son a young SPLA pilot residing in Gambella, whom I met at her place every time I went on mission. Obviously, such generosity generated speculation and rumors.

The above recollections have been shared because they highlight that there are some bad apples amidst the broad humanitarian community who should be named and shamed so that the image of the great majority of outstanding staff will not be tarnished.

Establishment of Dimma Refugee Camp

Reports were received of South Sudanese new arrivals in Keffa, close to the border, and that a site had to be identified to move them away from the border. I and Yalew, the driver, left for Jimma, where I met the administrator of the province, Colonel Kebede Gurmu, a former police officer who resented fieldwork and held himself in high-esteem. He drove with me to Mizan, where he directed the Awraja administrator, Aberra, to go with me. Aberra and I went to Bebeka farm, where we spent the night at the guest house in the middle of the farm at an elevated location with a breathtaking view. Apparently, the guest house was built to accommodate a visit to the farm by Fidel Castro, who, together with Mengistu Haile Mariam, spent a night there. I stayed in room number one, and excellent food was prepared and served by the resident cook. After breakfast, we drove to Dimma some thirty kilometers away.

The wildlife we saw on the way, including elephants and a variety of antelopes, was mesmerizing. As we approached Dimma, we were caught in the rain and our car got stuck in the mud. We got out and walked around shallow, undulating mountains, and down below the Dimma River running in the valley. The site had apparently been selected as a possible settlement for nationals being relocated from the drought-affected highlands of Ethiopia. We agreed on the spot of the site to be recommended for the establishment of the refugee camp.

Our car was finally pulled out of the mud by an Army Oural 4320 six-wheel-drive truck that was passing by. We drove back to Bebeka, where we spent the night, and left for Mizan in the early morning. We met the governor and briefed him at the hotel-bar where he was staying. We briefed him on what we considered to be an appropriate location in Dimma. I promised the governor that UNHCR would brief the minister of the Interior and also expressed our gratitude for the support I had received from him and his team.

In Addis, following briefings at the RLO, I joined the representative and his deputy to brief the minister of the Interior on the mission and its recommendations. Upon our arrival, we were ushered into the minister's office, when Minister Endale, full of smiles, took no time in informing UNHCR of what his team had done in the field, and that the government was proposing the relocation of refuges to the Dimma site, where a camp was to be constructed. The objective and tone of our visit to the minister changed, and we ended up thanking him for the government's moves and decisions. It was agreed that the high commissioner would visit the refugees as part of his mission to Ethiopia. It was apparent that the administrator had briefed the minister as to what he and his team had done, and what he was proposing. Well, as the saying goes, *the proof of the pudding is in the eating.* We thanked the minister and praised the governor for his recommendation.

High Commissioner Jean-Pierre Hocké visited Ethiopia and was taken to meet the new refugees. In the debriefing that was held at the RLO, Ray Fell shared with him a copy of our submission to headquarters for allocation of emergency funds. Hocké was supportive, and suggested that a team of experts from headquarters should come out immediately to assist. I suggested that we initiate the work, as we had already identified local experts. The headquarters experts could come at a later stage to evaluate the work and suggest whatever improvements, if any. The high commissioner and the head of desk traveling with him must have made the right calls to Geneva, as an emergency letter of instruction approving our submission was received by telex the following day.

I called upon Getachew Mahateme Selassie of the Ethiopian Red Cross Society-UNHCR unit to take a team from Itang, including the experienced health officer, Mulugeta, and to proceed to Mizan immediately. The team from Itang brought along emergency rations and medical supplies and food was diverted from the ongoing refugee feeding program. We all met in Mizan and traveled to where refugees had crossed into Ethiopia. The Red Cross team undertook a health assessment and provided intravenous (IV) drips to sick refugees, and food rations to the rest. We concluded that while those with critical needs required air transport, the great majority could be transported by trucks.

In Addis, we negotiated the free-of-charge use of four Russian helicopters that had come to airdrop relief items in the drought-affected north of the country. We agreed to pay for fuel, and the Russians airlifted those refugees with critical needs from the entry point to the Dimma refugee camp. Army six-wheel trucks transported the rest overland.

UNHCR recruited and deployed George Antonatos, who worked tirelessly with the Red Cross team to establish one of the best refugee camps in Africa, according to a Programme and Technical Support Service (PTSS) mission that visited the site two months later, involving Ms, Wairimu Karago from the branch office, and Rene Thiadens and Daniel Mora Castro. A tall and well-built local cadre of the Party, Shanko Gaganos provided liaison services with the Army for whatever support needed. SPLA fighters were not allowed in the camp that was secured by the local Army.

As a footnote, I have observed on several occasions that UN staff, upon assignment, assume or make-believe that a particular operation in their area of assignment was in fact started or initiated by themselves. No effort is made to either take note, acknowledge, or appreciate what their predecessors or the preceding team has achieved prior to their assignment. A good illustration: Following my assignment to Malawi, I visited Dimma while on home leave a year after my reassignment. I met the head of the UNHCR suboffice in Dimma, Mr. Donald Kwait, a Zambian with a Swedish passport. Donald organized a briefing for me with his staff and NGO partners, during which he explained how the camp was established and the role he and his team played in that. That statement brought an immediate reaction from the longest serving person in Dimma, Getachew of the Red Cross, who informed all those gathered that it was in fact the very person standing in front of them all that identified the location and brought him to the site. Most of the camp was constructed before my departure to Malawi. Donald thanked Getachew for his update, and continued to provide statistics and assistance package information. At no time, then or after, did he ask me about my experience in Dimma, or apologize for the wrong claim. At a later stage, I actually saw a recommendation from the representative in Addis for the promotion of Donald, claiming that he had established the camp. Donald was promoted, but he did not last long in the organization.

Assosa-Tsore Refugee Camp

Following the takeover of the Kurmuk area by SPLA forces, refugees were reported to have crossed over into the Assosa district. The Kurumuk incident was the first time the SPLA had moved north of South Sudan and carried out operations, which resulted later in the creation of the SPLM-North. I undertook a mission with Asfaha of the RRC-UNHCR Coordination Office.

We were met and hosted by Ato Getachew Ayele, who headed the Assosa office of the main RRC. While on a field mission to look at refugee border crossing points, we were turned back by the Army, reportedly exchanging fire with the Oromo Liberation Front (OLF) fighters. We were briefed on the OLF's frequent infiltrations into the Assosa district from the Sudan, and that they were trying to mobilize the local population against the government resettlement program. Movements in the evenings or early mornings in or out of Assosa were not allowed. We were briefed while in Assosa town that clashes between the SPLA and the OLF were too common along the border and inside the Sudan. It was alleged that the Eritrean EPLF and the Sudanese Army were backing the OLF, while the Ethiopian Army was providing logistics and other support to the SPLA.

Having visited the new arrivals in Ethiopia on various entry points, we met the local governor and agreed on the establishment of an emergency task force to coordinate the assistance program. I represented UNHCR on that committee, which included the RRC, as well as various government departments. A site some twelve kilometers southwest of Assosa-Tsore was allocated by the government, and the relocation of refugees from the various entry points commenced.

Given the strong RRC presence in Assosa, primarily due to

the implementation of the then ongoing government resettlement program, we agreed that the RRC-UNHCR Coordination Unit should assume responsibility for implementation of the Tsore refugee program. The refugee program initially relied on the RRC local office and the guest house. Food, shelter material, and health services were provided by the RRC. UNHCR recruited and deployed Mr. Brehan Haile Meskel, who had previously worked with Mr. Ramiro Lopez da Silva in the WFP-WTOE transport project, and who assumed responsibility for monitoring and reporting on the refugee program in Assosa. Upon his assumption of duties, and the recruitment of additional RRC project staff, the emergency task force disbanded and I returned to Addis.

Enduring moments from those days include the recollection of a small town, Assosa, where recent settlers and locals would venture in to buy essentials such as oil and soap, or enjoy local brews. The largest hotel in town was the Deriba Hotel, where we would stop over for food. While asking for breakfast or lunch, the young waiter would always run into the kitchen to ask the cook what was available. He would run back and inform us of the various food items that were under preparation, but would conclude by saying that unfortunately his mother, the cook, had gone to the market to get oil or some other ingredient, and would be back soon. We had to leave hungry on several occasions, or settle for bread bought from a shop next door and served with tea.

SPLA officers would also come for drinks in the evenings at the Deriba Hotel. South Sudanese military respected the civilian nature of Tsore camp and avoided it. However, I recall once, when we were at Tsore camp monitoring the setting up of various social service centers, a well-dressed and well-spoken refugee approached me, Brehan, and Getachew of the RRC, and informed us that the SPLA commander, Karibino, had crossed over from Kurmuk, Sudan, and was extending an invitation to meet with us a few kilometers away from Tsore. We accepted the invitation and followed our guide along a dusty road, through thick bushes, until we reached a cleared area with a dusty camp made of scattered temporary grass huts.

In the middle of the "military camp" was a well-built structure with thatched roof, and a shade next to it with troops, armed with AK-47s, who were lined up apparently to welcome us, the visitors. A flamboyant, well-dressed officer wearing a Sudanese general's official ceremonial attire decorated with a variety of medals came to welcome us and invited us to inspect the guard of honor. Anti-aircraft salvoes were fired in an apparent gun salute as part of the welcoming ceremony. The firing was so sudden and loud that some of us ducked to the ground. We were then ushered into the shade, where Karibino sat on a wooden highchair and lectured us on the recent successes of the struggle, and the many senior Arab generals he had personally killed. We were served food and warm whisky before being escorted out of the camp. The following day, we heard that an SPLA radio station had carried the news that a high-level Ethiopian delegation had met Karibino during a military graduation ceremony. Apparently, no mention of the UN presence was made, and we were grateful for that. Trying to keep humanitarian and protection support to refugees in an ever-changing environment involving armed belligerents was a challenge at the time, and still remains being so.

At a later stage, I learned that Tsore refugee camp was attacked at night and burnt to the ground by an OLF unit allegedly supported by the TPLF. Refugees and camp workers were scattered in the bush. A new site in Sherkole was identified, and a new camp was constructed from scratch, and the scattered refugees were gathered and resettled.

It is interesting to observe that there is no documented information readily available on Tsore camp. I could not find a single serving UNHCR staff member who had any information on the existence of the camp. For all intents and purposes, it was as if it never existed. That reality encouraged me to include my recollection of the domed camp, if for nothing else, for posterity.

SPLM–SPLA and the Game of Hide and Seek

The challenge of maintaining the civilian character of refugee camps and keeping SPLM military establishments separate and away from civilian refugee camps was a constant headache for all involved in the assistance and protection activities.

The SPLA viewed itself as a legitimate African liberation movement fighting Arab colonialism, and wanted to be treated equal with other liberation movements based in frontline states in southern Africa. We would have frank and candid exchanges with the Refugee Coordination Committee in Itang, which was supposedly elected by refugees to represent their interests. The committee was chaired by the former deputy dean of Juba University, and was composed of at least five PhD holders. The Refugee Coordination Committee chairman later on elected Dr. Amoun, currently a senior parliamentarian, who was later replaced by Taban Deng, who has now been appointed vice president of South Sudan, and has become a general.

These intellectuals saw themselves as freedom fighters, and even though they were not carrying arms, supported the SPLM-The Sudan People's Liberation Army (SPLA) whole-heartedly. They noted that refugees had the right to express their political opinion, which they considered a basic human right. The refugees were not active fighters but supported the struggle. The challenge was how to ensure that one does not crossover into the other realm while staying in Itang.

The SPLA, like the Eritrean liberation fronts (ELF and EPLF), the Oromo Liberation Movement, (OLF) or the Tigray Peoples' Liberation Front (TPLF), were known to get involved within the country of origin to assist and guide refugees across the border at specific points, and head to a particular location to seek asylum. The Sudan government provided a rear base for the various Ethiopian ethnic liberation movements, while the Ethiopian government provided an array of support to the SPLA.

Food supplies being diverted from the refugee camps further complicated the situation, as it was entangled with the selling of food and non-food items by refugees to buy legitimately what they needed. Refugee oil supplied by USAID, finding its way into the local market in Gambella town or shops, all the way back to Addis, was a common sight. Young boys doing group sports and staying together as unaccompanied minors was another feature of Itang camp that was subject to various speculations and scrutiny by various journalist missions to Gambella.

Like most refugee situations, the registration process could easily be implemented and monitored as new arrivals came into the camp. However, the ability to deregister departures remained a challenge. The inability to systematically deregister refugee departures from the camp for good can partially be redressed through a verification exercise. How frequently to organize and fund such an exercise was yet another challenge. The SPLA recruiting from amongst the refugees was constantly alleged but difficult to prove. We all suspected and knew, to a point, that it was happening. The alleged recruitment of refugees by the SPLA and food diversion had become the main talking point with the host government.

The inflation of refugee figures was inadvertently encouraged and supported by the UN arrangement that was in place, which asserted that refugee camps with less than twenty thousand would be fed by UNHCR through bilateral contributions. Any figure of refugees at one location above twenty thousand would qualify for a predictable and sustained food assistance through the WFP. The refugees, the SPLM, and the Government of Ethiopia preferred the WFP option, as it gave them flexibility and predictability. After all, the WFP did not deploy staff to monitor food distribution at field level.

The sale of jute bags was yet another lucrative incentive sought after by all parties. Jute bags bringing imported WFP grains would be sold locally to supposedly cover food handling costs. Refugee volunteers were used to handle loading, unloading, and distribution of food. The empty bags were collected and sold by the Refugee Coordination Committee, and the generated income was passed on to the liberation movement. Local officials were also known to be benefiting from the sales.

A Journalist's Mission that Nearly Went Wrong

Visit to refugee camps by international journalists was a common phenomenon at the time. The UNHCR encouraged it as part of its resource mobilization strategy while geopolitical considerations of the Cold War era, coupled with interest in the evolution of the Sudanese Peoples Liberation Movement, gave journalists an additional incentive to visit the country and refugee locations. The journalist missions were politicized, and created tense moments.

Of the various journalist missions I had accompanied to the South Sudanese refugee camps, one mission in particular stands out. A group of journalists from Geneva, New York, and Nairobi, numbering some fifteen in total, came to visit the South Sudanese refugee program in Itang in early 1986. The Itang refugee camp was the largest refugee camp in Africa at the time. In fact, the Itang camp had also grown to be the second largest "city" in Ethiopia, with a larger population than Dire Dawa or Asmara.

The journalist team was headed by the UNHCR public information officer, Ms. Maria Hutchinson. I joined the group in Addis, and we departed early from their hotel to the airport. The one-day mission was expected to return to Addis the same evening. Unfortunately, our chartered Ethiopian Airlines DC-3 plane departed late from Addis to Gambella, as the assigned pilot was reported sick and a replacement had to be found. A Boeing 707 pilot, who must have had a rough evening, and who admittedly had not flown a DC-3 for a long time, was assigned. The weather was bad and visibility was poor when we took off from Bole International Airport.

After flying for a couple hours, the pilot could not find the runway in Gambella, allegedly due to poor visibility as a result of low cloud cover. The co-pilot, when I went to the cockpit to check, claimed to have seen a Sudanese flag when the plane went under the clouds, and suggested that we could have crossed the border by mistake. Following a brief exchange not involving the journalists, we agreed that the pilot should return us to Addis. The pilot responded by confirming that he was returning, but might not have enough fuel. We flew back and landed at Jimma Airport for refueling.

While the pilot was discussing the next moves with his HQ, I had a tough time explaining to the journalists that this was not a staged act. Unfortunately for me, a small Dash-5 Ethiopian Airlines plane landed in Jimma. Upon inquiry, the journalists found out that the plane was returning from Gambella, and that the weather was clear there. That confirmed to the suspicious ones that the mission was being stage-managed to avoid the journalists from going to Gambella to visit the refugee sites.

I explained the situation to the pilot, and we jointly addressed our concerns to Ethiopian Airlines (EAL) headquarters. I argued that a return to Addis directly from Jimma would send the wrong message to the journalists and could negatively tarnish the image of the country. The EAL management agreed that we should try again. We also got their agreement to keep the plane overnight in Gambella at no cost to UNHCR. The captain pledged to fly under the clouds to best of his ability, as he was blaming the faulty compass on the plane for the mess-up.

We flew low and landed at Gambella's dusty airstrip, where the sky was clear. Upon arrival, I explained to the head of suboffice, Candida Toscani, what had transpired, and requested her permission to take the mission directly from the landing strip to Itang, even though they were hungry and thirsty. She agreed, and we proceeded in a convoy on the fifty-minute drive to the refugee camp.

In Itang, the journalists turned down an offer to be briefed by UNHCR, the Red Cross, and the RRC teams on the ground. I requested our local hosts to serve water, and gave the journalists the liberty to move around, talk to whomever they wanted, and return to base when they were tired. Scattered, tired, and covered in dust, they drank water and ate high-energy biscuits provided by the Red Cross feeding program. The journalists interviewed refugees and visited dwellings and social facilities all over the camp. One by one, they returned to the designated assembly point, exhausted. As the last journalist arrived, we departed from Itang.

We drove back to Gambella and spent the evening at the Ethiopia Hotel, where dinner was hosted by Candida. I received their apologies, and over dinner, together with Candida, we answered most of their questions. In the early morning, during the breakfast exchange, the head of the delegation from the UNHCR Public Information section at headquarters, the good-looking lady from the Caribbean, Ms. Maria Hutchinson, confided in me that the mission had been met by staff from the Sudanese Embassy at the Hilton Hotel in Addis upon their arrival. They were briefed and made to understand that the camps in Gambella were in reality an SPLA military base for rest and recuperation. They did not expect to see what they saw, and they were all satisfied that the refugee camp was, by and large, a civilian dwelling.

We flew back to Addis on the chartered plane, and the captain looked rested and more relaxed. He took the plane to a cruising altitude, which made the return smooth and not half as bumpy as that of the day before.

The Lost Boys of Sudan

The war between the SPLA and the Sudanese government, by the mid-1980s, had already claimed more than five hundred thousand lives and displaced huge numbers of people. Among these were at least twenty thousand children, mostly boys, between seven and seventeen years of age, who were separated from their families. These unaccompanied minors, who came to be known as the Lost Boys of the Sudan, trekked enormous distances over a vast, unforgiving wilderness, seeking refuge from the fighting. Hungry, frightened, and weakened by sleeplessness and disease, they crossed from the Sudan into Ethiopia, and some were ushered into existing camps of Itang and Dimma by the SPLA. It was a strange phenomenon to observe young boys who cooked and ate together, living in their own self-built string of thatched dwellings that replaced tents issued to them upon arrival. They played together and seldom mixed with the camp population. Those recruited to join the SPLA were taken out of the civilian camps in Itang and Dimma.

This extraordinary exodus had its origins in traditional forms of migration. After being initiated into manhood, young adolescent boys in southern Sudan have generally been mobile. Organized into small groups of their peers, they would leave home for a period to look after cattle. Or they might head for the towns or cities to go to school or to seek their fortune, before eventually returning home. During the war, this process escalated dramatically. Fearing they would be targeted as potential combatants, many boys left their villages and headed for cities such as Juba and Khartoum. Here, they hoped to find work or schooling, though as these cities became saturated with migrants, the boys often had to resort to begging or petty crime.

Motivated by the additional incentive of loss of their parents and their need to find food and safety from the conflict, an estimated twenty thousand boys from rural South Sudan fled to bordering Ethiopia and Kenya. Much of the travel took place by foot in large groups, with the boys traveling in single file lines. The journey from South Sudan to the nearest refugee camp could be up to thousands of miles. Travel ranged from a span of weeks to two or more years. Often, the children traveled with no possessions besides the clothes on their backs. The Boys often depended on the charity of villages they passed through, for food, necessities, and treatment of the sick. However, most of their travel was in isolated regions with minimal infrastructure. Groups of Boys were often organized and led by the oldest boy in the group, who could be a young adult, or sometimes as young as ten or twelve years old.

During this migration, the Lost Boys were extremely malnourished, as food was sourced through hunting, theft, and donations from villages encountered along the way. They were also vulnerable to heat exhaustion, pneumonia, malaria, and other diseases for which they had little means of prevention or treatment. Additionally, attacks by lions, snakes, and other wild animals were not uncommon. It is estimated that over half of the young migrants died along their journey due to starvation, dehydration, disease, attacks by wild animals and enemy soldiers. Conditions were made even more dangerous by the SPLA soldiers, who would attack the boys and forcibly recruit them as child soldiers. The SPLA estimated that twelve hundred boys were recruited from groups of displaced children, although they deny forcing any of them into conflict. Experts say the Lost Boys are the most badly war-traumatized children ever examined.

The survivors who reached the camps in Ethiopia started to lead a relatively peaceful life. But it was not to last. Following the change of government in Ethiopia in May 1991, they had to flee again, back to camps in the Sudan. This time, the journey was during heavy rains, and many perished crossing the swollen rivers, or were hit by aerial bombardment. Fighting erupted around them, and they, as well as children from other camps, were on the move once more, eventually heading for Kenya.

The journey of the Lost Boys was filled with suffering and unknowns, as the boys rarely knew the direction they were headed. They drew global media attention that engendered political and public support for the peace process in Sudan, and ultimately facilitated the resettlement of nearly four thousand of them in the United States.

A unique problem for the story of the Lost Boys is how the age and family structure dynamics of the camps changed with the influx of young people. The Lost Boys came to the camps without guardians or adult supervision. They immediately required housing and schooling, which changed the allocation of resources in the camps.

It is tragic that in 1991, the camps at Itang and Dimma were dispersed when the TPLF-led forces overthrew the Government of Ethiopia and most of the refugees fled back into South Sudan with the Lost Boys heading out to Kenya.

It is worth observing that in 2000, as part of a program established by the United States government and the United Nations High Commissioner for Refugees (UNHCR), approximately four thousand Lost Boys were offered resettlement in the United States. More also ended up in Australia, New Zealand, and other resettlement countries in Europe.

Although there is much attention directed toward the Lost Boys, common historical narratives often ignore their counterparts, the Lost Girls. Even before the conflict, inequalities between the Lost Boys and Lost Girls were manifested in the cultural practices of the Dinka and Nuer people. This marginalization heavily influenced their post-conflict recovery and integration in refugee camps and resettlement programs.

As mentioned above, upon their arrival in the camps in Ethiopia, the boys were placed into boys-only areas of the camp. Yet according to Sudanese culture, the girls could not be left alone, so they were placed with surviving family members, or adopted by other Sudanese families. Although these family placement practices provided security for young women, families often exploited the extra pair of hands at home. The girls were expected to fulfill numerous domestic responsibilities that were often taxing or even dangerous. The expectations of domestic work often prevented the girls and young women from attending school while in the camps, and even when allowed to attend, their housework often kept them behind their male classmates, who had time to study. In this way, girls were prevented from earning a formal education, further entrenching them in their inability to sustain themselves. Many girls were physically and/or sexually abused by their host families, raped by other refugees during activities such as fetching water or food rations, and occasionally, even sold as brides for profit. In each of these examples, the girls were taken in only as a potential profit or benefit to the family.

When the US resettlement program began in 2000, one requirement was that the children must be orphans. Because these girls had been living within a family unit for anywhere from nine to fourteen years, they were no longer considered orphans, and therefore were ineligible for the resettlement program. As a result, relatively few of the Lost Girls were able to benefit from the resettlement program to the US. Of the four thousand Sudanese refugees approved in 2000, only eighty-nine were women.

The Alain Peters Regime

Since my recruitment into the UNHCR, I had grown to appreciate the management style of the regional liaison representative, Mr. Nicolas Bwakira. He headed operations in Ethiopia, but also acted as the liaison to the African Union, thus the title Regional Liaison Office (RLO). He supported and encouraged locally recruited staff to act on par with international recruits. I remember Mr. Bwakira stating, in no uncertain terms, in meetings attended by his deputy, Ray Fell, myself, and many more, that what counted for him was the contribution of each staff member, and not his or her status. He would add: "If we were working in our home countries, we would be local staff."

Bwakira fought for the rights of national staff. I do recall the mission of Mr. Dan Conway, head of Division of Human Resource Management (DHRM), in 1985, where Mr. Bwakira had drawn UNHCR's attention to the fact that UNICEF had introduced the National Professional category in recognition of the professional work being undertaken by national staff. Conway's mission resulted in the introduction of the National Professional Officers (NOA) category in 1986. I and another colleague, Manikullehe Shiferaw, were among the first in UNHCR to be converted from the General Service to the National Officer category in 1986.

Following the reassignment of Mr. Bwakira, Mr. Alain Peters took charge of the RLO. It was soon clear that Mr. Peters was bringing a new type of management, which was based on loyalty, order, and respect of hierarchy. Africans, not nationals, were more equal than others. West Africans felt more at home than the others, while whites were treated with contempt and racism.

The weekly briefing of staff was chaired by Mr. Peters, who solicited opinions on participation of local staff in such meetings. The deputy representative, Ray Fell, explained that the meeting involved all professionals irrespective of grade, or national or international posting. My first conflict with the new representative was during one such meeting, where he informed us of a letter he was drafting to be submitted to the government to lodge a complaint about delays in getting security clearance for field travel, and he asked for our opinion. I shared mine, suggesting that we find out more about why a particular security clearance was being delayed before sending a protest. Mr. Peters abruptly suspended the meeting, and through his secretary, requested my immediate presence in his office. Upon going into his office, he explained to me that even the High Commissioner (HC) does not tell him in public that he was wrong, and wanted to know who I thought I was. I politely replied that I was simply sharing my thoughts, as requested by him. I suggested that he should not ask for views if those views were going to annoy him. Then I left.

During the following week's meeting, Mr. Peters rudely requested his deputy, Ray Fell, to stop taking notes while he was talking. Ray usually prepared the notes of such meetings, including the collective decisions taken. Most of us in the office could not comprehend or adjust to the new management style.

In a memo signed by Mr. Peters, I was transferred to the Ethiopian Return and Reintegration desk and told to hand over all South Sudanese refugees files to Sayio Saidi, who had served as the head of the Reintegration section until then. The other officer, Victor Nyerenda, made it clear to me that he had no job for me. I took it easy by coming late and leaving early from the office. Frustration was setting in as I contemplated other options, including leaving UNHCR.

During a mission by a team from headquarters to Gambella, apparently the then head of suboffice, Mr. Fabrice Gossan, had replied to some queries by the mission members, suggesting that they speak to Mengesha for better details in Addis. The head of desk from Geneva, Mr. Dan Fowler, briefed me on the developments in Gambella upon their return to Addis. Upon Fowler's request, I addressed some of the questions raised by the mission. Two days later, a note was issued reinstating me to my previous position.

It was an eye opener to observe that a change in the management of a UN office could bring about change in office relationships and management styles, as if a new political party with a different policy and agenda from the previous regime had come to power. The transition from one head of office to another amplifies that point. I did observe later that the Addis experience was not an exception. Incoming representatives will change management, and even immediately change the official cars and refurbish the office.

Dan Fowler, as head of desk, informed me that a submission had already been made and that my NOA post was being upgraded to a P4 international function. That upgraded post was to be filled by a newly recruited staff member from the DRC—Ray Chipanda. The other mission member, Ernest Chipman, confirmed the development and suggested that I consider reassignment to Malawi, as I could end up jobless. I agreed on the understanding that I would try it out for a couple months and decide whether to remain or return. My decision, if I call it that, to go international was thus based on developments that came about as a result of regime change in the country office management of the RLO.

The UNHCR Regional Liaison Office in Addis Ababa

Even though I spent significant time out in the field, my assignment and duty station as focal point for the Sudanese program remained at the Regional Liaison Office (RLO) in Addis Ababa. The *liaison* part signifies the accreditation of the representative in Ethiopia, and also the Organisation of African Unity. The office was located on the main Bole Road, in a building we shared with the European Union. The management structure was that the representative, Nicolas Bwakira, had a deputy, Ray Fell, who headed the Program unit, which in turn was subdivided into the East (Returnees from Somalia and Djibouti) and the West (South Sudanese and the North (Eritrea). I was the desk officer for the Program in the West. Community services were provided by a small unit headed by Manikulehe Shiferaw. The Administration, Finance, and Protection units were the two sectors that reported to the representative. The Protection unit had Nini Akiwumi, then Ernest Allison, and Wairimu Karago. Administration and Finance was headed by a Burmese, Mr. Kwa Zin Hla.

The office was vibrant and had a good hype to it. I received secretarial and program support from Hiruit Kassaye, who was respected and feared by most, as she gave each staff a label, which stuck. Kwa Zin Hla, who spoke a lot, was nicknamed "Zergaw," or "the stretched tongue," which has remained his call sign to date. The drivers, like their counterparts in any office around the world, had their own dynamics and characters. Some like Sirak, who attended the English School with me, had gone through a social transformation, as the family holding was nationalized during the revolution, and out of need and survival, had become a driver. Gorfeneh Girma fell in that same category. Others came from different backgrounds but were held together by the shared behaviors. Delivery of a letter to the Ministry of Foreign Affairs would take a whole day at times, and all had developed the art of telling convincing stories for either a delay or an absence from an assignment.

My schoolmate and driver, Sirak, was assigned to the representative. He had involved himself in a relationship with a demanding lady who owned a bar and was apparently difficult to satisfy. Sirak took the representative's Mercedes car for servicing on a Friday. It turned out the Burundi ambassador had noticed the car parked at the Langano lake resort, and asked Mr. Bwakira if he had enjoyed his trip there over the weekend. On Monday, Bwakira asked Sirak about the car, which he confirmed to still be in the garage, where he had taken it on Friday. Mr. Bwakira decided to fire Sirak for his wrongdoing and for lying. Sirak panicked and asked for my intervention, as I had also just been elected staff representative. I spoke to Bwakira and sought the support of his wife, Cyrilla, who was supportive. We convinced Mr. Bwakira to reassign Sirak to Gambella instead of firing him. That was done.

Friday afternoon barbeques at the office, and monthly parties at the representative's residence attended by all, remain a significant portion of my cherished memories of the RLO. Mama Desta, who served coffee and made breakfast on demand, was an icon of that era.

It is noted that in enormous and protracted refugee situations, local staff in the host countries had the opportunity to not only transition from General Service (GS) positions to the International Professional category, but also assume high levels of responsibility over time, including Country Representative. To mention but a few names of those who served with me as GS staff in Ethiopia: Aida Haile Mariam excelled in the organization to become the Representative in Ghana, West Africa before her retirement. Askale Benti had also become a reputable international senior logistics officer, while Abdul-Kadir Jamma served as head of suboffice in Herat, Afghanistan, and as representative in Malawi. Manikulehe Shiferraw served as head of field offices in South Africa, Tanzania, and Angola, while Girmai Wondimu became assistant representative for operations in South Sudan. Asfaw Legesse retired as a senior administration and finance officer in the UNHCR hub in Budapest, having served at various locations in Africa and Asia. Befekadu Berhanu excelled in finance and

IT, and retired as deputy director of the Division of Information Systems and Telecommunications (DIST).

Similarly, national staff who served in UNHCR operations in the Sudan and Pakistan have also grown within the organization's ranking system, and ended up assigned to international functions. Many have ended up in senior assignments, and the organization needs to be commended for recognizing the performance, experience, and contribution of these staff members.

The Passing of My Father

My father had developed breathing problems, and we all assumed he was having one of his usual asthma attacks. Upon arriving home in the evening, things were just not right, as Abune Indreas, who headed the Emperor Menelik Memorial Institute, was sitting next to his bed, and Father looked frail and was having difficulty breathing. In the morning, the family assembled, and we decided that he should be hospitalized. My brother Kassa came with two Ethiopian doctors, Dawit and Redda, accompanied by a visiting medical doctor from the USA. They examined Father and suggested that he be moved to the Black Lion Hospital for further examination and treatment. I joined Kassa and others by going to the hospital and renting a private room for father. Upon our return home to collect him, my other older brother, Yilma, met us at the car and simply said, "He is gone." I do not recall any other moment or incident in life that left me so stunned and shocked.

Father was buried on April 19, 1985, on the grounds of the Trinity Cathedral, with all honors and a well-attended funeral procession. Mourning lasted a couple days as relatives and friends were coming to the house to share their grief.

Engagement and Marriage

I first met my spouse to-be, Abenet Assegid, at the Itang refugee camp in 1985, where she worked as a nutritionist with the Ethiopian Red Cross Society. We started dating at a later stage in Addis. While I was contemplating an international assignment, we agreed to get engaged by signing an undertaking at the municipality in 1986. At the time, based on each of our families' understanding and dominant norms of society, going to the municipality and signing a commitment to marry was understood to be an "engagement." However, getting the certificate from the municipality, based on UN rules and regulations, was confirmation of marriage. Therefore, upon my engagement, I shared the certificate with the UNHCR administration, and Abenet was recognized as my spouse, with entitlement to travel with me at the UN's expense.

Malawi is also the place where I experienced firsthand the difficulties faced by international civil servants in bringing up a family in a remote location away from home. As mentioned earlier, according to the UN, I married my wife in Addis prior to my departure to Malawi. Abenet initially came and stayed with me in Ntcheu for a couple months, before proceeding to the USA. We met back in Addis during my home leave, and threw our wedding party and the official church wedding ceremony in 1988, which got our union recognized by our families and society at large.

Following our church wedding, I had to proceed to Namibia on mission, so Abenet stayed behind in Addis, and that was also the time I found out that she was pregnant. We agreed that she deliver in Windhoek, where the facilities were good quality. Abenet flew out from Addis to Angola and came to Windhoek on a returnee flight. My first daughter, Natena, was born in Windhoek Hospital. I do recall the head matron of that hospital suggesting that Abenet and our newborn be transferred by ambulance to a hospital in either Kata Tura or Comesdal, as the Windhoek Hospital was restricted to White use only. The suggestion was overruled by the doctor, who not only delivered my daughter, but had her moved to a first-class room, which had its own visitors lounge. Hospital staff was overjoyed and singing, "We shall overcome one day."

We returned to Malawi following a baptism stopover in Addis for our newborn daughter.

Endnote

1   Red terror and White terror: the Ethiopian Red Terror was a violent political repression campaign of the Derg against other com-

peting Marxist-Leninist groups in Ethiopia from 1976 to 1977. It was based on the Red Terror of the Russian Civil War, and most visibly took place after Mengistu Haile Mariam became Chairman of the Derg on February 3, 1977. It is estimated that over thirty thousand people were killed over the course of the Red and White Terror campaigns. The Derg labeled the EPRP's sporadic campaign of assassination of its members and supporters as the "White Terror," and promised, "for every revolutionary killed, a thousand counter-revolutionaries will be executed through the Red Terror Campaign.

CHAPTER FIVE

Again Out of Ethiopia

Malawi was my first international assignment with UNHCR, beginning in 1987. Following escalation of the Mozambique civil war, *Frente de Libertação Moçambique* (FRELIMO) versus *Resistência Nacional Moçambicana* (RENAMO), thousands of refugees crossed over into Malawi. I arrived in Lilongwe and was assigned to Ntcheu, where there was no UNHCR or any other UN field presence.

My recollection of Malawi was the generosity and welcoming nature of its people toward Mozambican refugees. In the central region of Lilongwe, Dedza and Ntchew districts, refugees literally crossed the road, which was built on the border, to seek sanctuary in Malawi. Given the linguistic and cultural similarities between the people that lived on either side of the border, refugees felt at home. Refugees were allowed to construct their dwellings in the areas of their arrival, which normally were farms of Malawians. There were no camps in the Central Region, as refugees settled in integrated villages with the locals. In most villages, refugees outnumbered locals with the Mozambican refugee population in Central and Southern Malawi exceeding one million by 1990.

Because of the integrated nature of refugee settlements, social

107

service provisions such as health, sanitation, water and education focused on expanding existing structures to absorb the additional new arrivals into the district and the host community. The District Joint Operations committees headed by the district commissioner, and involving UNHCR, NGO partners, as well as representatives of line ministries, met regularly and oversaw all aspects of planning and implementation. The district commissioners reported through the regional administrator to the Office of the President, which managed the overall coordination of the refugee protection and assistance program.

As refugees were granted access to district health facilities, the UNHCR program focused on increasing the structures and supplies needed for the health care centres to cater for the additional population. The district hospitals, as well as the outreach clinics of Dedza, Lilongwe and Ntchew more than doubled during my tenure as field officer covering those regions. The same approach was taken for schools, community centres and water points.

Malawi Under President Kamuzu Banda

Long before being assigned to Malawi, I had been reading a great deal about Hastings Kamuzu Banda, known for his strong anti-communist position on global and continental issues. I had been baffled by his pro-Western stance which had made him an ally of the Apartheid regime in South Africa, and a strong advocate of Israeli-South-African cooperation. He was also credited with having picked the name Malawi in 1964, when it broke off from the former Nyasaland.

I served in Malawi for over four years during the rule of, as he was known officially, "His Excellency, the Life President of the Republic of Malawi, Ngwazi, Dr. Hastings Kamuzu Banda." Banda, who exercised executive and legislative powers, headed the Malawi Congress Party (MCP), which was the only legally recognized party. It was that party which appointed him life president of the MCP, which was later ratified by Parliament, as President for Life of Malawi.

I first saw the president when all foreigners serving in the country were invited to attend the International Women's Day celebrations in 1988, at Blantyre Stadium. Close to some ten thousand women were either dancing or singing in the field or around the stadium. Kamuzu arrived in a black Rolls Royce, wearing a three-piece suit, matching handkerchiefs, and walking stick in hand. He went to the middle of the field and joined the women and girls in their thousands, wearing traditional long dresses with his picture printed in front and at the back, singing and dancing while occasionally wailing. He would attempt a dance and brandish his whisk, and the crowd would go wild and chant, "Kamuzu, Kamuzu," and "Kwacha, kwacha (dawn, or freedom)." He briefly addressed his embumba, flanked by Madam Kadzamira.

Madam Cecilia Tamanda Kadzamira was the official hostess of Kamuzu Banda. While she and Dr. Banda were not officially married, she served as the First Lady or official hostess for several years. During those years, she was the most powerful woman in Malawi. Ms. Kadzamira was fondly referred to as "Mama," or "Mother of the Nation." She was said to be the real power, and she headed various institutions, including the women's association.

Madam Kadzamira and her uncle John Tembo, formerly head of the MCP, were believed to control the Agricultural Development and Marketing Corporation, usually known as ADMARC, which ran the economy during my tenure. It had been set up to promote the Malawian economy by increasing the volume and quality of its agricultural exports to develop new foreign markets for the consumption of Malawian agricultural produce, and to support Malawi's farmers. With ADMARC being one of the largest landlords in rural Malawi, I also rented my house in Ntcheu from the organization.

Every meeting I attended in districts hosting Mozambican refugees, the price set by ADMARC on maize and fertilizers was the number one subject of concern expressed by inhabitants and managers alike. ADMARC was allegedly involved in the diversion of resources from smallholder farming to Kadzamira family estate holdings or affiliated members of the ruling elite. Malawians, who did not challenge the government in public at the time, would still quietly share their thoughts on the alleged corruption, abuse of office, and inefficiency in ADMARC, which would lead to the ultimate fall of the regime. Mama's influence had reached the point to where she was allegedly running the country upon my departure in 1991.

As a footnote, I would like to compare and contrast Malawi under dictatorship and upon my return on visit several years after the replacement of Kamuzu and the onset of democracy. Carjacking, robbery, or assault of any kind was non-existent during my assignment days. The major roads were well-maintained and clean. I left the keys to my house in Ntcheu with the resident helper, Nelson. I visited Malawi in 1995, and upon arrival at the Capital Hotel in Lilongwe, the registration desk requested that I leave valuables in the safe and limit my movements out of the hotel without an escort or the hotel taxi. Newspapers were visible all over town, and most carried front-page articles critical of the current government. My host from the Ministry of Local Government explained to me that articles critical of the government were the ones that sold. The drive from Lilongwe to Blantyre took double the time it took in the days of the dictatorship due to potholes and lack of maintenance. The contrast in the before and after makes one ponder about the onset of democracy in Africa.

Of the enduring memories of Malawi is the lifelong relationship I developed with friends such as Field Officer Joke Langenkamp, Protection Officer Teresa Cunha, Field Officer Chansa Kapaya, and Senior Protection Officer Seye Bajulaye.

DEPLOYMENT TO NAMIBIA

I traveled to assume my new assignment on mission to Namibia, from Malawi to Windhoek, through Johannesburg Airport. The onward flight to Windhoek was an internal local flight, with SWA being a South African colony. I arrived at Johannesburg Airport on April 2, 1989, without clear knowledge or understanding of developments on the ground in Namibia. Apparently, on April 1, 1989—D-Day for the peace plan—in the early morning, the South African Defence Force (SADF) had reported that heavily armed groups of People's Liberation Army of Namibia (PLAN) fighters had begun crossing the border and establishing positions in northern Namibia, in violation of the agreement that they should be confined to their Angolan bases. The South West Africa People's Organization (SWAPO) initially denied that it had violated the terms of the agreement, and claimed that its fighters had been going to turn in weapons to UNTAG, and had been attacked by the SADF. Apparently, a period of intense fighting had resulted in the deaths of at least 263 SWAPO freedom fighters and 27 South African troops.

Not being aware of the above situation, I presented my passport to the immigration official at the arrival desk. The officer asked if I was an Ethiopian, which I promptly confirmed. He dropped my passport under the desk and started asking me, in an aggressive and loud voice, to give him my passport. I politely reminded him that my passport was with him since I had handed it to him. What I did not know was that he had already alerted the immigration police, who came and took me to a side room and informed me that I was being detained for trying to enter the republic without proper documentation. There I was, later joined by another Ethiopian, Asfaha Bemnet, who had gone through exactly the same experience.

Both of us spent a couple days at the detention facility at the airport compound. Luckily for me and my detained compatriot, a Zambian colleague also on his way to Windhoek, was in the adjacent line and had observed what had transpired. He was apparently cleared, as Zambia was a southern African country and not communist oriented. That Zambian colleague, Cosmos Chanda, reported the incident to the UNHCR team that had come to meet us at Windhoek Airport. Later, I found out that the arbitrary detention was brought to the attention of the authorities, who had to instruct Immigration in Johannesburg to release us and put us on the next available flight. The situation in Northern Namibia was apparently under control, and the threat level had subsided.

As we were being ushered to an aircraft preparing to depart for Windhoek on the evening of our release, our passports were handed over. With a straight face, the officer explained that we must have dropped them while disembarking from the plane that

111

brought us into Johannesburg.

UNHCR's Role Within UNTAG

UNHCR was part of the UNTAG setup as part of Resolution No. 435 of the UN Security Council. The Resolution stated that all Namibian refugees or Namibian nationals detained or otherwise outside the country would be permitted to return peacefully and participate fully and freely in the electoral process without risk of arrest, detention, intimidation, or imprisonment. It also mandated UNHCR to assist the Special Representative of the Secretary General (SRSG) to ensure that "Namibians remaining outside Namibia will be given a free and voluntary choice whether to return."

Unlike for conventional voluntary repatriation processes, there was no tripartite agreement, but rather a general amnesty, successfully negotiated by UNHCR with the then administrator general, Louis Pinar, granting all returnees immunity from any criminal proceedings with respect to any criminal offenses committed by them either prior to or during their exile. Entry and reception procedures were agreed upon, the Voluntary Repatriation Form (VRF) was used as a valid travel document, and no immigration officer would ask any returnee any questions regarding their activities in exile, and that UNHCR and UNTAG CivPol and military would monitor immigration, health, and customs facilities.

UNHCR had also agreed that there would be no political activity inside or within the vicinity of entry points and reception centers. In practice, this turned out to be difficult to implement, as thousands would come to receive their leaders. The leaders, who also agreed not to use entry and reception facilities for their political work, would get off the plane waving SWAPO flags and singing revolutionary songs. Crowd management was one of the main tasks assigned to UNHCR officers who accompanied each returnee flight, and those assigned to entry and reception facilities. UNTAG military and police maintained a presence and provided security at all facilities. UNHCR was to plan and implement the repatriation of over forty-three thousand Namibian exiles, including the leadership of SWAPO. SWAPO had earlier claimed that the numbers could be as high as seventy-five thousand. The agreed entry points by air were Windhoek, Ondangwa, and Grootfontein. Entry by road, mainly for cargo, was designated to be Oshikango, Buitpos, and Venla.

I was fortunate to experience the leadership skills of Mr. Bwakira once again in Namibia, which contributed to the successful implementation of that program. I recall an attempt by a West African colleague to divide the UNHCR team into West and East Africans. He told me to my face to "Get out of my way, as we from the West have no time to waste." The attempt was squashed, and the colleague sent back. Another colleague, who insisted on maintaining two distinct groupings as Francophone and Anglophone, was also not extended. Building a cohesive team was vital, as all staff were on mission and had maintained a lien against their posts in their respective duty stations as Professional (P) or General Service (GS) staff.

A relatively unified solid team was established in a short period of time. Staff briefings included everybody, irrespective of grade or classification. All felt equally important toward the success of the operation. Cross-border relationship with colleagues, particularly Angola, were established in no time. The bondage was reinforced with the team on the Namibia side of the border sending items that were in short supply in Angola. For example, I developed a close relationship with Adey Makonnen, who was stationed in Lubango, by sending her onions upon her request ,as food items were in short supply in Angola. Similar gestures, though not initially planned, fostered a good cross-border working relationship.

Regarding his dealings with UNTAG, Bwakira offered office space to UNESCO and WFP, and provided them with secretarial support and radio communication equipment, winning them over to join the UNHCR team. Tadesse Negash of WFP, to this day, acknowledges how he felt to have been part of the UNHCR team headed by Bwakira.

For the record, UNHCR and WFP issued a common ID card for returnees to receive food, construction, and other reintegration supplies from designated outlets. We signed a common agreement with the suppliers and monitored implementation jointly. UNESCO staff worked on the education program from UNHCR premises as part of one team.

My logistics expertise was limited to a warehouse management course I undertook with WFP, and my experience in calculating and paying for grain, oil, and other non-food stuff brought in for South Sudanese refugees in Ethiopia. My experience in Malawi was also limited to field monitoring of social and food provisions for refugees. My job in Namibia, which I performed to the best of my abilities, included to "plan transport needs for returnees and cargo." I was able to train implementing agency staff in store management, recordkeeping, and introducing store documents. I took part in the allocation and delivery of all relief items to reception centers, central warehouses, and food distribution points throughout Namibia. I helped with arranging for returnee transport from entry points to reception centers, and from reception centers to final destinations, issuing transport tender, and assisting in the drafting of transport agreements with various South African companies. I also represented UNHCR on the joint UNHCR-WFP-CCN Procurement Committee for Food. I retain fond memories of the warehouse management courses I offered to storekeepers recruited by the church at reception centers, and the warm relationship that was maintained afterwards.

The planning of transport needs of returnees and cargo from countries of asylum involving aircrafts was not an area I knew much about. My supervisors kept encouraging me that I could do it. The Nairobi-based supply officer who also followed up with Geneva on contractual agreements, Jeff Groby, was supportive and encouraging.

UNHCR could have brought back the vast majority of Namibians from Angola and Zambia by road at a relatively cheaper cost. However, in southern Angola, the National Union for Total Independence of Angola (UNITA) and the People's Movement for the Liberation of Angola (MPLA) were at war. The roads from Zambia were almost unpassable, and the Caprivi was infiltrated by UNITA and their local supporters. The operation was to be conducted in a highly volatile political environment within six weeks, from June 12 to September 15, 1989, to enable returnees to register in time to participate in the election process.

Before I knew it, and given that the UK assigned logistics experts, who were either dragging their feet or were downright sabotaging the operation, I was called upon to get involved in the air logistics discussions—an area in which I had no exposure or expertise. "You can do it," Mr. Bwakira and my immediate supervisor, Ms. Karen Abu Zayd, told me, and I forged along.

In late May, I received a request for a UN flight from Windhoek to Luanda, Luanda to Lubango, and back to Windhoek. I consulted with UNTAG Air Operations and was made to understand that the only aircraft available to the UN fleet that could undertake the journey was a C-130 airplane rented by the UN from the Philippines, with its Filipino crew. In the process of arranging the flight, I found out that the list of passengers included only Mr. Bwakira, a Cuban general who served as liaison officer with UNTAG, and myself. Bwakira was to discuss a few outstanding issues with the SWAPO leadership, while I was to finalize the logistics arrangements for the return process, replacing the logistics expert consultant who had not shown up.

We undertook the flight, three of us seated on a canvas bench literally located behind the three crew, in a C-130 that was empty at the back. We had to fly out to sea, in conformity with missile avoidance protocols, before approaching Luanda, which extended the flight by a couple hours. As we landed, we were met by officials and ushered into limousines that took us straight to a guest house, which hosted several high-ranking Cuban military officers. Following a late lunch consisting of an assortment of cheese and ham, we indulged in toasting over chilled vodka, and discussed the mission with Angolan officials. We were driven in the late afternoon to the suburbs of Luanda, where SWAPO leadership was accommodated, and initiated our consultations.

The C-130 flight I undertook with Bwakira also stopped over in Lubango on the way back so we could meet UNHCR and field-based SWAPO leadership. My portion of the mission was to draft a return plan from Angola. As the Angolan government had instructed that we only use *Transportes Aéreos de Angola* (TAAG) for the return movement that cleared issues related to competitive bidding, and restricted the range of aircrafts to be used to the three available options—707, 727, and Antonov aircrafts.

With the help of TAG technical experts in both Luanda and Lubango, luckily for me, together with former Ethiopian Airlines (EAL) staff, who either knew me or my family back home, we were able to list the types of aircraft, their seating, and load-hold capacity. Landing strip lengths were determined which aircraft would go where on the three landing strips in Windhoek, Grootfontein, and Ondangwa, based on the information provided by the control tower in Namibia. We also segregated passenger and cargo flights.

The flight to bring back Sam Nujoma and the top leadership was the only exception, as Mr. Nujoma, the Head of SWAPO, informed us of his decision to use EAL for his return home. At his humble residence in Vienna, outside Luanda, Mr. Nujoma, wearing sandals, brought us, his guests a tray full of a variety of soft drinks. He spoke softly and was humble. I remember asking if we needed a clearance to use EAL from the Angolan authorities. The head of SWAPO smiled and replied, "You coordinate with EAL, and I will handle the Angolan authorities."

I shared the message upon our return with the then deputy head of EAL, Welde Gabriel. A couple days later, EAL confirmed the government's decision to release the latest Boeing 767 aircraft for the return of the top leadership of SWAPO. I was also informed that Namibian pilots, being trained in Addis Ababa, would be on the flight as passengers, but dressed in pilot uniforms for photo opportunities on the ground. I had cautioned that the pilots might not be allowed in, as they were not holding VRFs. I was assured that they would return to Addis with the aircraft. Contact with Ethiopian Airlines was easy, as it was transporting Pakistani peacekeepers to and from Karachi.

Once all transport arrangements were put in place, and during the six weeks of intense movements, I focused on the Windhoek entry point with returnees being referred to Dobra and Okahandja reception centers. From there, returnees received their first food and non-food reintegration packages, and were transported to their respective final destinations. The airport activity was intense at times, with several planes from Lusaka, Luanda, and Lubango landing at the same time. The Luanda flights did two shuttles in a day, while flights from Gaborone would arrive once a week. The odd flights from West Africa also brought returnees. The Windhoek tower acted as the national flight clearance center and kept track of planes coming into Grootfontein for the Northeast, and Ondangwa for the North. An expert from the UK was deployed to assist as my deputy.

One of the shortcomings of Bwakira was his love for telephone and radio communication. He would call the tower from his radio in the car and ask for passenger lists, or even suggest which flight should be given preference to land over another. To overcome the problem, and following various complaints, I requested his car to be taken in for servicing, and had the radio removed. I told him it was under repair and would be installed back soon. We installed the radio a day before the arrival of Sam Nujoma's flight.

The return of SWAPO officials was discussed with Dr. Nicky Iyambo, as he was designated by the SWAPO leadership, and had arrived earlier for that purpose. Upon the landing of the EAL 767 plane, with Sam Nujoma onboard—as instructed by Bwakira, who was standing with the UN Deputy Force Commander, Daniel Opande from Kenya—I went up to the aircraft, greeted Comrade Sam and his team, welcomed them back home, collected their VRFs from the escort, and requested them to disembark. The SWAPO leadership disembarked in an orderly manner, and I do recall seeing Mr. Nujoma kissing the ground once he had walked down the stairs. He was met by Bwakira, amongst other UNTAG dignitaries, as well as his mother and other family members. The Apartheid newspapers carried stories about how Comrade Sam threw up upon arrival, as the food onboard Ethiopian Airlines was not to his liking.

UNHCR and the Communist Takeover Conspiracy

Because of the highly charged political environment in Namibia, Bwakira was an easy target for those who wanted to discredit the peace process and the return of SWAPO. For starters, he was Black and an African. The head of UNTAG, Martti Ahtisaari, a Finnish national, in contrast, was presented as being a moderate and intelligent UN leader who was trying to rein in the radical communist and SWAPO stooges in the UN and UNHCR. Daily, the newspapers carried cartoons depicting that situation, for the duration of the repatriation and reintegration program. Bwakira treated the provocations with humor and the contempt they deserved, demonstrating his inner strength.

Ironically, that propaganda helped build his acceptance amongst refugees and the local population. Bwakira and UNHCR were singled out as being the Trojan Horse and the mastermind behind the communist takeover of Namibia. Or as being the puppet of SWAPO. In contrast, Martti Ahtisaari was portrayed as moderate and civilized. These can be illustrated by the daily cartoons that appeared in the *Dier Republikein*. The party in power was the Democratic Turnhalle Alliance (DTA). Its daily bulletin *Dier Republikein*, accused UNHCR and SWAPO of failing to account for higher numbers of refugees, which they had always claimed had been in exile. It accused SWAPO of having killed thousands in exile, and hence the discrepancy between those who returned and the reported high number of people who had been in exile.

The Voluntary Repatriation Form (VRF) issued to refugees was recognized as an identity document for purposes of voter registration. Voter registration took place between July and September 1989. Some returnees had misplaced the VRF documents, and UNHCR provided duplicates by tracing names and arrival date of the applicants. Duplicate copies always accompanied the flight manifests and were kept by UNHCR. The issuance of duplicate VRF forms was constantly denounced by DTA, accusing UNHCR of working in cohort with SWAPO to inflate the voter register.

During the buildup to the elections, UNHCR seconded some of its staff to UNTAG to be part of the monitoring team. Most of us remained with UNHCR and focused on the return of SWAPO cargo and the ongoing distribution of monthly food rations.

Returnee congregations for their rations were used by political parties for lobbying. The election campaign was full of energy, with the voting period running from November 7–12, 1989. The turnout was impressive, and some voters slept on the voting queues as a mark of their commitment.

Back to Malawi, and Change of Government in Ethiopia

I returned to Malawi upon completion of my mission in Namibia, and continued to oversee the three field offices in Central Malawi. The representative who signed my travel authorization to Namibia, Mr. Ray Mkanda, had died and his replacement, Dr. Yilma Mekonnen, was in post. National officers and other support staff were added to the previous teams, as the number of refugees had also increased.

In Malawi, I heard of the overthrow of the Derg and the seizing of power by joint EPLF-TPLF forces. The Ethiopian Airlines office also informed me that the family of former president Mengistu had flown to Harare through Lilongwe. During a telephone discussion with my mother, she informed me that she could not talk freely, as the "*adisochu*," or the *new ones*, were in her house. The new arrivals had also taken over the two houses next to hers that were inhabited by my two brothers, Kassa Kebede and Ayalew Kebede, who had left the country with their families a couple days before.

The news of armed fighters moving into my mother's house bothered me, so I sought permission and flew back to Addis from Lilongwe. I was met at Addis Ababa Bole International Airport by a UNHCR driver, Ato Tibebu Gobena. We drove straight to my mother's house and were stopped at the entrance gate by armed guards. They wanted to know who we were and what we wanted. I explained that I had come to visit my mother from Malawi, and showed my passport. A young fighter with a long radio antenna protruding into the air from his back took my passport and spoke to whoever was on the other end in Tigrinya. He only asked how many brothers and sisters we were, and I answered. The authorization to enter was given by the officer at the other end of the radio, and the gates were opened. Hundreds of young boy and girl fighters were scattered all around. I could see two tents that, one up front and the other at the back. Guns of all sorts and RPG launchers were kept in the open in bundles.

My mother was sitting in the living room, where there were no fighters, but a lady helper and relatives living with her. Following exchanges of greetings and briefings, I walked over to my brother Asfaw's place, which had a back door to Mother's compound. I met Asfaw, and we both agreed to jointly address our concerns regarding the occupation of our mother's compound by the EPRDF forces. We were informed that the commanding officer was staying in the house of Kassa Kebede, next door. We visited that house to explain our concerns to young officers, and asked whether they could help in relocating the troops out of our mother's compound.

I spent the night in my room at my mother's place. I was woken up early by her, as she had noticed troop movements and did not want me to be in harm's way. I got up and could see in the dark that troops were loading personal belongings and dismantled tents into two trucks. By dawn, the compound was literally empty, and they had withdrawn from my mother's place to a military base nearby. However, they remained in both Kassa's and Ayalew's residences.

We celebrated and rejoiced over them vacating my mother's compound. In the afternoon, a group of EPRDF troops, in single files, and arms carried casually over their shoulders, marched in and asked to see *Emama*, or *Mother*, as they called her. When Mother came out of the house, one by one they put down a parcel wrapped in brown paper and congratulated her for the return of her son, and thanked her for having hosted them until then. As they were leaving, I examined the parcels and found out that they had brought her portions of their rations, consisting of sugar, tea, coffee, and sardines. We were all moved by the gesture, which also demonstrated the genuine Ethiopian character, innocence, and decency the common troops had upon their arrival in Addis. The rank and file of the liberation forces that came into Addis were simple, principled, and disciplined. We were happy to return the favor, and invited all for lunch the following day, and served plenty of meat and drinks of all kinds.

How that army of liberation fighters was transformed over the years into what it became remains a mind-boggling phenomenon.

Mission accomplished, and satisfied with developments in Addis, I returned to Malawi.

Home in Malawi

At home in Ntcheu, Malawi, we had the support of Nelson and his wife, who resided in the service quarters of the compound. Nelson was a retired military officer who spoke perfect English and managed the house and the gardens. I had two guards and two gardeners. We hired an additional Ethiopian nanny to help Abenet, as our second daughter was delivered at the Adventist Hospital in Blantyre. Bringing up two daughters with no prospect for spouse employment, and the limited contact and recreational facilities, took its toll on the family, and particularly on my wife, Abenet, who was falling sick.

The compound we resided in was over fifteen thousand square meters. We had hired two gardeners and grew a lot of vegetables, including corn. We used to supply visiting colleagues fresh vegetables from the garden. The compound and the overall scenery were great. However, it was also boring, as social activities were limited, and even owning a television was not allowed by the regime. Having served at a difficult duty station for over four years, I informed the Africa Bureau that I felt that I was being condemned into exile by being forced to remain in Malawi as a field officer for life, mimicking President Banda.

CHAPTER SIX

First Assignment in Geneva

I was reassigned as desk officer at the Regional Bureau for Africa Desk 1 in May 1992. Upon arrival at the Bureau, I reported to the head of desk 1, Mr. Hubert Edongo, who informed me that my post had been discontinued, as the situation in Liberia and West Africa had changed. He suggested that I talk to the bureau director and the bureau admin officer, Ms. Marjon Kamara. My concerns were put to rest by Marjon, who simply told me to go look for an apartment, buy a car, and do the necessary things to settle myself, and that she would send for me at the Ethiopian ambassador's residence. The ambassador, Kassa Kebede, was my brother.

I took Marjon's advice and rented an apartment close to the office in Bude, bought furniture and a car. I was summoned by Marjon through my sister-in-law Adera Tsegaye. Upon arrival at the bureau, Marjon handed me a note signed by the director, assigning me the task of taking over the South African Repatriation unit in Geneva.

With UNHCR High Commissioner
Madame Ogata

Winding down of the South African Return and Reintegration Operation

I took over as head of the South African Repatriation and Reintegration unit in Geneva from Karen Abu Zayd, upon her reassignment in 1992. My assignment was to essentially wind down the unit in tandem with the decrease in activities in the field. The lingering issues were related to the closing of the reintegration accounts, as well as sorting out other residual activities.

As part of the project closure, I accompanied lead internal auditor, Mr. Galter, to South Africa, where we reviewed, amongst other issues, project expenditures. Over-expenditure was observed, and headquarters was informed accordingly. I participated in the debriefing the auditor gave at headquarters. In an indication that a meeting had been held before the briefing, I do recall Mr. Gerald Walzer, the controller at the time, informing the audit team that

124

he had consulted with High Commissioner Madame Ogata, and that the decision to act against Kallu Kalumiya, the UNHCR representative in South Africa, was that of senior management.

Kallu signed all the checks, which were prepared by his finance assistant, Zemzem Mohamed. There were no project, or even expenditure, control mechanisms in the office. Zemzem claimed to have been implementing her boss's decision, while Kallu argued that he had thought his program and finance units were monitoring the rate of implementation and ensuring that payments were effected in accordance with the letter of instruction received from headquarters. That incident also denied Zemzem's conversion to the professional international category.

UNHCR issued checks for over two million South African rands, over and above the agreement amount with the South African Council of Churches. As the issue was simply of mismanagement and not fraud, I had proposed to include the overpayment in a revision to the existing agreement. I was aware of the excellent political and public relations work Kallu had accomplished for UNHCR. He did not have program staff to watch his back. The controller refused to allocate the corresponding amount and demanded the representative be held accountable.

The bank acted as an implementing partner to the SA Council of Churches. The standard bank could not account for each check collected by beneficiaries sent to it by the church. The church submitted to the bank memos, usually signed by Reverend Chicane, forwarding a list of names. The bank effected payments without always ensuring that each person on the list appeared in person to sign a receipt. Moreover, besides the undertaking of the church, and the related godly trust, there was no cleared list of legitimate target populations. The matter was further complicated by the fact that the reverend was African National Congress (ANC) and the head of the church at the same time. His office decided who to put on the list. As UNHCR and the internal audit team could not act against the ANC or the Church, Kallu and the bank were sacrificed. The bank later returned the balance of under a million to UNHCR.

UNHCR's attitude and behavior toward the ANC and SWAPO

leadership were clear examples of unintended shortcomings. I also hold the view that there was nothing wrong in acknowledging that, in hindsight, some things could have been managed differently. We should have invested more into accountability-related issues with liberation leaders as they prepared to take over power. The argument that such capacity development was the prerogative of the likes of UNDP was neither here nor there. The UN system is such that the initial dealings with refugee or liberation leaders during the return and early reintegration phase of the operation was with UNHCR. Development agencies come in at a later stage.

The South African Repatriation unit was subsequently subsumed under the Southern Africa Desk V, headed by Mr. Willie Young. My last task dealing exclusively with South Africa was facilitating the conclusion of an agreement with International Office for Migration (IOM) for the voluntary repatriation of residual South Africans in exile.

General Service Staff in Geneva

Having relied on locally recruited staff to help me type and file my documents in Africa, I had taken the support for granted until my assignment to Geneva. The secretary assigned to the desk, Ms. Odiri Dafei, was from Nigeria. For starters, it was an eye opener to realize that most secretaries that were locally recruited were not from Switzerland. The income of some of the senior national staff was comparable to that of internationals, which was in sharp contrast to the situation in Africa or Asia.

My first encounter with the headquarters staff relations, or the Odiri phenomenon, was when I was instructed to urgently prepare a memo by the director, which I did, and requested Odiri to help me type it. Odiri took my draft and put it on her desk. As she was leaving, I interjected to her that the memo was urgent. She simply told me that she was going for her coffee break, and walked off. Upon her return an hour later, I tried to make the point that the director was waiting for the memo, which generated the reaction of, "Let the old man wait." In total disbelief, I brought the incident to the admin officer, who explained to me that the situation at headquarters was different from the field, and that there was not much that I or the bureau could do. Appeasement and bribery were the only options. The other was to become self-reliant. I opted to learn typing, and 'til this day, I am grateful to Odiri for leaving me no option but to type and file my documents.

Nelson Mandela's Visit to Geneva and the UNHCR Office

Nelson Mandela had direct and personal involvement with UNHCR, both before and after he took office. He was personally acquainted with the former High Commissioner for Refugees, Mrs. Sadako Ogata, as well as with other UNHCR managers, including former Africa Bureau Director Nicolas Bwakira, and Kallu Kalumiya, UNHCR's first representative in South Africa. This relationship was initially centered on the return of South African refugees, but broadened later.

UNHCR was the first UN agency that Mr. Mandela met with when he visited Geneva in 1990. When UNHCR first started negotiating with the Apartheid minority government for the voluntary repatriation of South African refugees, the African National Congress (ANC) was initially not supportive. Mandela personally gave his blessing for these negotiations to continue, and came at different points to support them.

A second formal meeting between the ANC, led by Mandela, and UNHCR on the repatriation process took place in Johannesburg a year later. The ANC reiterated its support for UNHCR's involvement in the process. UNHCR established an office in Johannesburg later that year, with suboffices around the country. It was the first United Nations office to be reopened in the country, and was supported and facilitated by the ANC.

Former UN High Commissioner for Refugees, Madam Sadako Ogata, was designated by the UN Secretary General to represent him at the formal launch of the Convention for a Democratic South Africa (CODESA) process, which negotiated a new constitutional dispensation for post-Apartheid South Africa.

Having been reassigned to Geneva, I saw Mandela during his visit to UNHCR headquarters in Geneva in 1992. As the senior desk officer covering South Africa, I was assigned the task of coordinating the reception party on the second floor where the Africa Bureau was located at the Centre William Rappard UNHCR headquarters. I arranged for my vocal and persuasive secretary of the desk, Ms. Odiri Dafei, to collect money from all Africans in the organization, and other staff. She did raise more than the target, and people were very generous. Having organized parties in Ethiopia, I placed orders from the duty-free shop based on the number of guests expected to attend. I ordered a crate of whisky, a crate of red wine, and a crate of white wine. Soft drinks were also ordered, and the cafeteria, situated on the roof, organized finger foods, while volunteers brought food from home. I visited the South African Embassy and asked if they could lend us pictures of Mandela, as well as South African flags for the party. They promised to make available their own pictures hanging at the embassy, and flags that would be brought in the morning of the party day.

In the morning, I was informed by the guard that fellows driving a van from the South African Embassy were looking for me downstairs. I went, and they gave us a couple pictures and flags. However, they also said they had brought us contributions for the party, which would also be a good occasion to introduce their products. They gave us several boxes of South African red and white wine, as well as boxes of sparkling rose wine and champagne. I thanked them for their gifts and requested the guards' assistance to take a box of each upstairs, but keep the majority in storage downstairs. In my mind, the disposal of the extra bottles in storage would be decided after the party.

UNHCR colleagues and invited guests will testify that the party turned out to be the mother of all parties organized by UNHCR. President Mandela briefly showed up and graced the occasion, accompanied by Madam Ogata. African music was blazing, plenty of food was served non-stop, and everyone was dancing, including senior managers, who were usually reserved. The celebratory and jovial mood was simply an unreserved demonstration of liberation and freedom by all staff.

What most guests did not know was that an hour or so into the party, the drinks catering team came up to me and informed that they were running out of wine. I could not believe what I was hearing. I requested more South African wine to be brought from the storage space downstairs. That up and down movement continued the entire evening, until all the stock in storage was depleted. Hundreds of bottles of wine and champagne were consumed. The case of whisky had only one bottle taken out, and even then, only half consumed, which also turned out to be by myself, assisted by two other compatriots I had invited. At that time, I realized that drinks being consumed at parties differ from country to country. Whisky was an Ethiopian thing, while in Switzerland people enjoyed wine. What saved the occasion was not my planning, but the generosity of the South African Mission. The remainder of the whisky became part of the stock kept at the bureau to be served at what was known then as the Organization of African Unity session, usually held late every Friday. All bureau colleagues and their invited guests would meet in the corridor of the bureau for drinks and finger food to relax before knocking off for the weekend.

The Angola Operation

I received an official communication signed by Sue Munch, chief of Recruitment, Career Development, and Placement, that the high commissioner had appointed me as senior desk officer (Desk V), to take effect on October 16, 1993. I was initially responsible for organizing and managing the desk's work related to South Africa, Malawi, Zambia, and Angola. In late 1994, I was charged with responsibilities for the planning of the Angolan repatriation operation. My focus on the Angola operation coincided with the appointment of Marjon Kamara as representative, taking up her functions in September 1994, in Luanda.

I undertook field missions and coordinated the putting together of the overall plan for the voluntary repatriation and reintegration of Angolan refugees from Namibia, Zambia, DRC, and Congo. The Repatriation Plan and the appeal document were to form the basis for the Regional Plan for the Angola situation, to be shared with donors and partners alike.

At the time, the warring parties in Angola—the MPLA

and *União Nacional para a Independência Total de Angola* (UNITA)—were engaged in negotiations convened in Zambia under UN sponsorship to restore peace in the country. Earlier, elections had been held, and UNITA did not accept the results, and therefore chose to go back to war. UNITA was occupying close to 80 percent of the country at the time. Negotiations had become protracted, and the UN had set a deadline of October 1994. The Lusaka Agreement was signed in the presence of dignitaries from all over, and the expectation was that refugees would return home since the parties had committed to peace.

UNHCR set out to establish the structure to support the voluntary repatriation operation. I went on mission to Angola to provide support in assessing requirements for establishing presences in the areas to which refugees were expected to return. The two main provinces of return were Moxico in the East and Uige in the North. Suboffices were set up in two provincial capitals: Luena in Moxico, and Uige in the North. In addition, field offices were established in M'banza Congo, Cazombo, and Lumbala Nguimbo. Travel to most of these places was by plane, as road travel was prohibited by the UN.

Tripartite meetings were held in the three capitals: Luanda, Lusaka, and Kinshasa. The representative in Angola, the country of origin, assumed the role of overall manager of the de-facto situational approach management, which was supported by the bureau.

The presence of the international community in Angola was heavy at the time. Hopes were high after the signing of the partial agreement, and there was gearing up for action, both humanitarian and reconstruction. Given the excitement, a fundraising roundtable event was organized in Brussels by UNDP and the European body. I attended that, together with Marjon Kamara. We held extensive discussions on the margins of the roundtable with various donor representatives, where we briefed them on the Angolan Repatriation and Reintegration Plan.

The roundtable and the exchanges we had remain notable events. The fruitful briefings and exchanges we had with one of the organizers of the roundtable meeting, the UNDP assistant administrator responsible for Africa, who later became Liberia's president, Ellen Johnson Sirleaf, was extended to a memorable dinner outing. I still vividly remember my excitement to see in the distance both Savimbi and Dos Santos walk together, holding hands. Over $1 billion were pledged at the conference, and hopes were high for both parties to agree to a lasting peace.

Unfortunately, the negotiations between the parties became protracted and were punctuated by periods of serious clashes between the two armies. The high insecurity and lack of movement on the ground saw a gradual waning of donor interest, which affected our voluntary repatriation operation. Lack of funding and insecurity resulted in the decision to scale down the operation, including the reduction of staffing levels, which were scaled down by 50% by the end of 1996.

With the Angola operation going nowhere, I became increasingly more involved in the Mozambican Return and Reintegration Operation planning. I focused on the countries of asylum and Peter de Clercq, another officer on Desk V, took responsibility for the country of origin, Mozambique. We worked as an excellent team and were able to compile a holistic document with the budget covering Mozambique as country of origin, and Zambia, Zimbabwe, South Africa, Swaziland, and Malawi as countries of asylum.

The Mozambique operation, though successful in the sense that the majority of the refugees, particularly from Malawi, simply walked back across the border and did not need much transport assistance, the operation lacked regional cooperation or coordination.

The appointment of Mr. David Lambo as coordinator, without line management responsibilities, allowed him to address donors in Geneva on the number of returnees and his field trip to Mozambique. However, David was not welcomed in Malawi by the representative, Dr. Yilma Mekonnen, who simply refused to work with him, and instructed his staff to do likewise. This was significant, as the majority of Mozambican refugees were in Malawi. Yilma worked more closely with the head of suboffice in Tete, Mr. David Kapya, who, as a seasoned diplomat, handled

Maputo and David tactfully, while working closely with Malawi.

The lack of any standards in terms of the returnee package to be provided in countries of asylum was also observed. Returnees from Swaziland were the most privileged, as Mr. Gary Perkins insisted and got his way by including house construction materials and hammers and nails for those returning from Swaziland. For the return journey, families were provided with food, which included roast chicken with rice, and fruit such as apples. Zambia and Zimbabwe offered cooked meals en route to reception facilities in Mozambique, while in Malawi, returnees were simply allowed to carry whatever they could from their houses. The few transported by bus were provided wet feeding and water for the trip back home. Zimbabwe, under Wairimu Karago, had developed a software, MozRep, to register returnee information, including intended places of return, to be used by all countries of asylum to share data with Mozambique to help plan accordingly for reception and reintegration. None of the other asylum countries utilized the system.

Unlike Angola, with the prevalence of peace and the international community's commitment, a huge amount of reintegration work was undertaken in Mozambique through Quick Impact Projects (QUIPs), which became the flavor of the day. I received notification that following a recommendation of the APPB, the high commissioner had decided to extend my standard assignment length for one more year as senior desk officer, through 1997.

Unfortunate Relocation from Centre William Rappard

Upon my first assignment at headquarters, I worked at Centre William Rappard at 154 Rue de Lausanne, Geneva, Switzerland. The architecturally stunning building was built in 1926 to house the International Labour Office (ILO). It was the first building in Geneva designed to house an international organization. In 1975, the ILO moved to Grand Saconnex, and in 1977 the Centre William Rappard was occupied by the Secretariat of the General Agreement on Tariffs and Trade (GATT), the UN High Commissioner for Refugees, and the library of the Graduate Institute of International and Development Studies. By 1995, the World Trade Organization (WTO) replaced GATT and became the main occupant of the Centre William Rappard upon the departure of UNHCR to its new headquarters.

It is only those staff members who had served at William Rappard that would appreciate the extent of the loss of moving. In the Africa Bureau, I had shared a room with Peter de Clercq, and later we were joined by Dominik Bartsch. We had a window opening to the rear garden, with a view of the lake. The cafeteria situated on the roof had a stunning view of the lake and the foothills of the Alps. The architecture scattered in the compound and walls, cedar trees planted by various leaders in the gardens all around were impeccable, and lunchtime strolls up and down the lake were refreshing.

In 1995, I was elected deputy chairman of the UNHCR Staff Council, with Nasir Ishaq as chairman. As deputy chair, I was designated to attend meetings on the relocation, which were chaired by Bjorn Johansen, head of the Relocation Task Force. I recall a month or so before the final move, we had gone to visit the new building in the presence of Madam Ogata. It was clear by then that the objective of housing all UNHCR headquarters staff under one roof was not being realized. Given former Yugoslavia operations, coupled with the Great Lakes genocide and displacement in Africa, the office staff had grown well beyond the six hundred or so that were to be accommodated. The new building looked like a prison from the outside, and was not half as attractive as the old one that we were abandoning. The environment around the building was also not attractive. Madam Ogata wanted her own building, I assumed. My query about the open space was responded to by Madam Ogata, who suggested that I visit the World Bank Office in New York, and that the open office space was the new direction the world was taking. She convinced all of us that the government had told her in no uncertain terms that expansion or construction in and around Centre William Rappard was not possible.

We had raised queries about the concept of open space, noise pollution, and stratification of desk and space allocation based

133

on the personal grades of staff. It was only D2s and above that would have their own room, while D1s and P5s would have a partitioning of a kind. The rest would be accommodated in open cubicles. Telephone calls and small meetings would be held in blocked cubicles located on each floor.

The move was an experience, as staff learned to speak quietly. Asking the likes of my secretary, Odiri, to keep her voice down was no easy feat. Privacy was a thing of the past. I had asked whether we could reverse the decision and remain in the old building if we were not all to fit under one roof.

Bjorn, who loved cracking jokes, said the HC could impose height restrictions on all staff to be recruited, which could give us the possibility of further horizontal partitioning, thus doubling the office space. Madame did not like the joke at all and simply left. The furniture for the new office was being provided by IKEA of Sweden.

One good Friday, we all packed our belongings and clearly marked our work unit. By Monday, we had moved into the new building to unpack.

At a later stage of my life, when I was assigned to headquarters for the second time, I observed that the WTO building was completely renovated, and an extension was constructed to make more office space available to accommodate an additional thousand staff members, and a conference facility with various meeting rooms. All that we had been told was not possible had become possible. Where the second car parking spot was once located outside the Centre William Rappard and across the road, is now a newly constructed building housing the World Meteorological Organization.

Project Delphi and the Short-Circuited Change Management Process

In late 1995, the high commissioner mandated Change Management Group (CMG) to undertake a comprehensive examination, known as Project Delphi, of how UNHCR conducts its business.

Under her guidance, the CMG initiated a reengineering process which mobilized and used inputs from the whole organization. The CMG had nine members: Karen Abu Zayd, Carolyn Coquet, Manuel de Almeida de Silva, Duncan Barclay, Tony Salmon, Jean-Francois Durieux, Ekber Menemencioglu, Izumi Nakamitsu, and myself.

Most of us did not know each other well, and did not fully understand the criteria for our selection. Madam Ogata, during our first meeting with her as a group, told us that we were selected by senior managers as being qualified for the task at hand. She also considered gender and geographic distribution. I was included as the African representative with program management background in the CMG, and observed that we all had varied experiences that covered almost everything the organization did. We were given a clean piece of paper to design and propose the best way forward for the organization "to remain relevant and do its duties in an effective and efficient manner."

We started off by going to Annecy for a week to brainstorm and figure out what was expected of us while getting to know each other better in the process. We took time to study earlier reports and recommendations that were pending. We read books on reengineering and management reform.

Earlier in our deliberations, we reached the consensus that the core process of what UNHCR does is broadly captured in operations, which includes all UNHCR actions that contribute to the resolution of problems and situations affecting refugees and other persons of concern. Assistance to refugees, internally displaced persons, returnees, or any other individuals of concern to UNHCR cannot be separated from other operational activities dealing with prevention, protection, fundraising, promotion, and rights advocacy. The aim of all these activities was to seek out, promote, and assist in the achievement of durable solutions to resolve an actual or potential problem. A set of guidelines, assumptions, and objectives had been identified as the basis for process design. The two main inputs to the operations process were people and money.

Focus groups to clearly design processes dealing with

operations, people, and money were established. I joined the Operations group, which included Jean-Francois Durieux, Ekber, Izumi, Mike Alford, Seyi Bajulaiye, Salvatore Ippolito, Harry Leef, Abdi Osman, David Rile,y and Kim Roberson. The People focus group consisted of Manoel de Almeida, Duncan Barclay, Tony Salmon, Chris Thorne, Hiromitsu Mori, Anne-Marie Kerrigan, Anne Gunning, and Tessa Williams. The Money focus group included Karen Abu Zayd, Caroline Coquet, Amin Awad, Karen Farkas, Filippo Grandi, Kai Nielsen, Fernando and Colette Turmel.

The lack of a clear and effective policy formulation and dissemination process, being one of the weaknesses of planning operations, was identified as needing corrective action. All focus groups carried out high-level process mapping. My focus group identified four core processes: program formulation, resource allocation, implementation modalities, and accountability. These were further subclassified into a number of second- and third-level processes. Similar work was completed by the Money and People focus groups.

A planning approach, which recognizes the need to identify a coordinated set of objectives and activities within both countries of origin and countries of asylum, was seen as both appropriate and necessary to the majority of UNHCR's operations, if durable solutions were to be identified and implemented. The success of this would depend on having operational responsibility, accountability, and authority. This situational approach was to guide field structures. Field presence would be based on specific refugee caseloads or caseload needs, which would be grouped together for effective and efficient management purposes. The situational approach to management was recommended as a dynamic approach which would allow UNHCR to plan for and organize resources to manage defined situations.

The Final Report of the Change Management Group was presented to the high commissioner and senior management on May 1, 1996. The report was endorsed, and a follow-up team set up under the patronage of Mr. Gerald Walzer, deputy high commissioner. I was briefly involved in the setting up of that change management body.

The Delphi Change Initiative was severely scarred when the high commissioner announced discontinuation of some two hundred positions at headquarters due to the prevailing financial situation facing the organization. This move was unfortunately understood by many to be linked to the Delphi proposal, "that the Headquarters should significantly reduce in size, as identified overlapping and duplicated activities are eliminated." The problem was that overlapping and duplicated activities were not yet clearly identified, let alone being linked to existing positions and functions that could be recommended for discontinuation.

The People focus group recommendation to set up a clear linkage between manpower planning and the Career Management System, which would make both the staff and the organization plan and agree on career prospects, was identified to be a priority. Planning human resources included an impact on recruitment, contract, and separation policies, all of which must be viewed in conjunction with a performance appraisal system, which would provide a credible and ongoing evaluation of all staff members. Existing staff rules would need to be revised, or UNHCR specific exemptions made.

Some restructuring and streamlining of processes were introduced, but resistance to change, particularly by the geographic bureau, was set to derail the change process. For example, while implementing the situational approach concept, the Yemen and Somalia situations called for restructuring. Middle East ambassadors and Arab League delegates were quick to visit the HC and express their concerns. The Middle East and North Africa Bureau was adamant that Yemen being managed with Somalia was a non-starter.

The need for a clear policy formulation and dissemination process did not appear to have been appealing to the high commissioner, who was happy with the information exchange taking place at the weekly senior management committee meetings. The vague management role and status of the Senior Management Committee (SMC) has remained and appears to be to the liking of subsequent high commissioners. The absence of a clear policy formulating and disseminating body within UNHCR remains the cornerstone of the preferred management style of previous and current high commissioner.

A summary of proposed next steps was provided but was not followed. The excellent support the Delphi team had received from the full-time services of a consultant, Jennie Barton, was also ended.

The short-circuited change initiative with in UNHCR, I later found out, to be similar to the various UN change initiatives launched by secretary generals upon their assumption of duties. The change objectives are seldom realized in full. But life continues.

CHAPTER SEVEN

Assignment to Southern Africa

The peculiarity of the regional office in Pretoria had been that, following the appointment of the then representative, Mr. Nicolas Bwakira, to the position of Director of Operations for South Africa in November 1996, the D2 post of representative was transferred and redeployed with the director without any new post being created to replace it. At the time, UNHCR's position was that the organization could not request for the creation of an additional position at the D-level, as the restructuring was to have been achieved without additional post creations. The request for the re-creation of the representative's position was also further delayed pending the resolution of a discussion with the Government of South Africa, regarding the implications of an accreditation of a UNHCR director and a representative both at the same location in Pretoria. The assignment note I received from staff service section on April 24, 1997, stated that "the High Commissioner has confirmed your assignment as Deputy Regional Representative in South Africa."

With my arrival in July 1997, and given the above impasse, the functions of the representative were subsumed by the deputy regional representative, and I continued to perform as head of the then Regional Office for Southern Africa (ROSA), which was separate from the Office of the Director for Southern Africa. Representatives in each country in Southern Africa, including my office, reported to the Office of the Director.

High Commissioner Ogata addressed letters to the ministers of foreign affairs of Namibia, Botswana, Mozambique, Swaziland, and Lesotho on June 5, 1998, outlining the restructuring of the Africa Bureau and indicating that my office would oversee UNHCR activities in their countries, and coordinate closely with "your Government and non-governmental organisations on continued implementation of refugee assistance programmes." The UNDP offices in Mauritius and Madagascar were also informed of the change, as UNHCR operated through them.

A reclassification request was submitted yearly as part of the Country Operations Plan (COP), or Country and Regional Operations Plan (CROP). Parallel, though, yet another high-level process of review of the management structure for Africa was initiated at headquarters level in March 1999. Following the endorsement by Senior Management of the Report of the Working Group on the New Management Structure for Africa, and in accordance with recommendation no. 12, the title Deputy Regional Representative was changed to Representative. The high commissioner approving the retitling acknowledged that the change was indeed "consistent with the actual functions and responsibilities performed by the present incumbent for the last two years." I was officially informed of the change in my functional title to that of Representative, effective July 1, 1999. A Personnel Action Form P35, No. 991650 was issued by the Staff Administration Section accordingly.

Complexities of the Work in South Africa

The UNHCR program in South Africa was different from any other on the African and Asian continents that I have been exposed to. I did realize early on that trying to meet the needs of thousands of refugees and asylum seekers scattered throughout the country, with the limited resources available to UNHCR, was impossible.

Collecting refugees into an encampment approach, while advocated by some local parties, was not an option.

In consultation with the Regional Bureau, the way forward was to use the limited resources available toward the creation of an enabling environment for refugees to move around and earn a living. Upon application for asylum, each new arrival was provided with a Section 41 permit, which allowed the applicant to move around and work to earn a living. The asylum process included an appeal option for rejected persons. Even though the process was to be completed in three months, given the tedious, legalistic, and protracted nature of the process, coupled with the lack of government capacity, the backlog regularly blocked the system, resulting in regular extensions of Section 41 permits.

Another dimension of the problem was the abuse of the Section 41 permit by non-refugees. The nationalities of asylum-seekers upon my arrival in South Africa included various Europeans, including German and Swiss nationals. Upon closer examination, we realized that tourists were going to the same Department of Home Affairs (DHA) to ask for an extension of their visa, but to avoid payment, would apply for asylum, as the Section 41 permit was given for free.

In order to overcome the various challenges, UNHCR ROSA became an active member of the commission which drafted the 1998 South Africa Refugee Act passed by Parliament, and was one of the most progressive acts in existence. The office dedicated resources by providing regular legal advice to the Department of Home Affairs (DHA) toward the establishment of a refugee status determination procedure. We also provided technical and human resources support to DHA, with a surge project to absorb the backlog in asylum applications. Additional legal experts in the field, drawn from the UNHCR standby roster, as well as IT equipment, were provided to the various offices of the DHA throughout the country.

My office got advice from the policy officer of the bureau, Mr. George Okoth-Obbo, who spent a significant time in various initiatives to assist the DHA. The initiatives were spearheaded by the senior protection officer, Mr. Bruno Geddo. We were able to form partnerships with Lawyers for Human Rights (LHR) to provide legal assistance to asylum seekers and refugees throughout South Africa. Indeed, the LHR acted as the UNHCR field presence, particularly in Cape Town and Port Elizabeth.

Another initiative we launched worth noting was conducted with the South African Human Rights Commission to undertake the public awareness Roll Back Xenophobia campaign. The campaign was needed, as xenophobia was growing in the country, and refugees and asylum- seekers were falling victims to wanton conflicts throughout the country. Former South African refugees, who had now returned and were in senior positions, were regularly interviewed, and addressed communities in various locations. Mr. Nyameko Barney Pityana, himself a returnee, and a former director of the World Council of Churches Programme to Combat Racism (1988–1992) helped us coordinate the campaign. A campaign compact disk was produced with the use of communication experts, and was widely disseminated using various media. A fundraising effort was made through local embassies, and significant contributions were received from the Swiss and US Missions in South Africa.

We were also able to access additional UNHCR funding from what was then called the Danish Special Fund, kept at headquarters and managed by the director and controller of the Resource Management Division. I and various colleagues from the office spent time with Community-Based Organizations (CBOs) to sensitize civil society in disadvantaged areas on refugee issues. Several events were organized around commemorations such as the World Refugee Day on June 20th, and the African Human Rights Day on October 21st. We solicited the support and endorsement of Nelson Mandela.

Beyond the various protection activities within South Africa, my office regularly provided legal and program advice and technical support to UNHCR liaison offices that reported to ROSA, in Mozambique, Botswana, Lesotho, Namibia, and Swaziland, on various aspects of the refugee status determination process, protection of refugees in camps and urban areas, and resettlement of stranded asylum seekers. We sent missions to

142

support UNDP offices handling refugees in the absence of a local UNHCR presence. I and the protection officer undertook various missions to Madagascar, where rioting by refugees demanding resettlement had become common practice.

Obviously, serving in South Africa at the time was a privilege that I cherish for life, as it also gave me the opportunity to personally observe at close range the transfer of power from Nelson Mandela to Thabo Mbeki. The coming into office of Mr. Mbeki gave UNHCR additional attention at the top level, as his wife, Zeleni Mbeki, had served as the UNHCR social worker in Lusaka, and Mr. Mbeki had benefited from the programs offered by the organization when he was a refugee in exile.

Impressions of President Mandela

As mentioned earlier, I had seen President Mandela in flesh and blood when he visited Geneva and came to the UNHCR office. However, that did not provide me the opportunity to have a one-on-one with this great leader, whom I had admired for a long time.

Following my arrival in South Africa, I got to see and greet the president on various occasions. When I first met President Mandela at the Union Building in Pretoria, in my first one-on-one, was at a meeting arranged by Reverend Chicane, where I had gone to seek his personal support and endorsement of the Roll Back Xenophobia campaign. The towering figure in my head was not tall, but even more humble and respectful than I had expected. I explained the campaign and he immediately assured me of his total support, and agreed to issue a vocal statement to be included in the CD to be launched. The CD had interviews with well-known former South African refugees talking about their time in exile, where they were tolerated and supported by host communities all over Africa and beyond.

During encounters at various functions, Mandela, in acknowledging his recognition of who I was, would ask, "How is Madam Ogata?" I would reply that she was well. I knew a close and trusting relationship between Mandela and Ogata was mentioned in her book, *The Turbulent Decade*. She visited South Africa at the beginning of her last year in office in 2000, and met with Mandela at his home.

My last official encounter with President Mandela was in South Africa in late 1999, when I wished him good luck with his endeavors after his retirement. The simplicity and magnanimity of this great man can be illustrated by him personally addressing his invitations and signing them. His last letter as president would read:

Dear Mr. M. Kebede,

It is a great pleasure for me to extend a warm invitation to you to attend the inauguration ceremony of the second democratically elected President of the Republic of South Africa, to be held on Wednesday, 16 June 1999, at the Union Building, Pretoria. I would be most honoured, should you be able to accept this invitation to an event that will play a critical role in strengthening the democratic order in the Republic of South Africa. It would be a personal pleasure for me to welcome you here on this special occasion. This event will also provide the opportunity for me to say farewell to you.

Signed by pen, yours sincerely,

Mandela

The Inauguration of Thabo Mbeki

President Thabo Mbeki became South Africa's second post-Apartheid president on June 16, 1999, taking over from Nelson Mandela, the man who, with unerring grace, steered it through a peaceful transition out of white supremacy.

Moments after Mr. Mbeki took the oath of office in Tswana, English, and Afrikaans, Mandela embraced his successor, and then both men turned and clasped hands high over their heads as the crowd roared its approval.

In his speech, Mr. Mbeki, then fifty-six, sounded many of the themes he has become known for, promising that change would come faster now for the millions of South Africans who lived in deep poverty. Mr. Mbeki called on all South Africans, black and white, to continue to work together for the rebirth of the nation, made possible by "the realization that we share a common destiny, regardless of the shapes of our noses."

The inauguration ceremony, attended by forty-five heads of states and governments, and hundreds of foreign dignitaries, was in some ways austere, taking only about an hour. But it was not without its glitches. I do recall that after Mr. Mbeki took the oath of office, five jets flew overhead, leaving a rainbow-colored smoke trail. Then three helicopters passed by, pulling huge South African flags. Then a Mirage fighter roared past, painted as the South African flag. When nothing further appeared, the master of ceremonies invited Mr. Mbeki to begin his speech. To our surprise, he protested, saying there were more planes to come. But the master of ceremonies insisted. When he was well into his address, three 747s finally thundered over, low and slow, drowning him out. The two outer planes bore messages painted under their wings. One of them reads "President Thabo Mbeki" and the other "Thank you, Madiba".

Mr. Mandela, who did not speak during the ceremony, greeted us as we were ushered in for lunch in tents erected on the lawns. I was seated next to the Ethiopian president, Negasso Gidada, whom I had known from the Gambella South Sudanese refugee assistance program days, as he and his brother were providing aid through the Lutheran World Federation (LWF).

The ceremony did not include the swearing in of a deputy president. The job was offered later to the leader of the Zulu-nationalist Inkatha Freedom Party, Chief Mangosuthu Buthelezi. We all knew that the move was intended to promote peace between the Inkatha Freedom Party and the governing African National Congress.

I recall the ceremonies were not without controversy. Statues of Apartheid-era heroes that are scattered on the lawn of the Union Building, where the ceremonies were held, were draped in green sackcloth. Officials gave various reasons, one point saying the statues were being hidden so as not to detract from the "ecstasy" of the occasion. White South Africans were reportedly upset by the covering of "history," which was compounded by the absence of white singers and bands that draw white audiences, like Springbok

Nude Girls or Nico Carstens.

The ceremony and free concert lasted all afternoon and into the night on the lawn in front of the buildings. Thousands of South Africans enjoyed the music, which included South Africa's best jazz, gospel, kwaito, and township jive acts, including Hugh Masekela, Brenda Fassie, Rebecca Malope, Bongo Maffin, and Boom Shaka. As part of Mr. Mbeki's African Renaissance theme, the organizers also invited many of Africa's best musicians, such as Angelique Kidjo and Papa Wemba.

The Passing of My Mother

I was working in my office in South Africa, Wednesday, February 24, 1999, when I received the sad news of the passing of my mother, who had been fighting periodic spouts of diabetes-related ailments. I made it to Addis Ababa a day after she was laid to rest in the family grave located at the "bale weld" church adjacent to the Trinity Cathedral. Upon arrival in Addis, I went to the graveyard with my brother Asfaw. We spent a couple days mourning at the family residence, before I returned to South Africa. The passing of my mother closed the chapter on the family home. As if that sad development wasn't enough, unexpected events started unfolding in South Africa that disrupted and curtailed my visits and connections with my home country for years to come.

Saga of Intrigues, Allegations, and Threats by the Ethiopian Embassy in Pretoria

Being active and visible, coupled with refugee work, has its challenges. Ethiopian refugees and asylum seekers, as well as various other African refugees, would regularly come to my office seeking either resettlement, family reunification, or assistance.

I was summoned by the Office of the Director for Southern African Operations in late September 1999, and handed a note he had received in person from the Ethiopian ambassador, Mr. Aman Hassen. The official note verbale, dated September 21, 1998, ref no. 04-3/36/98, stated: "The Embassy brings to the attention of

146

the UN regrettably, that Mr. Mengesha Kebede, a staff member of UNHCR in Pretoria, in breach of obligations he has undertaken as a UN staff member, has been found consistently involving himself in activities which undermine the political process in Ethiopia." It went on to say, "...the individual has been also constantly observed abusing the facilities and properties of the organisation to advance his political goals and objectives."

The embassy, while attaching a documentary evidence that allegedly proved the abuse, urged UNHCR to immediately halt "his dubious acts" by taking the appropriate disciplinary measures.

I requested to look into the allegations and provide my response. I responded in writing, expressing my shock and disbelief, as I could not comprehend the basis upon which the ambassador could have found me "to be consistently involved in activities undermining the political process in Ethiopia." Moreover, the so-called evidence of the note verbale did not make any connection whatsoever between the document and myself. From what I read, it appeared to be a newsletter published by an organization called the Ethiopian Community Organization in South Africa. I was not involved in either the deliberations of those organizations, nor in the production of their views.

I believed that the false allegations, if left unchallenged, could gain the appearance of being rooted in facts. I chose to believe that it did not reflect the official position of the Government of Ethiopia. Indeed, even as far as the ambassador himself was concerned, I noted for the record that I meet him occasionally, for instance at public functions, and at no time had he ever raised any of the matters contained in the note verbale. In all, I was left with no other conclusion than that the note verbale was, for reasons I cannot fathom, rooted in bad faith and sinister motives probably intended to achieve or advance personal political advantage. I felt I was taken advantage of by political appointees to mask or overcome shortcomings they may have had in the performance of their duties. I noted in my reply that "I also intend to draw the attention of the authorities back in Ethiopia regarding the unfortunate incident, and also seek their intervention to redress the situation."

Having reviewed my response, the Office of the Director for Southern African Operations responded in a note verbale to the embassy, stating that, according to applicable internal procedures, allegations have to be substantiated and supported by evidence, which has to be shared with the staff member concerned in order to enable the organization to fully investigate the information brought to its attention. In application of those rules, the embassy's note verbale was shared with Mr. Kebede, who replied to UNHCR's fullest satisfaction: "After careful consideration of the allegations contained in the Embassy's Note Verbale and the staff members' reply thereto, the Office of the Director believes that the allegations contained in the Note must have been based on information that did not correctly reflect the facts."

I contacted my nephew, Bekure Herouy in Addis, who was a former Foreign Ministry official, and sought his advice. He suggested that I address my concerns directly to the minister, and that the legal department was aware of the case. I wrote a letter to Foreign Minister Seyoum, stating that I was not involved in any activity to undermine the government, and that the allegations were tantamount to "searching for cow dung where cattle do not graze." I offered to appear in person and explain my situation, should he so desire.

Bekure confirmed in a telephone exchange that he had personally delivered the letter to the foreign minister. He later wrote to me in January 1999 that "as of date, no tangible/quotable measures have been taken." He recommended that I "cool off everything related to the issue, as it was vital for subsequent measures." He requested that I cease all contact of whatever nature with all Ethiopian Embassy personnel.

Notwithstanding my probing in Addis, the embassy, upon receipt of the UNHCR response, addressed yet another note verbale in late November 1998, indicating that the embassy "totally rejects the contents and inferences indicated in its reply. The embassy did not have, and still does not have, an iota of doubt on the veracity of the contents of its submission." It reaffirmed the embassy's unwavering position that "Ato Mengesha's activities

are still incompatible with the stand and conduct of UN Staff."
The embassy urged UNHCR to take the case seriously, as "In the
event that this individual's activities are not halted, the Embassy
will have no choice other than taking the matter up with higher
authorities for proper action." As per UN procedures, I was given
a copy of the note verbale for my comments.

My comment was that, in the absence of any proof or evidence
being provided, I was more mystified and deeply disturbed as to
what exactly may lie at the root of this campaign against me. I
had set out already in the note verbale, covering my reactions to
the first note verbale, that in the absence of any proof, I did not
know how to respond. However, I was particularly concerned by
the threat: "In the event that this individual's activities are not
halted, the Embassy will have no choice other than taking the
matter up with higher authorities for proper actions." Whatever
the intent of the threat, I needed guidance and protection from
the UN system to ward off whatever "proper action" the embassy
might be contemplating. I also noted that I was scheduled to
depart on home leave on December 5, 1998, and that tickets had
been purchased.

The UNHCR head of personnel administration, with a copy to
the assistant high commissioner, Mr. Soren Jessen-Petersen, and
the director of DHRM, Murphy, addressed an email to Bwakira
referring to the various exchanges concerning allegations against
me. In view of the tone and content of the letters of the ambassador,
"we strongly feel that it would not be prudent for Mr. Kebede to
proceed on Home Leave to Ethiopia." Thus, I was placed in a
refugee-like situation.

Nicolas Bwakira addressed a confidential memo to Soren
Jessen-Petersen, assistant high commissioner, on December 7,
1998, referring to their discussions, that it was his considered
opinion that the office should take up the matter with the Ethiopian
government at a level higher than the Ambassador: "I believe that if
the Minister of Foreign Affairs of Ethiopia attends the forthcoming
Khartoum Conference, the opportunity should be taken to raise
this matter with him and to clarify, among others, to what extent
this whole saga truly reflects the position and consensus of the

Government itself. I believe it would be necessary both to assure the Minister that as far as UNHCR is concerned, the staff member is innocent and also to extract assurance for Mr. Kebede's safety."

The subject matter was raised, and the foreign minister said he would look into the matter, as he had no information. Reportedly, Ambassador Konjit Sine-Giorgis, senior advisor to the minister, was asked to follow up.

Following their visit to the Ethiopian Embassy in Pretoria, on Friday, December 4th, George Okoth-Obbo prepared an extensive note for the file on a meeting between the director of Southern African Operations, Mr. Nicolas Bwakira, and the Ethiopian ambassador in Pretoria, Mr. Aman Hassan, at the Ethiopian Embassy. The note was shared with me and copied to the DHC, AHC, and Mr. Alejandro Henning, head of the Personnel Administration section.

The note recorded the ambassador, speaking emphatically, explaining that the note verbales submitted to UNHCR reflected the position and concerns of the Ethiopian government, speaking through him as its ambassador in Pretoria. The ambassador urged the director to "take action urgently to curb these activities, or else he would have no choice but to seek the appropriate actions of the higher authorities." He also added, "that issue was not a matter that the Embassy and the Government took lightly, when they were obliged to take the regrettable step of making a complaint against our own citizen."

A government, the ambassador said, "cannot make such allegations without facts." He added, as far as the Ethiopian Government was concerned, any Ethiopian "was free to express his or her opinion for or against the Government of Ethiopia, or even oppose it. "However, it was not the fact that Mr. Kebede had strong anti-government, which he has, but his abusing of his position and the facilities and resources of the Office, to carry out activities both inside and outside the Office to organise and facilitate the Ethiopian opposition in South Africa. Mr. Kebede was using the resources of the Office to advance his positions and views to undermine the Ethiopian Government." He concluded by making the commitment to provide further particulars and details as to the activities of the staff member, and would "be doing so shortly in writing."

The details to be provided by the government never materialized. Instead, the embassy resorted to spreading rumors about me, alleging that I was trying to organize rebel forces to reinstate a version of the former Workers' Party regime by overthrowing the current government.

Various publications started circulating in Amharic within the Ethiopian community in South Africa. One such publication, entitled "All Clouds Do Not Produce Rain and All That Smoke Does Not Burn," summed it all up by alleging that individuals, who had their hands soaked in blood of innocent civilians under the previous regime, were now active throughout South Africa. "Those individuals, like the former minister Bezuayehu Alemayehu, had been discredited and become non-effective. In realization of that fact, new players had surfaced to replace them. One such personality was Mengesha Kebede, who was seated in a comfortable position within the UNHCR, and was driven by the wild dream of bringing back the lost family power. Do not be fooled by his clever endeavors, as he is blinded by his drive for power at any cost," the publication warned.

Nega Alula Assumes Focal Role for the "Counter-Offensive"

The first time I met Nega Alula was at an Ethiopian-Embassy-organized fundraising and discussion event on the conflict with Eritrea. I recall Nega objecting to any suggestion that hinted at negotiations with the Eritrean government on giving Ethiopia the use of port facilities and access to the sea. He would emphasize that Eritrea was another country, and Ethiopia needs nothing from her. The irony was that Nega claimed to be the grandson of Alula Abanega, an Ethiopian war hero who fought off the Turks, Italians, and various other expeditionary colonial forces in what is Eritrea today. Nega, at the time, was the spouse of a diplomat, Meseret Telaye, for whom he was trying to lobby to get her a senior appointment. He took charge of the "counter offensive" by opening an office in Johannesburg and launching attacks against a shadow movement that did not exist. All embassy staff had to write an article denouncing my alleged political movement to show their loyalty. Such documents were distributed to Ethiopian refugees by the Johannesburg office. What a cheap position, to say the least, even though it clearly illustrated the inner workings of a government that tried to create a common vision that was not anchored in facts, but fiction. What matters at the end is the collective self-deception to classify issues into right and wrong.

The attempts to discredit and tarnish my image within the Ethiopian community did not have much impact. In fact, I was viewed as a hero amongst some refugee groups, and I was supported by community members who were equally baffled by the moves of the embassy. Most notable were a prominent Ethiopian personality who has long resided in Johannesburg, Gash Gizaw, as well as Haile Mariam and an Ethiopian expert funded by the European Union to assist the South African Ministry of Finance, Israel Kidanemariam, and his wife, Yemiseratch. As one of the anomalies of life, I also got to know and became close to Professor Minga Negash, head of the accounting department at the University of the Witwatersrand, Johannesburg. Minga approached me and informed me how he knew me from pictures and notes he had seen at a house in Chefebuki, where he had stayed as a team leader during the Development Through Cooperation, Knowledge, and Work Campaign in 1975–76. That was the house, where I spent summer breaks, as mentioned earlier, that was nationalized during the revolution, and was apparently serving as the head office of the regional peasants association.

Attempt at Meeting the Foreign Minister of Ethiopia in Durban

The UN High Commissioner Madam Ogata could not attend the Closing Ceremony of the 12th Summit Conference of Heads of State or Governments of the Non-Aligned Movement held in Durban at the beginning of September 1998. I was designated to attend on her behalf, which I did. At the Non-Aligned meeting, the Ethiopian delegation was headed by Foreign Minister Seyoum Mesfin, and included Ambassador Konjit Sine-Giorgis, his close advisor, and Ambassador Sahlework Zewde, currently the president of Ethiopia. Ambassador Konjit, whom I knew from when she was deputy ambassador to my brother Kassa Kebede in Geneva, literally would run away from me whenever she saw me. Foreign Minister Seyoum totally ignored my greeting gestures. The only warm greeting I received was from the Eritrean president, Mr. Isaias Afeworki, who was on his own and moved and interacted with others attending the conference, in confidence. In contrast, Minister Seyoum had a guard carrying his bag, who also spent most of the evening sitting outside his room guarding the entrance.

A mutual friend of mine, and Konjit, later confided that she was partially handling my case at the Foreign Ministry. Our go-between was convinced that she was using the case to get back at her former boss Kassa Kebede, whom she hated and wanted to hurt in any which way she could. The sad reality of vengeance and politics, as it is being executed in Ethiopia, and indeed elsewhere in Africa, where relatives are victimized through no fault of theirs, or for reasons not known to them.

I have recorded the details of the way I was treated by my own government while serving in South Africa to illustrate the extent to which insecure and undemocratic regimes go to destroy those they feel do not support their policy. Obviously, in comparison to my case, arresting or getting rid of perceived threats within the territory they administer appears to be straightforward and simple. However, the not-so-obvious time-consuming effort and significant resources deployed to address challenges they face, be it real or perceived, outside the country needs to be brought out and condemned. Coupled with this shameful behavior of governments, individual and insecure officials exasperate the situation by creating fake enemies they struggle against in order to conceal their shortcomings. Not deterred by this malicious mechanizations of the Ethiopian government, I continued to follow-up on various memorable aspects of my assignment as they unfold.

The Caprivi Liberation Movement in Botswana and Closure of the Osiri Refugee Camp in Namibia

Mistrust and suspicion were characteristics of the prevailing political environment involving Botswana, Angola, Namibia, and South Africa, which, as the regional representative covering most of these countries, I had to carefully navigate. The entry into Botswana of the Caprivi Liberation Movement coincided with the Namibian government's move to close the Osiri refugee camp and move Angolan refugees. The Caprivi Liberation Front and the San people were reportedly close to the UNITA movement in Angola, while SWAPO and the MPLA were strategic allies. The Botswana government historically had to navigate in order not to upset its South African neighbors, while simultaneously being involved in a border dispute with Namibia.

Of all the colonial geographic boundary-drawing absurdities, nothing fascinates me more than the Caprivi Strip, stranded as bacon meat sandwiched between Angola, Botswana, and Zambia. The German colonialists that ruled South West Africa in 1883, apparently wanted a road built on a strip of land to link the main colony to the Victoria Falls. In July 1915, South African forces invaded South West Africa and annexed the German colony as is.

In 1960, SWAPO was formed, and in 1964, the Caprivi African National Union (CANU) was formed and merged with SWAPO to present a unified front against South Africa. CANU was headed by Mishake Muyongo, who later became vice president of SWAPO. Mr. Muyongo split from SWAPO, alleging Ovambo ethnic group domination and discrimination. Muyongo went to Zambia, alleging a purge against Caprivians in SWAPO, but was detained.

After his release and return to Namibia in 1985, he formed the United Democratic Party (UDP), which joined the Democratic Turnhalle Alliance (DTA), and the main one in opposition to SWAPO.

The Caprivi Liberation Army (CLA) was formed in 1994, with the goal of self-rule for Caprivi. The Namibian government claimed that the CLA was allied with the Angolan UNITA movement. In October 1998, the Namibian Defence Forces had reportedly raided a CLA training camp that resulted in more than one hundred armed CLA men fleeing into Botswana. The ongoing government cleansing operation had displaced some twenty-five hundred civilians most of whom had entered Botswana.

I undertook a mission to Botswana to see the situation for myself and consult with the government on the next steps. In Gaborone, I learned that the Caprivi leaders, Mishake Myungo and Chief Boniface Mamile, accompanied by others, were sheltered in a compound in Gaborone. Field visits confirmed the arrival of destitute refugees who had to be relocated to Dukwe in order to be counted, for their needs assessed, and for them to be provided with protection and assistance. We separated the new arrivals into two groups and engaged in discussions with the government.

It has to be recalled that refugee matters in Botswana were administered under the Office of the President (OP). The OP coordinated refugee issues by chairing the Botswana Council of Refugees Executive Council, being a member of the Refugee Advisory Council, overseeing the running of the Dukwe refugee settlement through the Settlement Commandant, and authorizing the issuance of all refugee documents and changes of status. Therefore, all policy decisions pertaining to the social protection of refugees were controlled and authorized by the OP. Therefore, I had to meet the deputy president and seek his guidance and support. We agreed the refugees could be moved to Dukwe camp. However, the leaders in Gaborone were another kettle of fish.

The main NGOs providing services had been the Botswana Council of Churches (BCC), the Lutheran World Federation (LWF), and the Botswana Council for Refugees (BCR). UNHCR's role in the country was to support the government in providing protection to refugees, which it carried out mainly through providing financial support to non-governmental implementing partners. The BCR was established in 1975 as an implementing agent of UNHCR, LWF, and the World Council of Churches (WCC). BCR was mandated to provide counselling and social welfare assistance, as well as to facilitate the reception, protection support, settlement, resettlement and repatriation of refugees mainly from Angola, Namibia, South Africa, and Zimbabwe. The BCR was tasked with providing services, including medical care, as well as food, clothing, accommodation, and subsistence allowances for the fourteen or so refugee leaders sheltered in Gaborone.

While continuing consultations with the Government of Botswana, the Ministry of Foreign Affairs of the Republic of Namibia addressed a note verbale that a secessionist group led by Mr. Mishake Muyongo had committed horrific acts of terrorism in the Caprivi region of Namibia on August 2, 1999. In interviews to the international media, he stated, in no uncertain terms, that he is the leader of the secessionist movement, and he took full responsibility for the act of terrorism perpetrated by his supporters in the Caprivi region, which resulted in the death and injury of innocent Namibian citizens. Furthermore, the Namibian government noted the statement by the UNHCR Representative in Southern Africa, Mr. Mengesha Kebede, in an interview he gave to the Namibian Broadcasting Corporate Television (NBC TV) on August 3, 1999, during which he said: "If it is true that the Caprivi Liberation Movement Leader, Mishake Muyongo, is taking responsibility for actions in Katima Mulilo, it contravenes the conditions under which he gained refugee status in Botswana. In light of Mr. Muyongo's public support for the terrorist acts committed by his terrorist group, the Government of Namibia strongly demands that Mr. Muyongo's refugee status be revoked. Mr. Muyongo should be held responsible for the deaths of innocent Namibians and the wanton destruction of property."

The Government of Botswana, and indeed Mishake himself, argued that there was no evidence to suggest that he took part in the attack, or even organized the revolt. He claimed to be the leader of Caprivi, and that the incident being reported was only a manifestation of the built-in frustration of the people who wanted independence from the SWAPO rule and dictatorship. In fact, it was alleged that it was SWAPO forces that had attacked and pillaged villages along the border, resulting in the displacement.

Given the impasse and the exchange of harsh words between

the two governments, I undertook a mission to Namibia, where I discussed with the minister of Home Affairs, Mr. Jerry Ekandjo, primarily the Namibian government's proposal to move the Osiri refugee camp, and the possible return of Namibian asylum seekers, from Botswana. Given the intertwined nature of conflicts in the region, the Namibians had continued to be wary of the presence of Angolan refugees, including a few of the San people from across the border, in the Osiri refugee camp. They wanted the camp moved to an area away from major routes in the north, which happened to be a crucial environment for the livelihood of the San people of Namibia, who still survived as hunter gatherers. Chief John Arnold, leader of the San, had expressed that the self-sustaining livelihood of the San would collapse if twenty thousand refugees were moved there. The area was formerly known as Bushman Land and was home to some six thousand San people.

Human rights organizations and advocates of minority rights groups, like Survival International, were addressing their concerns to my office and the press. The SWAPO leadership had long maintained that a few of the San people, who served the South Africa Defence Forces as trackers during the war in Angola, had been taken to South Africa when the SDF pulled out. The president of SWAPO, Sam Nujoma, had accused South Africa of ulterior motives in resettling San in South Africa. He had claimed that they were being trained to carry out subversive activities in Namibia in a possible coordinated action with UNITA and the CLA. Therefore, any issue involving the San was viewed with suspicion.

Minister Ekanjo agreed to suspend the Osiri relocation issue until we resolved the challenge in Botswana, and work toward the voluntary repatriation of Caprivi refugees. The Namibian newspapers observed that the UN objection was voiced in a meeting held behind closed doors between the minister of Home Affairs, Jerry Ekandjo, his top aides, donor governments, and UNHCR. "A well-placed source said Mengesha Kebede, the Representative of UNHCR's Regional Office in Pretoria, told the minister at the tense meeting that donors might withdraw funding, if the Namibian Government went ahead with its plans."

Home Affairs spokesman, Mikka Asino, told the Namibians that a submission had been made to Cabinet on the proposed move to M'Kata. However, the plans will be put on hold for the time being. "While a feasibility study is carried out," Mr. Ekanjo requested UNHCR to urgently organize a tripartite meeting to facilitate the voluntary return of Namibian refugees from Botswana. The Namibian request was communicated to the Government of Botswana, which agreed immediately. A tripartite consultation was organized in Francistown.

Mr. Ekanjo came to Francistown with a sizable delegation and met with the Botswana counterparts headed by the minister of Labor on the establishment of a tripartite framework for the voluntary repatriation of Namibian refugees and asylum seekers. I represented UNHCR at that meeting, and we agreed on the launch of the return operation, as long as it was on a voluntary basis. The insistence that the leadership of the Caprivi Movement had to be handed over to Namibia for them to stand trial as terrorists was not acceptable to the Botswana government. In order to defuse the tension and provide the necessary asylum space for the majority of men, women, and children that had crossed over to decide freely on whether to return or remain in Botswana, the removal of the leadership and assurance that they will be kept away from the refugees and indeed the cutting of any links with movements in Caprivi was accepted as being a lesser evil. I consider my shuttling between the two delegations to find a common ground as being the most successful shuttle diplomacy effort ever undertaken by me. I remain proud of it.

It was clear that in order to rapidly defuse the tension that was building up, the so-called leadership had to be moved out of Botswana. The senior protection officer, Bruno Geddo, was tasked to urgently process their emergency resettlement and in coordination with the Regional Bureau and the Division of International Protection, and their cases were submitted to the Government of Denmark. They were accepted on the condition that they refrain from any political activity, and Myoungo and Chief Mamile, upon signing an affidavit to that effect, left for Denmark on a travel document provided by the embassy in Pretoria. The two leaders were joined by the chief's wife, a daughter, and a cousin.

A voluntary repatriation program for those individuals volunteering to return home was initiated immediately. I consider my actions in that operation to have been one of the most rewarding diplomatic undertakings. I take pride in the fact that I had contributed my bit at resolving conflict in a part of Africa, and avoided further blood shade and possibly war. I cannot think of more a gratifying undertaking in my line of work.

Lesotho Refugees Seeking Asylum in South Africa

One of the memorable, oversupplied, and fascinating refugee programs I have witnessed while serving in Africa would be that of refugees that crossed into South Africa from Lesotho, and the assistance they were offered.

In 1998, following parliamentary elections, an overwhelming majority voted for the ruling Lesotho Congress for Democracy Party, which won seventy-nine out of the eighty seats. However, following allegations of fraud, and after a failed lawsuit by opposition parties, widespread rioting broke out. Given the escalation in violence and looting, South Africa authorized the deployment of the Army to quell the violence on September 22, 1998. The operation was to "restore democracy and the rule of law." South Africa's first post-Apartheid war was ordered by the acting President Mangosuthu Gatsha Buthelezi, who was South Africa's third-in-command after Nelson Mandela and Thabo Mbeki. Buthelezi sent troops into Lesotho in September 1998, to protect the government of Prime Minister Pakalitha Mosisili, and called on SADC member countries to join in the deployment. Botswana participated by dispatching a token force.

As a result of the rioting and prevailing conflict, refugees crossed over mainly from Maseru, and sought shelter across the border in South Africa. The South African Deputy Minister of Home Affairs, Madam Lindewe Sisulu, called me at the end of September, and asked that I join her at Ladybird. We visited the refugee site just outside of Ladybird, on the way to Maseru, where some two thousand well-dressed and healthy-looking Lesotho asylum seekers were accommodated. Following random interviews, I confirmed that the arrivals could be considered as refugees on a *prima facie* basis. I found out that the government had already approved an emergency allocation, and that there was no need for UNHCR or any international assistance. This was news to me, as it has not happened then, or later, that I would be invited and told that my organization's material or financial assistance was not required.

I observed on the ground that Bloemfontein-based NGOs were active all over the "camp." The SADF had set up a heated tent village with the full complement of pit latrines and kitchens with cooking stoves. Various NGOs, the Red Cross, as well as the Defence Forces, were providing hot meals refugees could choose from. Eggs and bacon with porridge and milk were being served, while the other option was toast and roasted meat. Sandwiches and a variety of fruits were in abundance. I have never seen anything like this in relation to refugee feeding programs anywhere in the world.

I flew back to Pretoria and reported on my findings. The office sent a monitoring mission a couple weeks later to confirm the safe return of the refugees.

Relocation of Refugees in Mozambique

Mozambique will be remembered for its successful return and re-integration program, which benefited over 1.7 million of its refugees from neighboring countries. The country had acceded to the UN 1951 Convention relating to the Status of Refugees and the 1969 OAU Convention. However, it was not well-understood that the country also offered asylum for refugees, primarily from all over Africa.

Mozambique's generosity toward refugees was challenged by migrants using the same route and facilities as a transit route on the way to South Africa. Refugee status determination took place in Maputo, and there were a significant number of refugees in the country, assisted in two camps close to the capital, Maputo. The

Government of Mozambique was coming under pressure from the Government of South Africa to curtail the flow of asylum seekers and migrants. Most people assumed it was only Africans using that route. However, the great majority of migrants coming at the time included arrivals on chartered flights, posing as tourists, from Pakistan and some from India. The Asian migrants were well-organized and had their network from Durban to Mamelody on the outskirts of Pretoria. The Africans had to rely on traffickers and smugglers.

I visited Maputo to discuss a proposed plan by the Mozambican authorities to close two refugee camps in Boane district, about twenty-five kilometers west of Maputo, in order to exercise tighter control over asylum seekers. I would meet and exchange ideas on options with Mr. Fernando Fazenda, director of the government's Refugee Support Nucleus (NAR). UNHCR's position was not to relocate the refugees in the rural area away from Maputo, where some were attending school, and others were involved in small trade. A move away would deny them the opportunity of self-sufficiency and a durable solution through local integration.

The government wanted new arrivals, as well as old refugees, to be sheltered and catered for in just one center in the Nampula province in the north. Most of the refugees who entered Mozambique were from the Great Lakes region, and they crossed into the country over its northern borders with Tanzania, Malawi, and Zambia.

Fazenda would argue that this measure would allow the government to provide better humanitarian assistance to refugees, while at the same time ensuring more effective control over foreign nationals in the country. Like elsewhere, my government interlocutors never failed to allege that some refugees have been involved in crimes such as car theft, drug trafficking, and counterfeiting, as they were residing close to the capital.

Mozambique was just a stepping-stone. "They are using Mozambique as a corridor—their real destination is South Africa," Fazenda would argue. And it is easy to enter South Africa from Boane, because it is only a couple hours' drive away. But it would be much more difficult for people in a camp in Nampula, two thousand kilometers north of Maputo, to reach South Africa.

My plea not to move the refugees became even more complicated when I found out that the refugee camps had already been offered to Mozal for the establishment of an aluminium smelter joint project in what became the Beluluane Industrial Park. The project was a smelting facility that produces aluminium exclusively for export, and thus had to be near the port.

Mozal was a joint venture between major investors, BHP, Mitsubishi Corp, Industrial Development Corporation of South Africa, and the Government of Mozambique. The project was part of a recovery program led by the Mozambican government's active desire for foreign investment to help rebuild the nation after the country's civil war in the early 1990s. The Mozal smelter was officially opened in September 2000. It was the first major foreign investment in Mozambique, and the biggest private sector project in the country.

We had no option but to agree on the new camp for new arrivals, with the understanding that students enrolled in the capital, as well as self-reliant refugees, would be given the opportunity to remain in Maputo. In the final analysis, I have come to realize that governments were willing to compromise their position on refugee settlements if, and when, other national interests are considered more attractive.

Assignment as Acting UNHCR Representative in Tanzania

In January 2001, the high commissioner, Mr. Ruud Lubbers, addressed a letter to the then Minister for Foreign Affairs of South Africa, Mrs. Nkosazana Dlamini-Zuma, informing her that I will be leaving Pretoria shortly to take up "other important duties." Accordingly, he was proposing Ms. Bemma Donko of Ghana to replace me. I hand-carried the request to the minister, who was happy to observe that an African woman was being proposed to replace a male colleague. She instructed, on the spot, that her acceptance be communicated to the high commissioner as soon as possible.

While securing the agreement of the government to receive my

Tripartite meeting for the repatriation of Rwandan refugees involving UNHCR Tanzania and Rwanda

replacement, I was informed by the director of the Africa Bureau, Mr. Kolude Doherty, that my candidacy for Representative Liberia had been withdrawn, "as the organization needed my services in Tanzania." He explained to me that the new high commissioner wanted the representative in Tanzania to come to Geneva immediately and become his chief of cabinet. He had consulted with all, and it had been agreed that I replace her in Tanzania. I agreed, since the Tanzania option would give me the opportunity to be with my family, as Liberia was a non-family duty station.

Leaving my family behind in Pretoria pending my official accreditation, I proceeded to Tanzania in May 2001, and got to work with the excellent briefing and support I received from the deputy representative, Mr. Kai Nielsen. I visited all the field locations, and also found out that all had been informed of the transitional management arrangements put in place. Beyond the management of the office in Tanzania, I also got involved in the Tripartite Repatriation meetings in Rwanda and Burundi.

Sometime in October, I received a phone call from the bureau director, letting me know that the high commissioner had just informed him of his intention to appoint Chris Ache as his representative in Tanzania. He explained that Chris was in Geneva, waiting for his appointment to the UK, when the high commissioner visiting London had met with Tony Blair, who had suggested that he appoint Dawn Shepard as his representative. The HC had accepted, and upon his return to Geneva, had sought advice from DHRM, as to where he could send Chris. DHRM had informed the HC that Tanzania was vacant, as a new representative had not yet been officially appointed. The HC had agreed and requested that Chris be informed accordingly. Chris also called me, offering to buy the curtains I had reserved at the residence of the representative.

I was put in a dilemma, as I could not accept the prospect of being a staff-in-between assignment (SIBA), and I could not go to my country of origin, for reasons explained above. The South African authorities were also quick to point out that, as a former accredited official, I would have to regularize my stay under other immigration arrangements. Applying for asylum and joining the bandwagon of abusers was not an option for me either.

I expressed interest in moving to Geneva to assume a lower grade position to my previous assignment, as Chief of Section, Program Coordination, and Operations Support. I received my advanced reassignment to Geneva in November 2001.

In September, my family proceeded to Addis Ababa, where my daughters were enrolled at the Sanford English International School. I could not join them, as I did not have clearance from UNHCR, given the restrictions imposed upon me following the allegations levied by the Government of Ethiopia during my assignment in South Africa. However, as the standard assignment length (SAL) of the incumbent of the post, Robert Ashe, had not yet expired, I was put on special leave with full pay for two months, one week and two days, being charged to a vacant post as a senior officer in the then Central Southwest Asia, North Africa and the Middle East Bureau (CASWANAME). I took advantage of my presence in Geneva to get an excellent induction and on-the-job training, and briefing by Robert into the function of chief of Programme Coordination and Operations Support (PCOS), which I assumed in February 2002.

CHAPTER EIGHT

Round Two in Geneva

As chief of PCOS, I had the opportunity to look at all programs across regions and compare protection and assistance activities in my capacity as Secretariat to the Headquarters Operations Review Board (ORB) and Resource Allocation Committee. Part of the challenge the organization was trying to overcome was how to objectively review and decide which submissions from the field should be given priority over another. The country operations plans submitted to headquarters were closely examined by officers with designated geographic responsibilities.

The challenge facing UNHCR then, and now, is that the board or the executive committee, made up of member states, approves the annual budget, which unfortunately has never been, and will never be, fully funded. Therefore, the process of prioritization and reprioritization has become too frequent and makes the organization's management unduly bureaucratic. If member states could fund what they approve, the organization could do away with constant reprioritizations and cut-backs on its administrative and bureaucracy costs. Such a development could give its staff more time and effort to invest in working directly with and finding durable solutions for persons of concern. Pending the realization of that wish, prioritization continues.

I co-chaired various preliminary operations reviews with Mr. Roberto Meier, head of finance. We also had to scrutinize emergency and other submissions from the field for additional resources. We were not popular with the bureau, to say the least, and some, like the head of CASWANAME, had coined the term "Dark Forces of Evil" to describe our functions. Mistrust between the desk officers of the Regional Bureau and PCOS officers was clear and apparent. The DHC, as chairman of the ORB, appeared to have encouraged the division, as it served as a checks and balance of a divide-and-rule policy. The conflict and overlap were one of the driving motives for streamlining procedures, as advocated by the Project Delphi.

In comparing cross-region programs and trying to assess needs and impact, the need arose to further develop tools to assist in the standardized design of needs assessments and program formulation at field level. The need for quantifiable indicators for meaningful results-based management (RBM) was urgent.

We set the objective for the gradual rollout of RBM and the use of a logical framework (log frame) for planning that allows the systematic organization of operational goals, objectives, and indicators into logical relationships, using a matrix format. We were convinced that it would help operations teams design sound projects with an improved likelihood of success, and facilitate effective reporting.

A well-designed log frame can show project implementers whether or not they have achieved stated objectives and delivered planned outputs in an optimal manner. The following terms used in UNHCR's operations management documents reflect the principles and processes of RBM and the log frame:

- **Objective**: A statement of desired results and impact formulated at sector level for each program goal in a country operation.

- **Output**: A specific result delivered by the activities used to accomplish the objective. The delivery of an output must be under the control of UNHCR or an implementing partner, which is held fully accountable.

- **Indicator**: A unit used to measure signs of change toward the achievement of results.

UNHCR's operations management system (OMS) uses two types of indicators: impact indicators and performance indicators. Indicators should be disaggregated by age and gender, as appropriate.

- **Impact indicator**: A sign of changes in the conditions of target populations and their welfare. Impact indicators are set for objectives or goals.

- **Performance indicator**: A measure of performance toward the achievement of planned outputs. Performance indicators can be quantified and graded in terms of quality, and revisited within a planned time frame. Performance indicators are set for outputs.

In discussing improving outcomes of programmatic activities through monitoring and enhancing institutional accountability, it must be recalled that various initiatives were launched at the time between humanitarian organizations, agencies, and donors. Some have resulted in important work in developing performance standards and indicators relating to their respective contributions to humanitarian outcomes. Among others, the Executive Committee for Humanitarian Affairs (ECHA) and the Inter-Agency Standing Committee (IASC) launched an independent Humanitarian Response Review (HRR) of the Global humanitarian system (UN, NGOs, Red Cross-Red Crescent Movement, and the International Organization for Migration (IOM) to map out the gaps and make recommendations to address them. The review recommended the establishment and application of different sets of benchmarks at the level of the organizations (management benchmarks for preparedness and planning) and of the system (process and impact benchmarks for CAP and other planning models). At the various meetings, which I or a member of my team attended, we confirmed UNHCR's commitment to the delivery of quality protection and assistance activities, and to the optimal use of limited resources.

Hence, it has developed over the years a range of tools to enhance programming and accountability.

UNHCR has made great efforts in mainstreaming Standards and Indicators in the context of results-based management within the organization. We invested the necessary resources in a range of consultations, both at headquarters and in the field, to produce the first edition of the *Practical Guide to the Systematic Use of Indicators*. The guide was therefore developed to serve as a practical manual and reference tool for UNHCR staff and managers in the field, as well as for implementing and operational partners involved in program assessment, planning, design, management monitoring and evaluation. It would also prove useful for UNHCR staff and decision-makers at various levels who review and coordinate operations. This includes operations managers, resource managers, technical and policy officers, Regional Bureau, the Department of International Protection, and the External and Donor Relations Services. It was hoped that this guide, which contained detailed explanations and various tips, as well as references for further reading, would allow for the systematic, consistent and effective application of standards and indicators in refugee situations around the world.

The guide was also meant to be of interest to donor and host governments, members of UNHCR's executive committee, and other parties within the humanitarian community that support and monitor the activities and performance of UNHCR in carrying out its mandate.

This first edition was released with the understanding that it would be considered as work-in-progress toward achieving UNHCR's long-term vision of establishing and integrating standards and indicators into refugee protection and assistance operations. As such, it envisaged further refinement and fine-tuning based on feedback from the users.

The guide is divided into six chapters. Chapter 1 introduces the guide, providing background information and a definition of UNHCR's standards and indicators. Chapter 2 explains how the standards and indicators relate to UNHCR's results-based management methodology, and to its operations management system (OMS). Chapter 3 provides suggestions for systematic and reliable data collection. Chapter 4 describes how to use standards and indicators in the context of the UNHCR program planning, assessment, and design cycle. Chapter 5 describes how to integrate the standards and indicators into UNHCR planning and reporting documents. Chapter 6 presents the fifty-two core standards and indicators and their supplements, which explain standards and indicators in UNHCR operations.

This guide acknowledged that the set of standards and indicators included was not exhaustive. Nevertheless, it would provide enhanced quantifiable data for an increased number of situations, illustrating the well-being of the population of concern, as well as allow global comparisons between UNHCR operations.

Thus, through the use of indicators in the guide, UNHCR has a monitoring tool covering UNHCR operations worldwide. The snapshot of the well-being of refugees and returnees, which these quantitative indicators give, will need to be complemented with additional information from qualitative indicators, project-level indicators, detailed sectorial data, and various narrative reports.

The UNHCR guide benefited from the Sphere Project, the Good Humanitarian Donorship (GHD), the Active Learning Network for Accountability and Performance in Humanitarian Action (ALNAP), and the Humanitarian Accountability Project (SMA).

Upon completion of my assignment as chief of PCOS, my supervisor, Ms. Marjon Kamara, noted that the most notable of my contributions was "coordinating and overseeing the release of the first edition of the Guidelines on the use of Standards and Indicators in 2004." The guideline was released under the signature of the Assistant High Commissioner Mr. Kamal Morjane, who headed operations in the organization.

CHAPTER NINE

Assignment as Representative in Liberia

I took over the functions of UNHCR Representative in Liberia from Mr. Moses Okello, who had served the organization during the difficult days of the Civil War. He had indeed left a team and a well-managed office that made my transition pleasant. The presence of colleagues I had known earlier such as Adey Makonnen, Terry Ongaro, and Golam Abbas made my induction seamless.

In discussing the Liberia program, much attention is given to the Refugee Return and Reintegration program and the IDP program. However, it is not widely recognized that the country hosted Cote d'Ivoire refugees since 2002, when thousands had crossed and sought safety in eastern Liberia. The Government of Liberia had granted some twelve thousand Ivorian refugee status. The majority were living in camps and communities in Grand Gedeh, Maryland, Nimba, and River Gee Counties, which fell under the UNMIL Sector Four command.

Liberia also hosted residual Sierra Leonean refugees who had sought asylum since the Civil War in 1991. In mid-2004, UNHCR completed the voluntary repatriation operation for this population, after peace was restored in the country. However, 3478 Sierra Leonean refugees opted not to return home for a variety of reasons ranging from risk of revenge to forced female genital mutilation prior to being accepted into their communities of origin.

There were also some sixty-two urban refugees and asylum-seekers residing in and around Monrovia. They belonged to various nationalities: Algeria, Chad, Ethiopia, Iraq, Palestine, Rwanda, Somalia, the Sudan, and Uganda. Refugees in a country going through civil war reminded me, in a way, of my own situation earlier in Lebanon. As an example of the complex situation refugees go through in Africa, I was surprised to meet and interact with an Ethiopian refugee who came to Liberia in the early '80s, having crossed several countries on the way from his first country of asylum, the Sudan. As a young student, he had fled from the Red Terror campaign in 1976, in his country of origin. He was part of a group that was brought by traffickers to West Africa, from where they were told they could board a ship to the USA. He was stuck. Some had perished, and a few had moved on. He survived all these years in Ggbaraga town by selling charcoal.

Background to the Refugee and Internally Displaced Program

The civil unrest in Liberia had been one of the most destructive in West Africa. The first round of the war started in 1989 and ended in 1997, with the election of Charles Taylor as president, who subsequently failed to bring peace back to Liberia. The ensuing lack of reconciliation and economic progress eventually led to the emergence early in 2000, of a new rebellion in Lofa County, in the northwestern part of the country, led by a rebel group called the Liberians United for Reconciliation and Democracy (LURD). In March 2003, a second group called the Movement for Democracy in Liberia (MODEL) launched attacks against government positions in eastern Liberia. According to some observers and human rights groups, over seven hundred thousand persons may have lost their lives during the fourteen years of conflict.

As of December 2003, it was known that over 340,000 Liberians were in exile in neighboring countries, while an

172

estimated 500,000 Liberians were internally displaced persons (IDPs), of whom 325,000 were living in camps run by humanitarian organizations. The war in Liberia had a significant impact on most countries in the subregion, and was felt most strongly in Sierra Leone, Guinea, and Cote d'Ivoire.

As a result of concerted pressure from the international community, Charles Taylor relinquished the presidency and went into exile in Nigeria on August 11, 2003. His departure from office preceded the signing of a comprehensive peace agreement on August 18, 2003.

Following protracted negotiations, the formation of a National Transitional Government of Liberia (NTGL) was agreed in Accra. The NTGL, which took office on October 14, 2003, comprised representatives of LURD, MODEL, civil society, and all the major political parties. To support the peace process in Liberia, the Economic Community of West African States (ECOWAS) sent an initial peacekeeping force of three thousand, later to be joined by a larger force totalling fifteen thousand troops under United Nations command.

With the peacekeeping force fully deployed, and faction fighters disarmed, UNHCR increased its presence and activities, optimistic that adequate security would gradually be restored

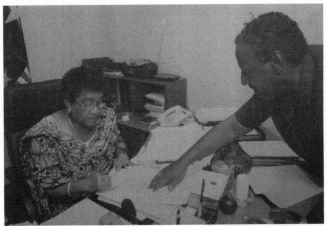

Me briefing the newly elected President of Liberia, Madam Serlif Johnson in the chapter regarding my assignment to that country

throughout the country. Based on these assumptions, UNHCR started planning for an organized voluntary repatriation of Liberian refugees, commencing in October 2004.

United Nations Mission in Liberia

The United Nations Mission in Liberia (UNMIL) was established by Security Council Resolution no. 1509 (2003) of September 19, 2003, to support the implementation of the ceasefire agreement and the peace process; to protect United Nations staff, facilities, and civilians; to support humanitarian and human rights activities, as well as assist in national security reform.

It has to be acknowledged that the peacekeepers were perceived as providers of hope, and UNMIL's contribution to Liberia has been immeasurable. It relentlessly supported every sector of the country's recovery: disarmament, demobilization, and reintegration; police and judicial reform; the conduct of successful elections; and the peaceful transfer of power.

The successful conduct of the 2005 elections would not have been possible without the assistance of UNMIL, and this endeavor on the part of the United Nations is worth noting. The backbone of UNMIL operations was the peacekeeping force which encompassed four brigade-sized formations, plus the force headquarters. Each formation was responsible for one of four sectors that the country had been divided into. Each sector contained a full range of combat units, engineering and medical support.

Sector Four Under Ethiopian Command

Sector Four was headed by an Ethiopian general, and the largest deployment in the sector were ground troops from that country. Ethiopia had three infantry battalions based in Zwedru, Tappita, and Greenville. Senegal had one battalion based in Harper. Health care for all was provided by two units from China and Senegal. The sector's engineering company was from China.

I had become close to the Ethiopian force leadership. Upon

my arrival in Liberia, General Kamal Geltchu was replaced by General Tsegaye Tessema "Patrice," followed by General Berhanu Jula, and then General Seyoum Hagos. The latter two generals in particular, with their senior management, were frequent visitors at my place. Each general served some eight months before being rotated back home.

During the social exchange with my visitors, it became clear that there was no such thing as a coherent and one UN military deployment, as each behaved and acted differently based on national standards of each battalion.

Lieutenant-General Chikadibia Obiakor of Nigeria, as the overall force commander of the United Nations Mission in Liberia, was followed by his replacement, another Nigerian, Lieutenant-General Joseph Olorungbon Owonibi. Both saw me as an Ethiopian over and above my UNHCR representational function. I would meet them at the weekly UN senior management meeting at the UNMIL headquarters, chaired by the SRSG, Mr. Allan Doss, a British national. Both had approached me at different times to suggest that my country consider deploying commanders who can easily interact with them and assume more command responsibilities. From their perspective, language limitations were hindering or limiting the Ethiopian role at UNMIL headquarters, which was made up primarily of Pakistani and West African officers.

I was treated with respect by Ethiopian troops, who were happy to see another compatriot heading a UN agency. During field visits, military escorts and guards were provided against my will. At times, I could not even go to the bush to take a leak without armed troops cordoning off that portion of the bush, which was extremely uncomfortable, to say the least. Most of those protecting me did not know my predicaments with officials of my government. It was indeed ironic that the very troops of the government that was asking the UN for my removal, were providing me personal protection and treating me as a VIP.

The commanders and senior officers of Sector Four would come over for drinks at my place, where we also celebrated every Ethiopian holiday with other members of the compatriot community. Monthly luncheons were also organized for all community members, at one restaurant or another.

UN standards and rules do not necessarily jive with national standards and values. One evening General Seyoum, his deputy, and two other officers came to my residence, where I offered them drinks, and the usual exchange continued. They had attended a UN one-day training on how to control the spread of HIV amongst the troops and the community. The call for abstinence and limited mingling with the community was controversial from their perspective. The allegation that UNMIL troops and police officers were engaged in transactional sex with Liberian women would generate the spontaneous reaction: "This UN of yours is crazy. How I tell my troops not to see or interact with women and the community, and maintain their loyalty?" An older colonel would recall that he had heard from Ethiopian troops who had participated in the Korea and Congo deployments, that women were brought for them to enjoy during their rest and recuperation period. Now, the same international community was trying to deprive them of enjoyment and fun.

I learned a lot from General Seyoum Hagos, who explained to me that Ethiopian troops were primarily freedom fighters who did not have the expected military discipline inherited from the colonial masters or graduates of respected military colleges. He often said, "We fight in the bush, we work with people, and we survive with the support of people." Hierarchy and military discipline were not respected much, as comradely greetings and exchanges across ranks were common. It is difficult to train and expect a guerrilla army coming from the bush to act and behave as troops recruited and trained to be soldiers.

Military parades and synchronized marches were not given much consideration. To my embarrassment, that was demonstrated at the Saclepea Stadium during UN Day celebrations, attended by UN senior management. Different units from the Sector Four deployment took part. The well-built Senegalese paratroopers branding their well-polished French submachine guns, with white gloves and matching handkerchiefs around their neck, passed in front of the podium in a well-choreographed and synchronized march. They were followed by well-dressed Chinese troops who wowed the crowds with a display of martial arts movements. Then came the Ethiopian Army which had a lack of synchronization and coordination which was amplified by their bright white gloves. Many of my senior management colleagues would look at me, with some making cynical remarks. I had to defend the troop's lack of coordination and synchronization by explaining how they were in fact the only proven fighters who might not march properly, as they were trained and tested in the bush.

The Ethiopian contingent in Liberia also underlined the irony in life one would come across in unexpected places. On a helicopter flight from Monrovia to Voinjama, a sector under the command of Pakistani troops, with the Deputy SRSG Jordan Ryan, Colonel Tekeste from the Ethiopian Contingent, saluted me and informed me that he knew me and my family in Addis. We could not discuss on the helicopter, as he was seated far away, and the flight was noisy. Upon arrival in Voinjama, I inquired about where he knew me from, and found out that he was the officer who had moved into my Brother Ayalew Kebede's residence in Addis Ababa when the EPRDF took power in Ethiopia. He was a military observer, and was still staying in that house vacated by Ayalew. My family in Addis confirmed to me at a later stage that he had come to inform them of my well-being in Liberia upon completion of his deployment on mission.

Finally, it has to be recognized that a UNHCR protection officer deployed in Sector Four, Ms. Biskut Getahun, brought refugee protection books translated into Amharic, on her own initiative, and offered classes to the Ethiopian contingent, which included human rights.

Lack of Discipline and Accountability Issues Behind Peacekeeping

The role played by UNMIL and the Ethiopian contingent contained therein has been exemplary and acknowledged by all. However, there were also some shortcomings that need to be flagged to further improve the situation.

The lack of discipline by so-called former guerrilla armies became too much. I recall that following a return field trip from Harper, through Zwedru, back to Monrovia, I was shocked to find the UN checkpoint unmanned. Upon hooting for a couple minutes, a young soldier wearing underwear and a t-shirt came out of a tent to open the barrier. The soldier was supposedly on duty guarding the checkpoint. I was upset by the lack of discipline demonstrated by the soldier, and I immediately asked to see his commanding officer. He called out, and the commanding officer came out in his underwear and a t-shirt as well. We had a heated exchange, as they informed me that it was hot, and that they were watching Liverpool play Manchester. I informed them that I would report what I saw to their headquarters. Both were baffled, and the only comment they offered was that they were surprised that I spoke Amharic. I did complain to General Seyoum, and since that day, all checkpoints were manned by well-dressed soldiers, who checked cars properly and saluted passerbys properly.

I was concerned by the repatriation of some four dead bodies of Ethiopian troops, and according to confidential reports, all had suffered from HIV. Issues around screening of troops before deployment were identified to be a problem requiring urgent redress. The allegation of the Nigerian Force Commander that Ethiopians were sending infected troops to get insurance payment did not appear to be well-founded. However, I understood that some officers would include HIV-positive soldiers to enable them to receive additional benefits, even though it was understood that Ethiopian troops were not getting their full monthly entitlements. Troops not being paid their dues, who collected, and how the amounts were accounted for and syphoned off remain a mystery.

I have observed in my years with the UN that countries with large military contingents deploy troops as peacekeepers partially motivated by the generation of foreign currency. Pakistan, Bangladesh, and Ethiopia, amongst others, belong to that category. The UN pays the monthly due of each soldier deployed at the rate of some $1,200. The maximum ever collected by soldiers returning home has never exceeded 70 percent. On top of the troop cost, the UN also covers the additional cost of arms, clothing, shoes, and belts. The cost of vehicles is also covered by the UN. In Liberia, Pakistan had deployed a significant number of road repair equipment, with some not in working condition, but all rented on a daily basis. The commanders of sectors, as well as senior officers at headquarters, and monitors, receive additional allowances.

The position of the troop commanders expressed to me with regard to sexual exploitation and abuse by peacekeepers warrants closer scrutiny, as it was not one problem faced by one or a few troop-contributing countries. West Africa has demonstrated the broad geographic distribution of the problem we face. The accountability of UN peacekeepers and oversight of the deployment is left to the governments of troop-providing countries. Unfortunately, residents in recipient countries cannot tell the difference between UN staff and UN military deployments. Efforts need to be made to bridge the gap, as oversight and accountability issues do linger.

UN Peacekeepers and the Lingering Ghost of Sexual Exploitation and Abuse

How to ensure accountability of UN peacekeepers remains a major challenge for the organization. Sexual exploitation and abuse of women by UN peacekeepers and NGOs in West Africa has been a source of major scandals, and international agencies are still struggling with attempts to install accountability measures.

In hindsight, and based on my involvement at a later stage with oversight, I realize that the UN has made, and continues to make, serious efforts to ensure accountability of its staff, but unfortunately has not been able to establish an effective justice mechanism under its control with regard to peacekeepers. Peacekeepers enjoy privileges and immunities as UN personnel, and further protection from internal repercussions from the UN is granted to troops supplied by member states through the organization's agreements with these states. Troop deployment agreements constrain the UN's accountability apparatuses by granting sole jurisdiction for redress to the states supplying the troops.

With no geographical jurisdiction, the UN has no citizens to comprise its own military, and thanks to reliance on member states for funding, it cannot afford to procure its own troops. Dependence is therefore placed on member states to loan their own armed forces to work for the UN. Unwilling to relinquish sovereignty over their troops completely, however, states are enticed to do so by signing agreements that allow the contributing country to remain the sole authority over their troops.

Bilateral agreements are made upon assurances by troop-contributing member states that they would prosecute soldiers for any offenses committed while working as peacekeepers. However, these promises are seldom proffered or pursued. Having signed away their right to prosecute their staff, and thus ensure justice, the UN has few options for ensuring that peacekeepers adhere to their role as protectors. Codes of conduct and verbal condemnation of behavior are insufficient in preventing Sexual Exploitation and Abuse (SEA). Without the threat of serious repercussions, peacekeepers continue to act with impunity.

Access to justice is further limited by the removal of processes for redress, as survivors suffer further from the invisibility of accountability mechanisms. Sexual offense allegations usually involve investigation and prosecution, if any, in the perpetrator's home country. Not only does this mean survivors' emotional trauma is extended by the absence of a sense of justice and ability to participate in the processes of justice, but the removal of the forum from the location of the offense means increased challenges for evidence gathering and witness summoning.

The United Nations tried to address a number of issues when it deployed the first all-female peacekeeping unit in Liberia. In January 2007, a 125-strong all-women police contingent of peacekeepers from India was deployed to Liberia. This is the only case of an all-women contingent that I am aware of. Traditionally, contingents have always been composed of men, and only a few women served with their male colleagues. And even then, in general service or administrative capacity.

These units, in theory, had increased the number of women in peacekeeping, and were reportedly providing better responses to local women's issues—especially in areas where sexual violence was a prevalent part of the conflict. They did inspire young girls to join the national police forces. This mission resulted in women peacekeepers, due to heightened expectations and stereotypes, being called upon to respond to crimes against local women, increasing their workload. As they were expected to take on all projects relating to women in the area, as well as regulate the behavior of their male colleagues, their mission was extended by several months.

The police unit hinted that women as best could work with other women, but one cannot help but remind the UN, and all observers, that separate has never been equal. The mixed-gender environment attempted in Liberia has been commended as being part of the UN commitment to gender mainstreaming. However, when we are talking about equality, it should be real equality. Referring to gender quotas and committing to mixed units is a better way to move toward gender parity—and not all-female units. It has also debatable if all-female peacekeeping units can solve all the problems related to women, peace, and security in the context of the UN. Faulty considerations of gender and power have reproduced problematic responses to a systemic challenge.

Women are seen as a quick fix to solve the UN's sexual violence problem. Diverting responsibility to women does not address the problem of sexual violence in peacekeeping operations, or help eradicate its causes. On the contrary, building sustainable peace will require work from both men and women, including peacekeepers, policymakers, humanitarian agency staff, members of community organizations, as well as the wider society.

As an alternative system to interrogating, investigating, preventing, and prosecuting SEA by UN peacekeepers, it is difficult not to link this issue to a failure of gender mainstreaming in peace operations—and examine the claim in the UN more broadly. The UN is consistently short of peacekeepers for various missions, but this does not mean that it must accept troops whose behaviors are far more serious than financial misconduct. For starters, if proper measures are not taken by national authorities to address and prevent such misconduct, then the countries involved must not be allowed act in any capacity that provides an opportunity for further exploitative behavior. The UN should name and shame such countries.

At the time I served in Liberia, out of 77,117 military personnel in UN peacekeeping, 1,640 were female, which is around 2 percent. It is clear that despite many appeals from the secretary-general and the Security Council, the UN has yet to achieve a gender balance, or to ensure the full and equal participation of women in peacekeeping. This state of affairs is also reflective of most member states.

One quick fix arrangement could be gender trainings in preparing peacekeepers to be deployed. The mandate should include gender training in peacekeeping missions. There are two main types of training given to peacekeeping troops: pre-deployment training, which occurs prior to deployment and is given in a troop's home country or region. And induction training, which occurs at the mission level. Pre-deployment gender training aims to educate troops on the basic values of the United Nations when dealing with men and women of the host population. Pre-deployment gender training should be broad and generic, incorporating a wealth of different examples, and cover specific information about culture and gender in the country where the mission will be deployed. Training should inform peacekeepers about the social and cultural context in which they will operate in order to help reduce unintended effects of their behaviors on the local population. Pre-deployment training is the responsibility of the troop-contributing member states. Unfortunately, not all countries apply the same policies and priorities in these trainings, and the levels of training can be substantially different from one country to another.

Many of the top troop-contributing countries (TCCs) are developing countries, where there might be few resources for providing troops with adequate training and resources, especially with respect to gender issues. Nevertheless, there are a considerable number of training centers, particularly in the global south, that conduct capacity-development activities

Finally, while discussing peacekeeping and sexual exploitation and abuse, it had be noted that the calls for reforms of the United Nations in general is growing louder by the day. However, there is little clarity or consensus about what reform may mean in practice. Both those who want the UN to play a greater role in world affairs, and those who want its role confined to humanitarian work, or otherwise reduced use the term "UN reform" to refer to their ideas. The range of opinion extends from those who want to eliminate the UN entirely, to those who want to transform it into a full-fledged world government.

Recent secretary-generals have presented numerous ways to implement new reforms. However, the proposed reforms appear to be limited in scope and coverage, as they remain constrained by the UN structure dominated by the permanent membership of the UN Security Council, which reflects the power structure of the world as it was in 1945. The big powers, who talk of reform and change, do not appear to be ready or willing to give it up their monopoly for the common good. Instead, they continue to hide being a smoke screen slogan of demand for change and reform of the very body, while in reality, they continue to incapacitate the organization to consolidate their hegemony. The rise of China as a superpower might not change the status quo, as it also remains a member of the UN veto club. The world may have to wait for the rise of middle-income countries to either meaningfully change the UN, or replace it with a new global peacekeeping structure.

The Liberian Return and Reintegration Operation

In 2004, it was foreseen that close to 100,000 Liberian refugees would repatriate spontaneously, or through facilitated voluntary repatriation. A further 154,000 Liberians were expected to repatriate in 2005, while about 65,000 were to return home in 2006. Reintegration programs were to continue throughout 2007.

I was assigned as representative in Liberia on August 1, 2005. My assignment coincided with the December 2005 agreement of the Inter-Agency Standing Committee (IASC) to establish the cluster leadership approach in non-refugee humanitarian emergencies. UNHCR accepted to lead the Protection Cluster, as well as the Camp Coordination and Camp Management Cluster (CCCM) for conflict-induced internal displacement and shelter. The IASC also agreed, initially, to apply the cluster approach in the DRC, Uganda, and Liberia.

Regarding the refugee program, UNHCR coordinated all aspects of the return and initial reintegration efforts. Upon my arrival, some two hundred thousand Liberian refugees, who were registered with UNHCR, were living in camps and urban centers in various countries, while eighty thousand registered internally displaced persons were in camps in and around the Monrovia area. Unknown numbers of unregistered IDPs were occupying public buildings in Monrovia.

In order to expedite the refugee return program in a coordinated manner, I visited UNHCR offices in Guinea, Sierra Leone, and Cote d'Ivoire. Having cooperative and willing UNHCR partners, particularly in Guinea with Stefano Severe, and in Sierra Leone with Emile Segbor, we were able to put in place a de facto situational management approach in order to accelerate the voluntary repatriation process. The return process was treated as one operation, where returnees and their personal belongings were transported from countries of asylum to their final drop-off points inside Liberia. A common mass information campaign was launched for all countries, sending one message to all refugees and returnees alike.

Road-building equipment and expertise would come and assist from Sierra Leone and Guinea to improve access inside Liberia. The cooperation and coordination efforts were recognized by the bureau, and indeed UNHCR as a whole.

In an effort to secure sustainable return, and in collaboration with other UN agencies, local and international non-governmental organizations, and the donor community, UNHCR initiated reintegration programs in keeping with the 4R (Repatriation, Reintegration, Rehabilitation, and Reconstruction) principles. The aim was to develop effective links between start-up reintegration projects and long-term development goals. A key element of this strategy would be the community participation approach through sectorial activities and community empowerment projects (CEPs). Communities would be given the opportunity to fully participate in the planning and implementation of programs in their localities. Programs would endeavor to address the needs of all displaced people, and not target particular groups. However, the programs would be geared toward areas with high numbers of returnees, including both refugees and IDPs, and address the specific needs of such communities. The CEPs would form an effective basis for the introduction of community-driven development (CDD), funded by UNDP and the World Bank, throughout the entire country, beginning in 2005.

Refugee and IDP returns merged and became one program in rural areas, from where internal and external displacement took place in the first instance. It is a cherished memory that UNHCR constructed several schools in returnee areas, involving returnee labor, where UNICEF provided the equipment and teaching materials. UNDP rehabilitated the schools and community water points, and WFP provided food for laborers and school feeding programs. Notwithstanding logistical constraints, it was a commendable coordinated community-based recovery activity.

Ellen Johnson Sirleaf Elected President

Madam Ellen Johnson Sirleaf was sworn in as Liberia's President on January 16, 2006, becoming Africa's first elected female leader. In a video recorded for UNHCR, she appealed to refugees, saying, "your government wants you home." I was positively surprised to learn that Brownie Jeffrey Samukai Jr. had been appointed as the minister of National Defence of Liberia. He took office as part of President Ellen Johnson Sirleaf's Cabinet.

When I first met him in Tanzania, I was aware that he had military and police background. He had accompanied me on several field trips to Mwanza, Ngara, and Ngoma. He was the head of UNHCR's field staff and security setup. I was aware that he had served as a security officer with the United Nations in East Timor, before joining UNHCR as Head of Staff Safety and Security in Tanzania. That acquaintance did come in handy to help me expedite things whenever they were blocked in one bureaucratic structure or another. When we both exchanged greetings whenever we met, referring to each another as *sir,* in a respectful manner. This mutual respect and formality signified the change in our relationship.

World Refugee Day 2006

On December 4, 2000, the United Nations General Assembly, in Resolution No. 55/76, decided that beginning in the year 2000, June 20th would be celebrated as World Refugee Day. In this resolution, the General Assembly noted that 2001 marked the 50th anniversary of the 1951 Convention relating to the Status of Refugees. It is commemorated to honor all refugees, raise awareness, and solicit support.

African Refugee Day had been formally celebrated in several countries prior to 2000. The Organization of African Unity (OAU) had agreed to have World Refugee Day coincide with Africa Refugee Day on June 20th.

Each year, on June 20th, the United Nations, the United Nations Refugee Agency (UNHCR), and countless civic groups around the world, host World Refugee Day events in order to draw the public's attention to the plight of millions of refugees worldwide who have been forced to flee their homes due to war or persecution. The annual commemoration is marked by a variety of events in more than one hundred countries, involving government officials, humanitarian workers, celebrities, civilians, and the forcibly displaced themselves.

UNHCR designates the theme for each World Refugee Day. The theme for the campaign in 2006 was Hope. Liberia, with ongoing refugee and IDP returns and reintegration programs, was chosen accordingly.

High Commissioner Antonio Guterres arrived on the evening of June 19, 2006, in preparation of World Refugee Day to be commemorated the following day, June 20th. I met him at the airport, together with the deputy head of UNMIL and the humanitarian coordinator, Jordan Rayan, as the head of UNMIL was out of town. I introduced myself jokingly as his representative, as I had not met him since his appointment a few months back. Driving back, I offered Guterres the option of moving into Mamba Point Hotel, where he was booked. Or, if he considered himself a friend, that he could actually stay with me at my humble residence guest house. He confirmed himself to be a friend, and I took him home, where I briefed him on the program over dinner prepared by Prince, the cook. Having inquired about his likes and dislikes earlier with Athar, his chief of staff, I served him dark chocolate after dinner, which he visibly enjoyed more than the meal.

In the morning, after breakfast, he asked if I had access to the Reuters financial portal. I told him that I could get him the UN exchange rate, not realizing then that he wanted to know the ups and downs of each major currency in order to determine if the organization was facing an exchange gain or loss at any given time, which I also later found out to be his daily obsession. Gains were for him to dispose of as he pleased, while losses had to be immediately covered through a review of programs.

On June 20th, and as part of the program, the high commissioner and his entourage departed early to the Mano River border bridge between Sierra Leone and Liberia. We walked across the bridge, accompanied by the Deputy SRSG and media representatives.

We met Emile Segbor, representative in Sierra Leone, with some two hundred returnees standing in front of trucks that brought them to the border. Several children dressed in *Hope* T-shirts met the high commissioner, who took two boys by their hands and led all of us over the Mano River border bridge to their Liberian homeland. This symbolic and picturesque undertaking was captured by international journalists, and printed by various newspapers around the world.

Earlier, as part of the program, I had agreed with Emile that he would sit with the high commissioner on the drive back to Monrovia in the armored vehicle deployed by UNMIL for our senior guest. The plan was for Emile to brief the HC on the repatriation, and also get to know him better. Unfortunately, Mr. Guterres had other plans. He jumped into the back of one of the trucks with Liberian returnees. I climbed onboard, together with the impeccably dressed Emile, with black suit and tie.

At the back of the moving truck, the high commissioner tried to start a conversation with three families. It turned out to be humorous, with one of the drunk heads of family interrupting the discussions rudely by asking all to shut up because he was trying to sleep. The two UNMIL armed Filipino commandos, who had also jumped on to the truck, stood at the back and observed. The trucks arrived some forty minutes later at the Sinje transit center, where the returnees disembarked. The delegation was briefed by African Humanitarian Action (AHA) staff, who took the HC around and showed him the cafeteria, the medical screening facilities, and treatment centers, as well as the place where returnees traveling long distances would spend the night before heading to their home villages.

The World Refugee Day celebration continued in Sinje Town, where Liberian President Ellen Johnson Sirleaf joined Mr. Guterres in a commutative, colourful ceremony. The day was also the launching of the year-long campaign called Ninemillion.Org, which aimed to deliver education and sports programs to nine million refugee children around the world, through awareness and fundraising. The campaign was supported by corporate partners such as Nike and Microsoft. Colourful sportswear, T-shirts and durable balls were distributed to returnees, who put on an excellent football game at the school football field. In the evening, the president hosted a dinner banquet at the palace.

The following morning, the high commissioner had a staff meeting in the office. I explained to all that I was, in fact, an SIBA pending his departure, and gave other staff the opportunity to brief him and move around with him. The only absentee from the staff was the newly appointed deputy representative, who stayed away, as she did not want to shake hands with the high commissioner.

Sudden Religious Conversion of the UNHCR Deputy Representative

The deputy representatives function in Liberia was advertised, and I was advised to account for gender considerations and geographic representation in the selection process. UNHCR Liberia was said to have too many Asian and African males. With the encouragement of the bureau, I interviewed Ms. Christine Neveu, who was a senior officer in the Emergency Service section at headquarters. I submitted my recommendation for her appointment as my deputy, replacing Golam Abbas. She was well-versed in program management and had experience from all over Africa and Asia. She was French and very white.

A couple months later, Christine came to assume her new functions, and was picked at the airport by a driver who brought her to my office. I got up to greet her and shake her hands and was shocked by the reaction I got. She screamed, "Don't touch me!" I then noticed that she was wearing a long skirt, and her hair and part of her face were totally covered. She informed me that she had converted to Islam, and that her religion does not allow her to do certain things. Upon inquiry, I found out that she had been deployed to Pakistan for a month or so during the conflict displacement response operation. She had met a UNHCR local staff member with whom she had developed a relationship. As he already had a wife and children, she had agreed to be the second wife and live by the strict interpretation of the Holy Book, the Quran.

The following days were difficult, to say the least. She could not go to the field, as she did not have a brother or husband accompanying her. She complained that all drivers were male and Christian. I got an Ethiopian Muslim staff member, Halimu, to help, as the two knew each other from Jijiga years back. Halimu gave up, and informed me that Christine was too radical for her liking.

At the UN senior management meeting chaired by SRSG Alan Doss, he informed me that he will be talking to the Pakistani colleague I had sent to him to recruit. He wanted to know from me, his strengths and weaknesses. As I was not aware, I told him I would check and get back to him. He shared with me a letter from my office addressed to him and signed on my behalf. Upon inquiry, I found out that the Pakistani husband from UNHCR Peshawar was in Monrovia, and that she was trying to get him employed by the UN without my knowledge. I called her and cynically asked if her religion allowed such acts behind my back. I also reminded her that Liberia was a non-family duty station, where spouses are discouraged, given the volatile security situation. She reacted negatively to my comments and stayed away from the office, reporting sick for a couple days. When she decided to show up, she would come late to the office because she "had to prepare breakfast and feed her husband," as that was her duty. She refused to attend functions at the president's palace, because "alcohol was being served." She would not come into my office to discuss work-related issues, as she would allege that her religion calls for a neutral witness to be around whenever she met with another male. I tried to talk to her and assist in any way I could, but it was to no avail, as she was convinced otherwise. She would argue back that the UN was a Christian-Jewish organization that had no room for Muslims.

I called for help from the mediator, Chris Mougne. Christine agreed to go to Geneva and consult on the next steps. She never returned, and later I found out that she had left the organization. Raouf Mazou, another male African, was sent to Liberia to perform that function.

Enduring Impressions of Liberia

Prior to my arrival, I had an impression of Liberia, and particularly Monrovia. As a young boy in Ethiopia, I had heard of Ethiopian diplomats being assigned to London, Paris, or Monrovia. My Liberian colleagues in UNHCR had also painted a picture of a glamorous place ravaged by war. All African strategic literature during the Cold War recorded the significance of Liberia-based US stations for communications and other activities by NATO and the US. Upon arrival at the airport, what I saw, even with the scars of war, was not what I expected. My impressions of Monrovia as the London of Africa were shattered.

I found it strange that, even though people are close to one another, they speak loudly in English, which I had a hard time following. In the evenings, various generators would be turned on at the same time, which initially created a problem in regard to falling sleep.

The people were warm and social and enjoyed partying. I inherited a Liberian cook, Prince, who helped maintain my apartment and do the laundry. He had been with two previous representatives, Augustine Mahiga and Moses Okello. He was an excellent cook, and in my first report back to colleagues in Geneva, I had summed it up by observing that Prince was out to kill me. After a three-course dinner, he would put tea and the "night cap" in a covered tray next to my bed, which included various delicious finger food items to munch on whenever I woke up. Breakfast would include an array of fruits, eggs, and porridge served together with cornflakes and milk. He enjoyed throwing parties, which came in handy, as he helped organize the lovely evenings we used to have with colleagues downstairs in the garden. He would take my music set down and get a couple women to help him cook and serve dinner. He also acted as the DJ. The cost for throwing such parties was cheap by any standard.

Driving around in Liberia from one end to the other, I was mesmerized by the greenery and beauty. It is mind-boggling that the country, which has rain for several months, and looked fertile and green, did not grow tomatoes, which had to be imported by Lebanese traders, and was sold at the supermarket at exorbitant prices. As part of the reintegration of refugees and IDPs in Lofa County, we exerted a lot of efforts and resources to encourage farmers to grow rice and vegetables, which were not successful, as the seeds were consumed.

While driving out of Monrovia, small boys would sell meat, or "bush meat," as my driver Mawolo would explain. The meat, or the dead animal, being sold came in various shades and shapes. I would constantly ask Mawolo what type of meat it was. Is it wild pig or some kind of antelope? He would reply, "Neither," and smile. Following a couple of my naggings to know what it was— as I had been briefed that Liberians enjoy dog meat—and over time, he must have gotten so fed up with my queries that he simply stopped the car, and in a well-composed and polite manner, told me, "Boss man, anything the Lord has created and is not human flesh is bush meat." That settled the case.

Liberian food is simply tasty and fantastic. Upon departure,

Meeting with the UN Humanitarian Coordinator, Jordan Rayan and UNHCR Representative in Guinea, Mr Stefano Severe, to coordinate the return of Liberian Refugees.

I had put on the weight to account for it. The hot and tasty "no-small-boy" soup, and the various concoctions of jollof rice with greens still makes my mouth water when mentioned. Indeed, I still look for restaurants serving such food wherever I go.

The Return and Reintegration Program and UN Coordination

As mentioned above, prior to my arrival, UNHCR had been facilitating the voluntary repatriation of Liberian refugees. Assisting UN coordination was facilitated and enhanced by the people-to-people contact and relationships that were established between the agencies. In Liberia, Alan Doss of UNMIL delegated most of the humanitarian work to his deputy, Jordan Rayan, who also served as humanitarian coordinator. He relied on UNHCR for all refugee information, and would invite me to join him whenever he went to visit IDP camps, as UNHCR was responsible for Protection and Camp Coordination and Camp Management (CCCM). We met in the evenings and would resolve any issues over a drink. He helped with the release of UNMIL equipment and trucks for road construction, and the return movement of IDPs, organized by UNHCR.

The UNDP representative, Steven Ursino, was a respected manager and an excellent cook of Italian food. There was also an excellent team spirit with WFP, particularly Representative Louis Imbleau, which facilitated enhanced cooperation and made the work enjoyable. Because of the attitude and behavior of the country manager of the World Bank, Luigi Giovine, the bank was considered by all as being an integral member of the UN Country Team. Keith Wright and Rozanne Chorlton of UNICEF made UN meetings enjoyable by throwing in humor when needed. In short, the team spirit that prevailed made possible coordination and cooperation amongst the various UN agencies and programs.

Pushing the Limits of Protection

The majority of Liberian refugees were transported and provided with repatriation packages consisting of food and domestic items. Houses were constructed for returnees with critical specific needs. The majority returned from Guinea, Sierra Leone, and Cote d'Ivoire to the Liberian counties of Lofa, Bomi, and Maryland. The areas of return were devastated by the Civil War, and most infrastructure had been destroyed.

Regarding IDPs, since November 2004, UNHCR had supported the resettlement of over three hundred thousand, most of them to the same refugee return locations of Lofa, Bomi, and Grand Cape Mount. The areas of return of IDPs and refugees became the focus of UNHCR Liberia. The IASC and the UN Country Team endorsed a decision that UNHCR should assume lead responsibility for the wider protection role.

The challenge in enforcing IDP and returnee protection was highlighted during a field visit, when we were briefed by UNHCR Saclepea staff how an alleged rapist had escaped from the Gbarnga prison, having punched a hole in the wall of his prison cell. During a visit to the so-called prison, we observed a weak structure that had been erected in haste, and had collapsed when punched by an inmate. Moreover, the judiciary did not have a place to assemble or adjudicate such alleged criminal cases. In discussions with

UNDP and UNMIL, we discovered that recovery and development funding was not yet available, as this was determined to still be the emergency phase. As UNHCR, we decided to do what we could under our protection lead role, and started constructing prisons and courthouses in most capitals of the major counties of return. To my surprise, the UN, UNMIL, the Government of Liberia, and the donor community supported our initiative, and funding was provided.

To facilitate refugee return movements, and also provide access to IDP resettlement locations, UNHCR got involved in major road repair work using contractors hired from Guinea, as well as funding fuel and running costs of UNMIL engineering units from the Pakistani and Chinese contingents. Repair of the road from Monrovia to Lofa, and the border with Guinea, as well as the road linking Saclepea to Harper, totalling over 150 kilometres, was carried out by UNHCR. In 2006 alone, UNHCR Liberia spent over $54 million under its annual and supplementary programs.

On January 9, 2007, I received a letter from the director of the Division of Human Resources Management, Merida Morales O'Donnell, informing me of the high commissioner's decision to appoint Ms. Renata Dubini as the new representative in the Republic of Liberia. She enclosed a letter addressed to the minister of Foreign Affairs, signed by the HC, requesting the government's approval. I delivered the letter, and following various consultations, Foreign Minister George W. Wallace Jr., wrote a confirmation letter to the HC on March 2, 2007, accepting Ms. Dubini's appointment.

CHAPTER TEN

Round Three in Geneva

The previous two deputy director functions covering Central Africa, including Chad, the East, and the Horn, encumbered by David Kapya and Seyi Bajulayie respectively, were merged into one, and I assumed that function. I joined the bureau in September 2007, as the substantive deputy, and oversaw the development of strategic direction and oversight for UNHCR programs in East Africa, the Horn, Chad, and the Sudan. Since the desk teams I inherited were good, there was not much that was demanded of me. As deputy, I represented the bureau at various forums in the absence of the director. I undertook various missions in the field to better understand and discuss objectives with the representatives who reported to me.

I was lucky to have Patricia Seri as my secretary and assistant. The bureau still had strong personalities such as Odiri, who one needs to make sure are kept on your side. The networks of such individuals have an outreach throughout the organization resembling a mafia structure. You just do not antagonize any member of that grouping if you want a peaceful term.

I took advantage of that assignment to sort out the long outstanding issue of allegations brought against me in South

Africa by the Government of Ethiopia. I recall that in 2003, the UNHCR Branch Office for South Africa had addressed a letter to the government referring to the meeting on December 4, 1998, between the UNHCR director of Southern Africa Operations and the Ambassador of Ethiopia in South Africa, Hassen. During the meeting, the ambassador agreed to provide, in writing, further details relating to allegations against me. Over four years had elapsed, and no evidence had been provided regarding those allegations. Meanwhile, both the ambassador and myself had taken up assignments outside South Africa. Given these circumstances, the UNHCR addressed a letter to the embassy, indicating: "UNHCR believes that the allegations should be considered as unsubstantiated and that the issue considered closed." UNHCR has never received a reply.

In consultation with the Administration for Refugee and Returnee Affairs (ARRA) director, Isayas Wolde Giorgis, who was also deputy chief of security, and my long-time friend from the Gambella days, Ato Ayalew Awoke, I decided to break the impasse. I was made to understand that my name was no more on the wanted list. With their reassurances, I went on an official mission to Ethiopia to visit the refugee program, as it fell under my purview as deputy director of the Africa Bureau. I had requested to visit South Sudanese refugee and Somali refugee locations, as I was involved in both regions in my previous life.

Upon arrival at Bole International Airport in Addis, I was met officially by government protocol personnel, who took my passport and ticket, and had me driven to the VIP lounge. I was met by UNHCR and ARRA at the VIP lounge and served drinks before being driven to the Hilton hotel and accommodated in the presidential suite on the top floor. Welcoming drinks and flowers were placed on two tables. The following morning, I was flown to Mekelle, and then to Shire for a state banquet dinner hosted by the local government. I visited Shimelba camp and met with Eritrean refugees. I was driven around to see the border area and some locations where bitter fighting took place between the Ethiopian and Eritrean defense forces.

I was kept at the best hotel in town, and my host had to

remind me that I was given the same room Meles slept in a week before, when he had come to attend a TPLF celebration. As we were boarding the flight back to Addis, I was seated in the VIP lounge with a general, who I was informed to be the deputy force commander, and was also traveling to Addis. He had two armed escorts. As we were about to board the aircraft, the general went ahead of me. At the checkpoint, he was told that he could not take his lighter onboard, and it was taken from him. I voluntarily surrendered my lighter before being asked to do so. To our surprise, I was told to keep it. As we landed in Addis at the VIP lounge, the general came up to me and asked who I was, and if I could light his cigarette. I told him who I was, and he left unimpressed. The treatment I received, I took to be a message that the government had dropped its earlier demands, and that this was a turning point. Thus, after over eight years of exile, I started coming in and out as I pleased. Trying to settle my hotel bills in Shire and Addis, I was simply told by the desk that I was the guest of the government, and that all my expenses had been taken care of.

Departure Difficulties at Khartoum Airport

I traveled to Uganda, and together with the UNHCR representative, Stefano Severe, toured the program in the north of the country. From Arua, I then crossed over to South Sudan at Nemule, where I was met by a guard of honor, as the commander was claiming to know me from the Gambella days in Ethiopia. I took the UNHCR plane to visit several offices before reaching Juba. In Juba, the representative, Ann Encontre, and her deputy, Girmai Wondimu, briefed me on the program. I spent a memorable evening with a former UNHCR colleague, Barnabas, who had become the controller for the government.

I flew to Khartoum the following day, and then to Darfur to observe firsthand the complexities and challenges we faced in that region. At the WFP guesthouse in Al-Fashar, we spent a couple memorable evenings with colleagues and partners, enjoying abundant smuggled whiskey from Chad. The dry and arid land, with watermelon and fruits piled up in the local market, were in sharp contrast to the rainy and evergreen Liberia. Looks could be deceptive at times. I did not expect to see as many fruits and vegetables in the market in arid Darfur.

My Sudan visit remains memorable, as on the way out, the immigration officer at the Khartoum Airport asked how I had entered the country, which I explained with pride. He gave me back my passport and asked if I could direct him to the page showing immigration stamps to confirm I'd entered as I claimed. I then realized, in the reception fanfare, I was welcomed by the Army and had bypassed entry formalities. Chris Ache had to talk to the deputy foreign minister, himself a Southerner, who understood the situation and intervened.

However, the clearance process took some time, and my flight departed. I had to take another one, which took me through Addis to Amsterdam. I could not disembark in Addis, as the ground time was only one hour, and Royal Dutch Airlines (KLM) crew explained that they would be penalized if they let me go down. I left without even calling my family, and that remains my shortest visit of home.

Visiting Refugees in Djibouti

I undertook a mission to the UNHCR program in Djibouti, in December 2008, and visited the two refugee camps at Ali Adeh and Hol as well as the transit center at Loyada. The visit was sentimental, as the two camps were the first locations from where I participated in my first ever UNHCR exercise to return and repatriate Ethiopian refugees some twenty-five years before.

During my mission, I was hosted by Madame Ann Encontre, the UNHCR representative, who made all the arrangements for me to meet with refugees, the president of the Republic, the US ambassador, and the head of the Office National d'Assistance aux Réfugiés et Sinistrés (ONARS), Mr. Hassan Omar.

Djibouti is proud of its seaport, which forms part of Djibouti-Ville. The port handles import and export commodities mainly for landlocked Ethiopia, and is the main revenue-generating activity for the government, as agriculture production is minimal. At the same time, most of the fresh produce consumed in Djibouti arrives by train and trucks from Ethiopia, which are the same trucks and railway cars that transport imported products from Djibouti. The interdependent link between the two countries is clear. The large number of trucks from Ethiopia waiting to enter the port area, and the hustle and bustle in the suburban shanti town that has sprung up to provide food, drinks, accommodation and other services to the truck drivers remains a fascinating memory for me.

The actual number of refugees at the time was some twenty thousand, mainly Somali refugees, and two thousand Ethiopians in the two designated camps. Djibouti officials claim that tens of thousands of additional refugees were living in the capital, Djibouti-Ville. Besides refugees, more than a hundred thousand people—mainly Ethiopians, Eritreans, and Somalis—migrate through Djibouti every year.

About one hundred Eritrean military defectors were kept separately at a police barracks in Negad, and UNHCR had completed its evaluation of the deserters and found seventy-three individuals to qualify for resettlement. I did raise the subject with the US ambassador.

Former Ethiopian troops languishing in the refugee camps, by contrast, had no resettlement prospects, as most resettlement countries were not interested because they did not want to harm the relationship they had with the government in the country of origin.

I recall that the Somali refugees I spoke to all claimed to have fled their country because of persecution by Ethiopian troops. This remains stuck in my mind, as I did not expect to hear such claims.

One of the new developments since my earlier mission to Djibouti which caught my attention was the new five-star Djibouti Palace Kempinski hotel, with several swimming pools, a private beach, a full-service spa, offering 320 accommodations, with modern amenities. That luxurious setting became even more spectacular and memorable when one evening, upon my return to the hotel, an official banquet had been organized by the government for naval officers and military attaches stationed in the country. I have never seen anything like it before, or after, as all were white-dressed and decorated naval officers from all over the world, appearing to compete for who had the best uniform. They were all over the lounge and the seafront terrace: US, UK, French, Chinese, Turkish, Iranian, Pakistani, Indian, Egyptian, Italian, UAE, and Japanese were amongst those I recognized.

The naval show of presence reminded me of the strategic importance of the country and what to expect in the years to come. French colonial forces had remained present since the territory (the last in Africa) gained independence from France. The June 1977 agreement between the two countries laid down the conditions for the stationing of French forces at Lemonnier— under a defense agreement to secure the country's independence from the threat of being absorbed by either Ethiopia or Somalia. France has guaranteed the independence and territorial integrity of the Republic of Djibouti since independence.

Given Djibouti's strategic location by the Bab-el-Mandeb Strait, which separates the Gulf of Aden from the Red Sea, and controls the approaches to the Suez Canal, the country has become a desirable location for foreign military bases. Camp Lemonnier was abandoned by the French and later leased to the United States Central Command in September 2002, and renewed in 2014 for another twenty years. The French Foreign Legion is still stationed in Djibouti as one of the largest French military presences abroad. The country also hosts the only overseas Chinese support base, the only overseas Japanese military base, and the Italian national support military base. The hosting of foreign military bases not only grantees the country's independence, but is also an important source of revenue for Djibouti's economy, as most countries pay significant amounts for rental of facilities.

The small but strategically located country will continue to play a significant role in regional and global geopolitical ramblings for years to come.

Departure of the Bureau Director

While in the bureau, news came of the director, Ms. Marjon Kamara, being offered an ambassadorial post in New York by the Government of Liberia. Marjon informed us that she had accepted the offer, and that the high commissioner had also agreed to the move. The HC was looking into a list of three to decide who would replace her. I was left to act, pending the appointment of a new director. I learned that the list of candidates included myself, George Okoth-Obbo, and Arnauld Akodjenou.

I moved into the director's office as acting director and represented the bureau at all levels accordingly. One of my memorable recollections was that I found in one of the drawers under the director's desk, the twenty-five years' service recognition gold pin for me, which she did not get the chance to give me, as she was waiting for the next bureau party.

During a bureau party, I requested for the longest serving staff member in the Africa Bureau, Mr. Roger Pellet, to do me the honors and perform the recognition ceremony on behalf of the organization by pinning the gold pin on my jacket, which he did. That was appreciated by me, Roger, and indeed the bureau staff. It gave me a sense of respect for those who had served the organization, and what it stood for most of their adult life.

One morning, the HC called me to inform me that the Troika, HC, DHC, and the two AHCs had discussed the need for a senior officer to replace the retiring Guenet Gebre-Christos to assume the Representative function in Pakistan, and that the Troika was unanimous that I was the man for the job. I politely informed the HC that I still had over two years of SAL to go in Geneva and would prefer to stay and perform my deputy director function. He argued that he does not see me as a deputy, and requested that I consider the appointment.

A couple days later, the DHC, after a resource allocation meeting in his office, asked me to stay on, and casually informed me that I was being considered for a D2 promotion by the Troika. They were simply waiting for my reassignment to Pakistan to implement the decision. I realized then that the carrot-and-stick approach was being utilized to influence my decision.

The HC, following a discussion we had on the Chad and Darfur situation, asked me to remain in his office, and briefly mentioned that he was agreeing to the AHC protection, Erika Feller's request, to bring young blood with new ideas to lead DIP. He hinted that she was frustrated and was not happy with George. Because of that, he was considering moving George to the Africa Bureau. I informed him that I would be delighted to work with George. He abruptly turned down my suggestion and started rubbing his eyes with both hands. I knew that gesture to be an indication of his nervousness, as I had observed before, and later, the eye rubbing ritual during a tense situation.

Before leaving the room, I informed him of my choice to stay with the bureau, which did not mean that as a good soldier, I would not respect his final decision. He announced my appointment as his representative in Pakistan the following day.

Volker Turk was brought in to head DIP, and George was assigned as director of the Africa Bureau. I worked with George for a couple weeks, pending the receipt of the agreement of the Government of Pakistan regarding my appointment as representative.

The circumstance and manner of my assignment to Pakistan simply illustrates the absence of a clear career path, and the projection one can follow above a certain grade level. Senior managers are at the disposal of the secretary general of his undersecretary to be assigned to whichever post deemed to be in the best interest of the organization. Refusal to obey reassignment is dreaded, as it would inevitably lead to marginalization and abandonment. For well over a decade of my last assignments in UNHCR, I have been appointed to functions that were not in my trajectory, or for which I had not applied. In a way, I am grateful and consider myself privileged to have been recognized and assigned.

CHAPTER ELEVEN

Off to Pakistan

Replacing a long serving and well-respected Representative in Pakistan, Guenet Guebre-Christos, was no easy task. Both of us coming from the same country of origin did facilitate the transition in a way. People would ask where I was from, and upon responding, "Ethiopia," the reply would be "Oh, from Madam Guenet's country." And I would nod.

My assignment to Pakistan turned out to be a pleasant surprise. I found the country to be beautiful, with breathtaking topography, and its people warm and welcoming. Rich in history and culture, the intriguing political establishment that strove to make one guess next moves added to the excitement and challenges of working there.

Pakistan is one place nobody really understands, including locals, trapped between worlds and pulled in different directions between the Americans, the Chinese, radical Islam, modernism, nuclear-armed army, unbelievable nature, ISIS and India, and millions of refugees and IDPs. Given the cultural similarities, particularly food and hospitality, I concluded shortly after my arrival that if ever I decided to live outside Ethiopia, it would have to be in Pakistan.

The political posturing, obsession with being outdone by India, the dominant role of the military, and the modern state, intertwined with tribal values, are fascinating and can be observed in the daily ritual at the border with India. While attending a refugee meeting in Lahore, I was invited to the Wagah border gate closing ceremony as the guest of honor. The image of fancily dressed, tall and well-built border guards on both sides of the border performing the daily ritual of posturing dance, with the constant closing and opening of the gate is fascinating. The crowds gathered on either side, chanting opposing patriotic songs and slogans, culminating with the lowering of the flag and the shaking of hands by the show leaders at the border. I observed tourists on the Indian side of the border taking pictures, which, given the prevailing situation in Pakistan, was considered dangerous and unthinkable. I was ushered to the border gate and introduced to the Indian side commander, who shook my hand, saluted me, and walked me in and out of India before I knew what had happened.

The warmth of the people, the cultural similarities, and the quality of life were manifested daily by the head of the refugee office in the Ministry of Ministry of States and Frontier Regions (SAFRON), Mr. Imran Zeib. He was an intriguing gentleman who enjoyed quality drinks, and was conversant on any topic. He enjoyed luxury and was a feudal, in a sense, with Afghan peasants working on his property. Mr Zeib was an expert on Afghanistan and Afghan refugees, having worked on this topic for decades. He made my stay in Pakistan pleasant, and I am pleased to have him as a friend.

UNHCR Representative in Pakistan

UNHCR has had a long-standing and strong operational presence in Pakistan since the Russian invasion of Afghanistan in 1979, taking care of over three million Afghan refugees. It had long-established field presences in both Peshawar and Quetta, and was well-known by the local people and local authorities before the arrival of other UN entities.

By the summer of 2009, Pakistan was dealing with some 2.3

million IDPs out of the Swat Valley in the North-West Frontier Province, now known as Khyber Pakhtunkhuwa, following months of bloody incursions and armed conflict between the Pakistani Army and the Pakistan wing of the Taliban. UNHCR had been called upon to lead the Protection, Shelter, and Camp Coordination and Camp Management Clusters in the IDP operation, mainly in the North-West Frontier Province. The IDPs, mainly older persons, women, and children, had had to leave their homes, seeking refuge in various makeshift communal shelters.

On its part, the Government of Pakistan designated a government counterpart—the Provincial Disaster Management Authority (PDMA)—to coordinate humanitarian delivery to IDPs. Within six months, well over two million IDPs had returned to their homes.

While humanitarian organizations were striving to increase their capacity at provincial and capital levels, several security incidents had taken place, some of which had far-reaching consequences. In June 2009, a senior UNHCR national colleague was gunned down at an IDP site in Peshawar. The same month, a truck bomb exploded right into the Pearl Hotel in Peshawar, killing dozens of people, including several humanitarian staff, among them a UNHCR colleague on mission from Belgrade. Three additional major security incidents occurred in Islamabad, affecting the US Embassy, the Marriott hotel, and the WFP country office. The situation became untenable, resulting in the UN Department of Security and Safety (UNDSS) declaring Pakistan as a "non-family duty station for the United Nations." Consequently, international schools had to be closed and evacuation of non-essential UN staff and dependents ordered.

Over the next couple years, UNHCR, alongside the Government of Pakistan, and international and national humanitarian partners, would be engaged in a protracted humanitarian program for IDPs in camps and in urban settings. Access and security of UN and NGOs to IDP sites became challenging.

The government and people of Pakistan truly appreciated UNHCR's gesture in reaching out to millions of people in need who had lost their homes and livelihoods following the floods in

2010. Meanwhile, UNHCR continued to work closely with the Pakistan and Afghanistan governments in finding lasting solutions for the millions of Afghans in Pakistan. Voluntary return of Afghans to their home country obviously remained the preferred and viable option. Tripartite meetings to facilitate and coordinate the refugee voluntary return were regularly held in Kabul and Islamabad. Meetings in Kabul also included UNHCR Iran. The UNHCR representative in Kabul at the time, Ewen Macleod, was a regular visitor to Islamabad, where a small liaison unit reporting to his office was accommodated.

To the credit of the Pakistan government, Afghan refugees have been largely treated in many ways like Pakistani nationals, with the inclusion of education, public health services, local trade, and agriculture.

Throughout this turbulent time, UNHCR remained steadfast in overcoming multiple complex refugee and IDP situations, thereby maintaining its relevance in the country.

Floods Hit Pakistan

In late July 2010, Pakistan was engulfed by a natural calamity and flooding disasters affecting as many as twenty million people, including refugees and IDPs. It was yet another humanitarian front requiring UNHCR and others to provide immediate humanitarian assistance. The floods in Pakistan began in late July 2010, resulting from heavy monsoon rains in the Khyber Pakhtunkhwa, Sindh, Punjab, and Baluchistan regions of Pakistan, which affected the Indus River basin. Approximately one-fifth of Pakistan's total land area was affected by floods, with the Khyber Pakhtunkhwa Province facing the brunt of the damage and casualties with 90 percent of deaths in that province. According to Pakistani government data, the floods directly affected about twenty million people, mostly by destruction of property, livelihoods, and infrastructure, with a death toll of close to two thousand.

The Pakistani economy was harmed by extensive damage to infrastructure and crops. Damage to structures was estimated to exceed $4 billion, and wheat crop damages were estimated to be over $500 million. The total economic impact may have been as

Dealing with the flood response with Angelina Jolly and UNHCR Deputy Representative Khassim Diang. Addressing the UN Staff in Islamabad.

much as $43 billion.

A new humanitarian response architecture, led by a newly designated humanitarian coordinator (former UNICEF country representative), supported by a team from the Office of Coordination of Humanitarian Affairs (OCHA), was quickly established to manage the situation. To support our appeal for the Pakistan floods, Angelina Jolie, UNHCR's Goodwill Ambassador, agreed to come for a short visit. With Imran Zeib, one of my deputies, Khassim Diagne, and the head of suboffice Peshawar, Ahmed Warsame, we planned to take her directly to the most affected province, which also hosted the largest Afghan refugee population. Angelina liked the suggestion.

Coinciding with the floods, Lady Valerie Amos was appointed as the UN undersecretary general and emergency relief coordinator from September 2010 to May 2015. Lady Amos was in charge of overseeing all emergencies requiring UN humanitarian assistance.

Unaware of the visit of the newly appointed undersecretary

general and emergency relief coordinator, Lady Valerie Amos, I arrived at Islamabad Airport to receive Angelina and rush her off to Peshawar for the night, as planned and cleared with the government, and based on her request. At the airport, and to my surprise, the UNICEF representative, David Kanja, who also acted as humanitarian coordinator, was standing with OCHA colleagues in the VIP lounge. I was baffled and wondered how he knew of Angelina's confidential mission. As we were trying to find out what the other side was doing at the airport, the Foreign Ministry Protocol Head of Department came and loudly asked if "Mr. Kebede of UNHCR" could kindly follow him into the limousine car parked by the door of the VIP lounge facing the runway. I did, and we drove up to the parked Emirates plane, then boarded and went to first class, where I met Angelina with her escort and ushered them down the plane, into the parked car. The protocol officer took her passport for processing as we were driven to the president's VIP lounge for Angelina to change into a local attire for the drive to Peshawar. I do recall seeing an African lady on the plane, but did not know who she was at the time.

Following the change of attire, we left the presidential VIP lounge. To access the UNHCR vehicles, we had to go through the other VIP lounge. With a police escort, we swiftly proceeded. The police were clearing the way for us, and unfortunately the UN team standing with the African lady that had arrived and was brought by bus, was pushed aside to make way for Angelina and her escort. David called out my name and suggested that I apologize to the African lady, who was apparently shoved out of the way by one of the police leading Angelina's entourage. David introduced the lady to me as being Lady Valerie Amos. I was surprised, as I did not know that the lady was in fact the black African I had seen earlier on the aircraft. As a member of the UN country team, I had not been informed of her visit. The following days, unfortunately for Lady Amos, Angelina took all the limelight and attention of both local and international media, and definitely Pakistani officials.

We drove off to Peshawar and spent the night at the UNHCR Suboffice and guesthouse, hosted by the head of suboffice, Ahmed

Warsame. The following morning, after breakfast, we visited refugee and IDP locations around Peshawar. Angelina's arrival in-country was officially announced, and the field visits gave photo opportunities to the public information unit and selected press teams organized for the visit. Following lunch, we drove back to the Serena Hotel in Islamabad.

Meeting with Prime Minister Raza Gillani

I had requested a courtesy call on behalf of Angelina, with the Prime Minister Yousuf Raza Gillani, who accepted but insisted that the courtesy call was to be followed by dinner at the palace, and that I was also to accompany our guest. The dinner involved the prime minister's wife and children, but no other government official. It turned out to be a photo opportunity for the prime minister and his family with Angelina. I sat in a corner, observing the various poses and was not asked to join in any photoshoot.

During dinner, Angelina took out a note, which we had reviewed earlier and requested the prime minister's personal involvement, amongst others, in securing the extension of the proof of residency for Afghan refugees. He emphatically agreed to follow-up, and told her to consider it done. He thanked her and UNHCR for joining in the flood relief exercise, which he said was appreciated by both the people and the Government of Pakistan.

The following day, Angelina met with staff at the branch office, the minister of SAFRON, and held a press briefing in the UNHCR compound. Her plea to support the UNHCR appeal for the flood response got worldwide coverage. She also announced a significant personal contribution toward the UNHCR appeal.

Lukewarm Support by the Emergency Relief Coordinator

The emergency relief coordinator, either annoyed by the reception she received, or for reasons unclear to me, never supported the UNHCR program in the flood response. She was well-spoken but clearly lacked experience in humanitarian field work. She wanted

Tripartite meeting between UNHCR Government representatives in Pakistan and Afghanistan in Kabul

to please all, and relied heavily on headquarters' intervention to resolve local issues. I recall the High Commissioner calling me on two occasions to consult me on the possibilities of cutting back on the UNHCR budget contained in the joint appeal. On one occasion, I found out that the Office of the Emergency Relief Coordinator had called the assistant high commissioner, Janet Lim, who in turn had brought it up at a Troika meeting. The second was a direct phone call to the high commissioner by Lady Amos. On both occasions, the high commissioner supported my position that the budget had to be determined based on needs and in consultation with the UN team on the ground, and should not be dictated by headquarters. Whoever was complaining to Valerie's office did not have the courage to raise the issue with me locally, where I had the support of the majority of the UN country team. I had my suspicions, and I still think I know who.

The suggestion that all agencies divide the cake equally was a point I resented, as capacities and the ability to deliver were not equal. The absurdity was not seeing or understanding that, unlike the Haiti emergency or elsewhere, UNHCR had a strong presence in the flood-affected areas of Pakistan because of years of involvement with refugee protection and assistance programs. Rather than using the relative advantage UNHCR had, the emergency relief coordinator insisted on other agencies doing it.

210

The ability of UNHCR to deliver was not because we were better, but because we had teams on the ground, stocks of non-food items in our warehouses, and sufficient partnerships to move faster than anyone in KPK, FATA, or Baluchistan, which happened to be the most affected regions.

Donors, who realized this, were diverting money from one agency to another. For example, Japan gave UNHCR an additional $60 million, which had been pledged to others for shelter construction. In 2010, we received $171 million toward our flood response appeal. The UNHCR component of the joint appeal 2010–11 was fully funded by the time of my departure from the country. Due to the standing arrangements we had with suppliers, we were able to procure and distribute over 155,000 family tents for emergency shelter in a couple months following the floods.

A few UN country team members also did not understand that UNHCR was using its clear and visible support for the Pakistani people in order to galvanize support for the asylum space for Afghan refugees under its protection mandate.

Either through divine intervention or pure luck, the couple of awkward situations that arose were resolved in UNHCR's favor. One incident was when Lady Amos, while visiting Pakistan, removed my name from the list of participants to accompany her to meetings with the government in Islamabad. I was informed of the arrangement for her meeting to go to the KPK, and that I would attend when she met the provincial authorities. Valerie had brought a BBC team to broadcast and film her visit. I met her with Ahmed Warsame in Peshawar, and had a meeting with the provincial officials in the governor's office. Most speakers who took the floor spoke positively about the work of UNHCR, and Valerie's body language indicated that what she was hearing was not to her liking. Her field visits, which were being filmed and arranged by the local government, were projects that were predominantly being implemented or completed by UNHCR.

As scheduled, she sat under a tree, overseeing an IDP camp to give an interview to the BBC. During the interview, flies and bees were interrupting her, apparently attracted to the perfume she was wearing. I had to fill in for her, which I did with no hesitation.

A Parallel Humanitarian Coordination Mechanism

Unlike Liberia, and many other places where the UN operates in Africa, the UN coordination mechanism had a challenge in operating in Pakistan. Each agency was invited on its own merits to attend the coordination meeting by the Pakistan National Disaster Management Agency, (NDMA). The NDMA took the lead in coordinating the response efforts. The Provincial Disaster Management Agencies (PDMAs) in the affected provinces were coordinating efforts at the provincial levels under the overall supervision and guidance of the NDMA.

The first challenge observed between the NDMA and the UN coordination mechanism was the lack of understanding on the number of IASC clusters to be activated. The Government of Pakistan wanted to limit the number of clusters to be activated to four key clusters—food, water and sanitation, and health and early recovery—while the UN insisted on eleven clusters. The UN agreed to reduce the number of clusters to seven, which was used in the initial response plan in August, but was increased to twelve when the revised appeal was launched in September. Recruitment and funding of cluster coordination outfits at the national and provincial levels were considered too heavy and costly.

Information sharing was yet another challenge, as there was no common reporting format used by the different organizations involved in the response. NDMA and OCHA discussions on that subject, at each meeting I attended, could not be conclusive. Moreover, the number of NGOs reporting to the NDMA was far greater and varied than those engaged with the UN. Consequently, precise and consolidated data did not exist, affecting not only monitoring, but also the humanitarian systems programming in terms of identifying precisely what had been attended, where and by whom. Much time was spent at meetings to gather and corroborate such information.

While the UN, under the overall guidance of the humanitarian coordinator, was trying to put together its consolidated appeal, the government would issue its own requirements, which would consider the UN and other NGO submissions. The government also had significant funding sources that were not accessible to the UN, particularly from governments such as Saudi Arabia, Iran, and the Gulf States. Islamic religious institutions throughout the Gulf and the Middle East were donors to Pakistan. China was yet another donor and partner to the Government of Pakistan's bilateral appeal.

I do recall that the government had blocked the UN consolidated appeal, which was launched following the personal intervention of our high commissioner, who had raised it with the prime minister and General Nadeem. It was from the car, when we left the prime minister's office, that Mr. Guterres called Valerie and informed her of the go-ahead he had just secured. General Nadeem and the high commissioner shared mutual admiration and respect. The HC, who visited Pakistan twice during my tenure, on both occasions requested a one-on-one meeting with General Nadeem, which testifies to the amicable relationship they enjoyed.

The need for political intervention by either the secretary general or the UN high commissioner, with the appropriate contacts in the host country government remains a prerequisite for the successful implementation of humanitarian action by the UN team and the NGO community. The high commissioner's intervention with General Nadeem illustrates that reality. Simply drawing the attention of member states that they are signatory to this or that convention, or coordination and delivery mechanism, in itself does not suffice. The UN, and indeed the international community, needs to learn from that in order to address the needs of the affected population without resorting to political entanglements and possible sanctions that could impact the government, but does not meet the needs of the population.

UNHCR's Unique Standing in Pakistan

UNHCR's unique standing in Pakistan was not well-understood by the UN country team or the various coordination mechanisms put up to ensure coherence and coordination. UNHCR has maintained a presence in the country since the mid-1980s, dealing with Afghan refugees who were primarily located in integrated villages along the border of the KPK, the Federally Administered Territory, and Baluchistan. When the floods hit and the UN coordination mechanism was rolled out, most of the facts on the ground were not considered.

Taking a helicopter ride with General Nadeem to Waziristan, to visit conflict-displaced IDPs, or undertaking a field visit with Ahmed Warsame, head of suboffice Peshawar, to the Federally Administered Territories to visit Afghan refugees, would be reported as being a breach of UN rules and reported to New York. On both occasions, the HC had called me to hear my side of the story. Regarding the first report, I told him that General Nadeem had invited me to join him, together with the head of the National Red Crescent—a retired Air Force commander and a USAID representative from the US Mission—in a helicopter ride to visit displacement sites in Waziristan. Regarding the second, I confirmed that I and Ahmed Warsame had visited refugee sites in the Federally Administered Territories, accompanied by the refugee coordinator, Imran Zeib. I enjoyed that mission, given the warm reception we received from refugees welcoming our visit. In accordance with African and Asian hospitality, sheep were slaughtered and roasted to welcome us. They tolerated me relaxing, while Ahmed would pray with our hosts. On both occasions, the HC understood and endorsed the action taken.

In order to overcome such misunderstandings, I explained to the head of UNDSS, during his mission to Pakistan, that UNHCR had to work in UN no-go areas in the Federally Administered Territories, including Waziristan. He suggested that we address a letter requesting exemption, which we did. We obtained an exemption, which allowed UNHCR staff to proceed with their work in these locations.

Another complaint brought to the attention of the HC was our insistence on maintaining UNHCR logos on our vehicles. That issue was resolved when the HC visited Pakistan and met staff in Peshawar, and local field staff explained to him that putting UNHCR stickers on cars to identify them as such made them feel better protected. The refugee agency logo offered more protection than unmarked vehicles, which could be targeted as belonging to the CIA or other such entities. UNHCR and its logo were known to refugees and nationals in those territories. As the UN, and indeed any other configuration, we need to realize strict adherence to rules might not work for all at all times. The ability to recognize the need for selective flexibility is a better way forward.

Accounts to be Closed

The Soviet–Afghan War was a conflict wherein insurgent groups, known collectively as the Mujahedeen, fought a nine-year guerrilla war against the Soviet Army and the Democratic Republic of Afghanistan throughout the 1980s, mostly in the Afghan countryside. The Mujahedeen were backed primarily by the United States, Pakistan, Iran, Saudi Arabia, China, and the United Kingdom. The conflict was a Cold War-era proxy war. About one million civilians were killed, and millions of Afghans fled the country as refugees, mostly to Pakistan and Iran.

Afghan insurgents received massive amounts of support through aid, finance, and military training in Pakistan ,with significant help from the United States and United Kingdom, as well as being heavily financed by the Gulf Cooperation Council countries.

It was known that Soviet Union and Democratic Republic of Afghanistan Air Force jet fighters and bombers would occasionally cross into Pakistani airspace to target Afghan refugee camps in Pakistan. The existing bomb shelters and camouflaged dome-shaped storage facilities in refugee hosting areas in Pakistan stand testimony to that period. The sight of anti-aircraft batteries being stationed in refugee camps, as well as open recruitment and training of fighters, is told by elder refugees. It is safe to conclude that the civilian nature of the refugee camps was severely compromised at the time. The neutrality of UNHCR, WFP, and other humanitarian organizations operating in the refugee locations appears to have also been compromised, to say the least.

Various reports confirm that several channels were used to funnel funds, arms, and other humanitarian assistance to the

Mujahedeen in Pakistan, further blurring the distinction between humanitarian assistance and military support. By the war's end, more than $20 billion were funnelled through Pakistan to train and equip the Afghan Mujahedeen militants. The covert and overt support has left behind some unresolved issues.

Leftover money from the sale of jute bags in the '80s and '90s was held by SAFRON in a high-yield bank account. The money, which was kept in local currency, was dispensed by the government in agreement with UNHCR, as apparently agreed with WFP earlier. I was not briefed about the existence of the account until I was invited by the minister of SAFRON to attend a meeting of the committee that approves expenditure under that allotment. The minister had called that particular meeting to approve bonuses for refugee commissioner staff at both the provincial and capital levels. Even though I was promised on various occasions, I was never provided with details of that account.

Moreover, I was made to understand that there was yet another account kept in joint custody in a high-yield investment account, with the original source of money allegedly being UNHCR, in the late 1980s and early 1990s. I wrote a letter requesting the UNHCR controller to share any information that could shed light on the matter, but I never received a reply. Nothing exists in UNHCR to explain where the money came from, or its purpose.

In order to pragmatically end that story, I suggested to the ministry to close both accounts and transfer the money to the Refugee-Affected and Hosting Areas (RAHA) account to be recorded as a contribution by the Government of Pakistan. That decision was pending upon my departure. However, both outstanding issues gave a glimpse as to what could have transpired during the early days of the Afghan refugee influx into Pakistan, and would benefit from closure.

Refugee-Affected and Hosting Areas Program

The Refugee-Affected and Hosting Areas (RAHA) program was introduced as a response to the political, socio-economic, finan-cial, and environmental consequences associated with hosting

Afghan refugees for four decades. To alleviate the burden on the host communities and promote social cohesion, in 2009, the Government of Pakistan, through the SAFRON, and the Economic Affairs Division (EAD), in partnership with UNHCR and a consortium of other UN agencies, initiated the RAHA program.

The RAHA program constitutes the cornerstone of the implementation of the multi-year regional Solutions Strategy for Afghan Refugees (SSAR) in Pakistan, and remains the principal responsibility-sharing platform for maintaining temporary protection space, mitigating the impact of the protracted refugee presence, promoting social cohesion, and enhancing community acceptance of Afghan refugees in Pakistan.

By linking vital humanitarian and development interventions that benefit both refugees and their host communities, RAHA serves as the central delivery platform for the implementation of whole-of-community resilience-building measures in Pakistan. This constitutes an effort to move away from prolonged dependence on open-ended humanitarian aid (care and maintenance) by enhancing social cohesion and developing empowerment, resilience, and productive capacities of both refugees and their host communities through targeted investments into national public service delivery systems such as health, education, social protection, and infrastructure.

Since 2009, the RAHA program has implemented approximately 4,260 projects worth $220 million, benefiting around 12.4 million individuals, of whom 15 percent are Afghan refugees. These RAHA projects prioritize five main sectors of interventions: education, health, livelihoods, water, and infrastructure. These include projects aimed at improvement or construction of additional public-school facilities and infrastructure, enhancement of public health care services, provision of medical equipment to health facilities, provision of clean drinking water, rehabilitation or construction of streets and roads, construction of flood protection walls, social protection projects, as well as provision of technical and vocational skills trainings and livelihoods interventions.

In the first phase of the RAHA initiative, which started in

2009, the program received around $136 million in contributions of the total requirements of $140 million. UNHCR had invested approximately $36 million in community-based interventions in areas hosted by large numbers of Afghan refugees.

What made the RAHA program interesting was that it provided longer term planning for development options in comparison to the yearly UNHCR care and maintenance projects. Moreover, it did not divert money from the ExCom approved annual budget of the organization. Excellent support for the program was provided by GTZ-BMZ experts bringing their own funding. The approach, including its international solidarity component addressing all aspects of current or former refugee hosting communities, is a good example to be replicated elsewhere.

CHAPTER TWELVE

Round Four in Geneva

Sometime in May 2011, the high commissioner called me in Pakistan and talked to me about Cote d'Ivoire and the change of government. He also mentioned that the new government had requested the withdrawal of Abou Moussa, a former UNHCR colleague who was reportedly close to the former government. The incoming government wanted UNHCR to know that they had no squabbles with the organization, but with Mr. Moussa as an individual. Further to that development, then inspector general of UNHCR, Mr. Arnauld Akodjenou, was being appointed by the secretary general to be his deputy special representative for the UN operations in Cote d'Ivoire. The HC had consulted and wanted to appoint me to the position of inspector general. My immediate reaction was that the IG was not in my trajectory, as I still considered my strengths to be in the operations management area. He suggested for me to think it over, and said that he would call later.

My former deputy in Pakistan, Khassim Diagne, had already moved to headquarters, where he was serving as head of the secretariat, dealing with external relations, including ExCom. Khassim shared with me a letter that had already been sent to the Ambassador of Egypt, Mr. Hisham Badr, who was the chairman of the Executive Committee, informing him of the high commissioner's intention to appoint me to the position of inspector general. As was the procedure, the ambassador had circulated the HC's intention to Executive Committee members and Standing Committee observers through Ms. Catherine Walker, secretary of the Executive Committee. I soon realized that the high commissioner's request that I consider the IG position had reached a point of no return. In fact, I received a congratulatory memorandum regarding my appointment as inspector general, from the ambassador and the Permanent Representative of Morocco, Mr. Omar Hilale, who assured me of his government's full support and cooperation. A similar letter followed from the Ambassador of Algeria. I realized then that it was a done deal.

It was brought to my attention that it was a policy for a senior D2 colleague, who has a couple years to go before retirement, to be assigned to the IG function, with the understanding that he or she will not assume other managerial functions in the organization, as they would have had access to personal and confidential information concerning staff. The high commissioner's letter to the chairman of the ExCom had also mentioned: "In reviewing all eligible senior (D2) personnel, Mr. Kebede stood out based on his proven competencies related to a wide range of UNHCR functions, his diverse and longstanding experience with UNHCR both in the Field and at Headquarters, and his outstanding managerial skills and personal qualities." Having read that submission, I knew the IG was going to be my last assignment in UNHCR.

The mandate of the Inspector General's Office (IGO) comprises three functions: inspection of field offices and headquarters' units, investigations of possible misconduct by UNHCR personnel, and ad hoc inquiries into grave violent attacks on UNHCR personnel and operations. Ad hoc inquiries into other incidents that could directly impact the credibility and integrity of the UN refugee agency, can also be carried out by the IGO at the high commissioner's request. Well, given the access to information and the need for confidentiality, I cannot dwell much on the fascinating and diverse discoveries regarding the various allegations brought against staff. Suffice it to say, it was much more complex, diverse, and interwoven with conflicting values and cultures examined against standards set up in the UN staff rules and adherence to the code of conduct expected of international civil servants.

Roster of Investigators Hosted by the DRC

During my tenure as IG, we tried to push ahead and give NGO partners the ability to investigate wrongdoings of their staff. Efforts at strengthening UNHCR-NGO cooperation on third party investigations were made by conducting workshops for national NGOs, whenever an investigation team visited a particular country. Dedicated workshops were also organized in Bangkok and Tunis. One of the glaring gaps we were able to identify was the lack of capacity by many local and regional NGOs to conduct investigations. In an effort to partially address the problem, we set out to establish an NGO Investigation Specialist Roster (NGO-ISR). My office signed an agreement with the Danish Refugee Council (DRC) to host the roster, and UNHCR provided the financial resources to implement an Investigation Specialist Roster comprising persons with substantial and specialized investigative backgrounds and experience, who are available, at short notice, to carry out investigations into allegations of NGO staff misconduct.

I presented the subject during the UNHCR Annual Consultations with NGOs in 2014. I addressed NGO concerns about being skeptical of the need for DRC to investigate their staff. I had to explain that the DRC was simply serving as a platform that administers the roster on UNHCR's behalf. The DRC will not investigate any NGO staff, as that was not the purpose or intention of the roster. The roster would be available to UNHCR, UNHCR's NGO-implementing partners, and NGOs serving the humanitarian community. Its objective was to ensure that allegations of misconduct were expeditiously pursued, and the necessary investigations carried out. Most NGOs had pointed out that they did not have the capacity or the expertise to conduct investigations regarding allegations of wrongdoings by their staff.

The roster was simply to address that need and offer financial support where needed.

The ISR was fully operational and consisted of fifteen specialized investigators, including French, English, and Arabic speakers, all able to conduct investigations and travel to the field at short notice. All requests to the ISR for specialized investigators to conduct investigations into alleged misconduct by NGO staff or contractors should be submitted through an online request form. Complaints by NGOs regarding possible misconduct by a UNHCR staff member can be reported to the inspector general's office.

The roster was not utilized by NGOs to the extent expected, as some remained skeptical, or simply feared the findings could be used to undermine their organization. The other challenge was getting the necessary resources from the annual UNHCR budget or dedicated earmarked funding from interested donors. In addressing the 66th session of UNHCR's Executive Committee on October 9, 2015, I stated: "In order for the aforementioned initiative aimed at increasing accountability of UNHCR partners to be successful, the IGO requires your support. The sustainability of the NGO Investigation Specialist Roster depends on availability of dedicated funds to ensure that investigations into allegations of misconduct of UNHCR's partners are carried out in a timely and professional manner."

During a follow-up meeting with friends of the IGO, the representative of the US Bureau of Population, Refugees, and Migration (BPRM) was quick to agree with me on the importance of the initiative, and pointed out that priority should be given to it by the senior management of UNHCR as well, and the necessary budgetary allocation made in support of the program. In short, donors considered it a priority activity, and UNHCR should prioritize the issue and make the resources available to the IGO from their regular annual contributions.

My submission for sufficient allocation for the initiative did not receive the required additional budgetary support requested. Instead, I was asked to prioritize from within the IGO budget, which would mean cutting back on the organization's own investigative capacity, determined to be below standards in the first place. Ironically, the same donors or member states that would cry out about sexual abuse of refugees and IDPs by NGO humanitarian workers did not consider putting the capacity at the disposal of those willing to look into such allegations as being worthy of dedicated financial support. Not extending an agreement with NGOs whose staff were alleged to be implicated in one wrongdoing or another was the prudent and preferred way of saving face by UNHCR, with the tacit approval of donors. That remains tantamount to condoning such actions, and sends the wrong message to perpetrators.

Efforts Toward the Establishment of an Internal Oversight Directorate

The initiative to establish an internal oversight directorate within UNHCR was undertaken before my arrival. During a short briefing I had with Arnauld Akodjenou, the outgoing IG, he shared with me a copy of a letter dated June 30, 2011, that he and Ms. Karen Farkas—then controller and director of the Division of Finance and Administrative Management—had addressed to the high commissioner on the establishment of internal audit services within UNHCR. They were seeking the HC's endorsement of this, as well as the creation of a task force to work on an implementation plan in that respect. Bringing together all oversight services—Inspection, Audit, Investigation, and Evaluation—under one directorate was explained to me as being the job at hand.

The in-housing, though logical, turned out to be more complex, bureaucratic, and cumbersome than I had initially been made to understand. I undertook a mission to New York in March 2012, to consult all concerned UN Secretariat entities regarding UNHCR's intention to establish in-house auditing. I also wanted to learn more about how other UN agencies and programs were handling oversight in their respective organizations, and to also learn what could be adopted as good practice.

I held official meetings with agency offices responsible for audit, investigation, and evaluations (UNDP, UNICEF, UNFPS, and OIOS). In addition, two meetings were held with oversight management entities of the OIOS, the secretary of the Fifth Committee, and the Committee on Programme Coordination. I also met the IRC internal oversight officials to examine how big international NGOs were handling oversight. That mission afforded me the opportunity to learn that there was no one standard oversight system in the UN, and there was a lack of common understanding of services and terminology. What is defined as being *inspection* in one, is labeled as *evaluation* in another. Therefore, UNHCR had to tailor its own oversight mechanisms. Regarding oversight mechanisms in place in the various UN agencies—the Secretariat, Programs, and Funds—the notions of working toward UN coherence, common service, consistency and UN standards and practices were not applicable.

In a meeting with the USG for Internal Oversight, Ms. Carman Lapointe, on March 20th, I got a hint as to what was to come. Ms. Carman expressed her support toward the in-housing initiative, but also expressed a degree of confusion about the nature of UNHCR's governance structure. She noted the independence of UNDP, UNICEF, and UNFPA, but saw UNHCR only halfway there. The confusion over the status of UNHCR was further drawn to my attention by Ms. Sharon Van Buerle, secretary of the Fifth Committee and CPC, who recalled the nature of UNHCR as a hybrid that was partly independent but still in receipt of regular budget funds.

In May 2012, the Board of Auditors (BOA), UNHCR's external auditors, undertook a review of the organization's internal audit arrangements. The BOA recommended that UNHCR undertake a comprehensive appraisal of options for the provision of internal audit, and develop a full business case and timetable for the implementation of the preferred option. In August, the IGO, in collaboration with ODMS, commissioned an independent study to review the current internal audit arrangements and examine options. The study concluded that the preferred option for an organization the size and complexity of UNHCR "would be to create an internal audit capacity in-house." The study concluded that a modified MoU with OIOS for the transition period would be necessary. I appraised the high commissioner in a memo on November 23, 2012, and got his feedback on November 27th, agreeing that we undertake the second phase of BOA recommendations on the option of in-housing. Given his obsession related to costs, he recommended that the audit and inspection service should be merged, including from the functional point of view. The structure should be light and as flexible as possible.

In March 2013, a subsequent study, setting out the development of a business case for the in-housing of internal audit, was completed. The high commissioner approved the establishment of a task force to steer planning and discussions on the establishment of an internal audit service.

In the meantime, the head of UNHCR's legal affairs section, Frits E. Bontekoe, wrote to the high commissioner in March 2013, through the deputy high commissioner, Alexander Aleinikoff. Legal affairs, having reviewed various documents, reached the conclusion that regardless of whether UNHCR is indeed a part of the secretariat, GA resolution 57/287B, combined with others, confirmed UNHCR's prerogative to decide its own internal oversight mechanism and relationship with OIOS.

In July 2013, UNHCR officially informed the undersecretary general of the Office of Internal Oversight, Ms. Carmen Lapointe, of its decision to make internal audit part of its internal oversight mechanism. UNHCR wanted to discuss arrangements for the transition period. It was expected that the transition would be completed by early 2015. UNHCR also recruited Mr. Egbert Kaltenbach, the retired head of the UNHCR audit service, and informed OIOS that he would consult with them and assist in putting together the transition agreement.

Constructive Ambiguity

The tone and support from OIOS started wavering when Mr. David Kanja, assistant secretary-general for the Internal Oversight Service, was assigned to follow-up on the transitional arrangements to be put in place pending UNHCR's total in-housing of audit. Mr. Kanja must have considered the move dangerous to his own career, as the in-housing would have reduced his supervisory and functional responsibility by half. Egbert was having difficulties with Kanja, who insisted that OIOS should continue providing audit services until such a time the General Assembly decided otherwise. He repeated that position to me when he visited UNHCR headquarters in November 2013.

UNHCR went ahead and drafted a transition MoU and shared it with OIOS for comments. Mr. Kanja objected to the main emphasis being on an eventual in-housing of audit, and a merger of the inspection and internal audit functions. The OIOS comments on the draft agreement repeated the argument that OIOS provides internal audit "in accordance with relevant provisions of the Financial Regulations and Rules of the United Nations." Moreover, GA Resolution No. 48/218 B states: "The purpose of OIOS is to assist the Secretary General in fulfilling his internal oversight responsibilities in respect of the resources and staff of the organisation." The fact that UNHCR, an organization that had an over $3 billion budget then, received a contribution of some $45 million that was being used to block in-housing. Even then, legal opinion had confirmed that there were no ground for that argument.

The newly recruited UNHCR controller, Ms. Kumiko Matsuura-Muller, got along with Mr. Kanja. They exchanged visits between New York and Geneva, and both were vocal in highlighting the incompetence of previous UNHCR controllers, who did not have the right skills, as they were not certified chartered accountants. A couple weeks after her arrival, Kumiko concluded that the financial accountability and oversight mechanisms she found in place to be lacking in many ways. She was going to introduce IPSAS as the new accounting system, and did not consider the timing of in-housing of audit to be appropriate.

On several occasions in my presence, Kumiko would vigorously argue against in-housing, and would advise the high commissioner that UNHCR had benefited from the confusion that prevailed, and should actually maintain the audit status quo. She argued that having an internal audit, or falling totally under the secretariat, would give donors the added capacity to scrutinize UNHCR closely. She was convinced that the organization's finances were so badly managed that a closer scrutiny would be disastrous. The current prevailing confusion being allowed to linger was in fact the best option forward. UNHCR benefited from being neither here nor there.

Toward the end of 2014, I sat down, one-on-one, with the high commissioner to exchange views on further strengthening my office in preparation for my expected departure on retirement in mid-2015. We had a frank exchange on a variety of issues, and we agreed that we would both leave UNHCR at the end of 2015. In that regard, he was extending my retirement date from June 2015 to December 2015.

The high commissioner, having considered the response from OIOS and the argument presented by Kumiko, had concluded that the prevailing "constructive ambiguity" regarding internal audit should continue for the duration of his tenure. It could be picked up by the incoming high commissioner, should he wish so. However, we should finalise a MoU with OIOS, ensuring the merger of audit with inspection. He also wanted the internal audit coordination and support services moved from DFAM to the IGO.

As part of his vision on the way forward, he supported and encouraged me to move ahead with the OLAF recommendations and the professionalization of the investigation function, the recruitment and placement of investigation experts, and further strengthening the strategic oversight-risk management function recently introduced in my office. He also supported the establishment of an online complaint mechanism, and the establishment of the roster of investigators to be used by UNHCR and NGOs.

Observing my facial expression, he advised that I let it go: "I and you will be leaving soon. The incoming HC and the IG will look into the matter. I will also defer the appointment of the new IG to the incoming HC." He later informed me in November 2015, that he had agreed with the Troika for Claire Bourgeois, who had just returned to UNHCR from her humanitarian coordinator role with the UN "to head the IGO for a transition period of three months." I was pleased to observe that most of his recommendations were either completed or set in motion prior to my retirement.

OLAF Recommendations

The European Anti-Fraud Office (OLAF) had conducted a study of oversight in UNHCR and made several recommendations long before I came to the IGO. The high commissioner had picked up on the need to professionalize the investigation function and the streamlining of inspection from that recommendation. I represented the IG at the fifteenth conference of international investigators, held at Riva Del Gaarda in Northern Italy, in mid-October 2014. The conference consolidated my belief that investigators were a specialized breed with their own language, acronyms, and culture. I briefed the gathering on UNHCR's drive at professionalizing the investigation function with the recruitment of experts, including the head of Section. The European body appreciated the UNHCR move in that direction, and assured me of their continued support in that regard.

To be honest, what I recall most from that conference was the beauty of rural Italy. I have been to Rome, Milano, and southern Italy on several occasions. However, what I saw was simply breathtaking. We were staying at the Du Lac et Du Parc Grand Resort, and would go out for dinner to the various castles scattered in the mountains around the lake. It was stunning, where history is interwoven with natural beauty. The cost of the conference was all covered by OLAF, which included a bit of tourism by bus. I understood that the head of OLAF, and our host, were Italian and from that part of the country.

CHAPTER THIRTEEN

Retirement and Final Recollections

A retirement farewell party was organized for me by UNHCR colleagues in the cafeteria at headquarters, with a live band and a variety of food partially catered by the cafeteria, and most provided by staff and an Ethiopian corner laid down by compatriots. The turnout was great, and the farewell speeches were delivered by various colleagues. My long-time friend and colleague, George Okoth-Obbo, gave a memorable farewell speech, followed by the high commissioner, who also presented me with a thank you letter on behalf of the organization.

I was happy about the farewell speech made by George, who was then the assistant high commissioner for Operations. George Okoth-Obbo is one of the closest friends I have had in UNHCR. He is meticulous, hardworking, and humorous. On various occasions he has supported and stood by me. His strength also comes from the supportive lady next to him, his wife, Esther, and his lovely children, Calevin and Vanessa.

We partied and danced 'til late in the evening, as this chapter of my life came to an end.

As I reflect on my past life, which I have tried to capture in this

Natena to my right and Helina on the left

autobiography, I acknowledge how I have been blessed to have had a privileged upbringing, followed by experiences in various parts of the globe, full of ups and downs, but ultimately rewarding and fulfilling. I was born into a well-to-do family and brought up well-provided for in an affluent and protected environment. My family offered me the best educational opportunities in both the modern and traditional aristocratic contexts. I grew up in the late 1950s and '60s as an "elite" teenager in the cosmopolitan mix that was the Sanford English School. And at the same time, as was customary, sheltered in the family compound, isolated from our neighborhood, without much engagement with broader society.

My upbringing had its advantages and disadvantages. I gained the ability to easily mix and get along with people of different nationalities and ethnicities, and this smoothened my social interactions during my university days and beyond. However, there were also unintended disadvantages that do not appear obvious, but that had an impact on my life as well as, I assume, on several others in my situation.

The first disadvantage was that I did not grow up knowing my home environment at the grass roots level, and did not get many chances to freely communicate with people outside my limited family and social circles. The Sanford School prided itself in its diversity, but that diversity was almost entirely a matter of nationalities, race, and gender. With respect to class and social hierarchy, the school was not heterogonous at all. The campus was comprised of children of moneyed businesspeople, diplomats and other expatriates, high-ranking government officials, and professionals. There were no students from the less fortunate segments of society.

As Sanford School tended to cultivate liberal attitudes, it left us students in the paradoxical position of wanting to advocate on behalf of the peasants, the working class and the poor, while being unable to relate to that experience, or even hold a meaningful conversation with anyone in that category. I now realize that I had been promoting a radical revolution without understanding the full extent of its impact on society in general, or on my own social standing and wellbeing down the line.

In short, I grew up sheltered from the realities of the poverty in my neighborhood—a realization which has come to haunt me. Upon return home following my retirement, I found our original compound had been dismantled and reduced, as most of the property had been nationalized during the revolution. It was populated by new settlers residing in shanty dwellings, which in turn provoked a sense of isolation. In my neighborhood, the change had brought down the privileged class to be poor, on par with the rest of the population. It is evident than less fortunate benefitted from the so-called revolution.

My sense of disconnect became even more pronounced when I listened to newfound friends of my age group discuss their individual experiences during the revolutionary days of the mid-1970s, especially during the Red Terror or the literacy campaigns, and how these had shaped their world outlook and impacted their psychic makeup. I was away studying in Lebanon during both periods, but still I somehow felt as though I were a traitor who had avoided the main challenges facing my generation back home.

The political implications and contradictions did not stop there. My privileged education had not only ushered me into the upper classes, it had also trained me for the life which I was expected to lead. Most of my generation was expected to put our higher education in service of the nation.

I had advocated for change and revolution without understanding what it meant in practice, until I began comparing my experience with that of other friends from humble backgrounds, who went to government schools. They stood for the revolution not only as an ideology, but they also believed that it would level the playing field, and that their social class stood to benefit from it in real terms.

Over time, and in an effort to fit in, I learned to adapt to various cultures and political beliefs. I became even more adaptive by moving from one country to another as if I was born and raised in one country by parents who came from elsewhere. Having a more fluid sense of self offered me greater flexibility in tailoring my responses and behavior to different social situations. For instance, in my time in Lebanon, I befriended many Palestinian and Lebanese comrades, thanks to this adaptability to any environment. It has become second nature for me to embody our values whenever I rejoin my family at home, and reflect another set of values when abroad or with friends of different backgrounds and nationalities. I believe I have learned to relate to various cultures without compromising my deeper authenticity.

Indeed many of my generation and I have stood against oppression and exploitation, even if we did not face them ourselves as individuals. Such a stance, in turn, increased our susceptibility to radical ideas, which we drew from the revolutionary theories from the likes of Marx and Lenin. In Lebanon, where I went to study, standing with the oppressed, or supporting the cause of the Palestinian people and the Ethiopian revolution spearheaded by aristocrats and the middle class, was yet part of that outcome.

I regret that I did not share the collective experience and psyche of my generation of countrymen. On the other hand, I do feel lucky not to have witnessed the atrocities committed during the revolutionary days in the country. However, I did live through a civil war in Lebanon, which was more vicious than any of my contemporaries could imagine. My experience in Lebanon remains my own. I have found it difficult to share with my compatriots, who either feel I am making up stories of irrational conflict and sectarian violence, or show little interest in the matter. This is a paradox of my life in retirement. My profoundly traumatic experience in Lebanon was marked by the worry of being killed for being in the wrong place at the wrong time, being caught in a random exchange of artillery fire, or suffering as collateral to the continuous random explosions and suicide bombings.

What scared me the most was the thought of being killed for no reason, and being buried in an unmarked grave somewhere in Lebanon, with nobody back in Ethiopia having a clue as to what had happened to me, or where I was unceremoniously laid to rest. That is the time that I realized that having an idea of where and how one is to be buried was essential to our human psyche, an indication of our inner value regarding death and the afterlife.

Some of the scariest moments of life in Beirut during the Civil War were during the various ceasefires. The wary quiet usually resulted in one or two sleepless nights, not knowing how and where the ceasefire would be broken, or how, in turn, that would affect me and my friends. In a way, the raging war had its frontlines to be kept at a distance, and we knew from where to expect shelling and how to avoid its consequences. Ongoing fighting allowed us to pinpoint where the belligerents were at any given time. The ceasefires, which usually lasted a day or two, denied us the ability to predict what was going on the ground before the truce was to be broken. The ceasefires denied us the ability to anticipate next moves by the belligerent forces. In fact, the only time I visited the school's psychiatrist and asked for help was as a result of a prolonged ceasefire where I could not sleep.

The regional and geopolitical context of the Lebanese Civil War, coupled with the vibrant political environment on campus at the American University Beirut (AUB), have greatly shaped my world outlook, my support of the Palestinian cause, as well as my acceptance of the change process in Ethiopia. My skepticism and fear of ethnic federalism being derailed in Ethiopia stems directly from my observation of the irrational evolution of ethnic and religious divisions in Lebanon, and the devastating human suffering brought about by years of civil wars with no end in sight. Trying to address the misery of the displaced in Africa, and examining the root causes, only augments my anxiety toward the future of my country and its ethnic federalism, if not properly addressed.

A constant theme in my life, extending from my childhood to adolescence to my international civil service career, has been the constant turmoil in the political process within Ethiopia, and its direct or indirect impact on my wellbeing. Revolution and attempted coups, coupled with the targeted government threats I faced while serving in South Africa, remain part of my life.

International Civil Service

Working as an African UN civil servant, particularly in my own country, I have experienced firsthand the prejudice and oppressive attitudes and behaviors of some expatriate colleagues. Nationally recruited staff serving in their own country continue to be treated as second-class staff with limited privileges and entitlements. The professional contribution of locally recruited staff to the work of the organization has received some acknowledgement and recognition of late. However, equal treatment appears to be some ways off. That state of affairs, in turn, tends to foster an imbalanced power relationship between national and international civil servants in the same location. The stratification offers a few radical or racist internationals an opportunity to exploit that situation, which needs constant attention and redress.

Part of the inbuilt racism and the tendency to look down on locally recruited staff could emanate from the reality that most of the humanitarian and development work being undertaken by the UN is targeting the least developed countries. The Western countries, and a few Asian nations, that contribute financially to most of the UN budget appear to have that condescending donor mentality.

Serving as an international staff myself, in Africa and Pakistan, I observed and experienced the advantages and shortcomings of employment in the UN, notably in UNHCR, which has a staff rotation policy. On a personal note, rotating from place to place made keeping a family together challenging. The strain put on family life by mobility is not fully recognized and managed, as it results in unintended consequences. I have observed firsthand that many international civil servants, including myself, raise children who belong everywhere and nowhere. Children are offered the best international schooling, but in reality, are not anchored at home in one place. They grow to like the country of their ancestors without knowing how to live there. In contrast to my experience, my sisters and brothers who never left the country have been able to raise more predictable and stable families.

In contrast to the above shortcomings, I have traveled around the world and consider my life and efforts to have been worthwhile in terms of acquired exposure and experience. And more significantly, it has been a privilege to have contributed to efforts at making the life of less fortunate and needy human beings more bearable. Saving the lives of refugees in Malawi, or contributing to the return and reintegration of the internally and externally displaced by conflict in Ethiopia, Angola, Zambia, Namibia, Afghanistan, and Liberia, amongst others, or responding to the needs of the flood-affected population in Pakistan, have been rewarding and fulfilling. These undertakings have made me to realize the relevance of humanitarian organizations such as UNHCR in meeting the needs of conflict-affected populations.

Notwithstanding my overall satisfaction, I believe that the humanitarian response setup has its own shortcomings. The inability of the international community to designate one focal organization for the protection and delivery of relief to the displaced has resulted in a coordination mechanism that is far too cumbersome. Inordinate time is spent in coordination meetings. This limitation also blurs the lines of responsibility and accountability, thus delivery is neither efficient nor effective. As humanitarians continue to respond to the needs of conflict-displaced populations, the UN, in sharp contrast, continues to fail in its primary function of maintaining world peace and security.

UN Reform

The issue of UN reform continues to be an ongoing interest and concern throughout my career and beyond. Attempted reforms and constant restructurings appear to be a common trend in both the UNHCR and the UN. Ever since I joined UNHCR in the early '80s, there have been many calls for reforms and change initiatives that tend to come and go as seasonal variations of the flu. Everyone agrees on the need to reform the UN, with little clarity or consensus about what reform might mean in practice.

I have witnessed various short-circuited change processes within UNHCR, with cyclical centralization and decentralization being championed by the ever-changing top leadership and management of the organization. I took an active part in the UNHCR change initiative in the late '90s, only to realize our suggestions were sidelined by top management, who preferred not to risk change, but rather continue with cosmetic adjustments and business as usual.

I do recall in 1997, when Secretary-General Kofi Annan assumed office, he took immediate steps in an effort to improve the functioning of the UN by building on reforms already instituted by his predecessors, with new reform proposals. For example, he oversaw the implementation of the UN System Common Premises and Services in the Field program, which co-located various agencies into one building, including sharing of common services. It worked particularly well in Pretoria, South Africa, where I was personally able to experience and recognize its positive outcome.

Dismantling the Department of Humanitarian Affairs (DHA) and replacing it with the Office of the Emergency Relief Coordinator headed the list of the most disappointing aspects of UN Secretary-General Kofi Annan's reform package in mid-1997. Giving in to USA-UK pressure to designate an official of the British government as the UN Emergency Relief Coordinator to be supported by a coordination office was an unfortunate development. I consider the cosmetic adaptation of diplomatic and coordination machinery that displaced more serious rethinking or restructuring of humanitarian action shortsighted, though considered prudent at the time.

There are operational and political implications for Blue Helmets, as discussed earlier, be they more traditional peacekeepers or more robust peace enforcers. The central challenge for peace operations and humanitarian action remains how to get the various units of the so-called UN family, along with a host of recently adopted NGO subcontractors, to function more effectively as a system, rather than as a loose collection of independent actors with separate mandates, budgets, priorities, and programs. I was of the opinion, and still believe, that the consolidation and streamlining of the various actors would be the ideal way forward.

For starters, the UN should designate one agency with the mandate to manage both external and internal displacement caused by both conflict and man-made disasters. One agency should be responsible for all the logistics aspects of food and non-food provisions, instead of designating one for food and another for the cooking utensils. Such a move would not only be cost-effective, but would also ensure predictability and accountability. The current situation of bringing all actors, UN and NGOs, into a coalition of the willing with no accountability is no solution but a temporary holding position.

The credit column must also include the phenomenal aid, relief, and development efforts. Many UN agencies operate in the harshest of circumstances, saving the lives of millions. Is it always sound value for money? No. Frequently not. But agencies such as UNICEF, the UN Development Program, and the UN High Commissioner for Refugees, are irreplaceable in delivering aid at scale. Often, they succeed despite the UN bureaucracy and the bickering and interference of its member states. Not all UN agencies have hit these heights.

In December 1997, the General Assembly adopted changes by consensus, improving the efficiency of UN activities in the areas of development, humanitarian relief, human rights, and peacekeeping. Since then, the UN has gone through reforms in various areas with the changing global situation, under the terms of Annan, Ban Ki-Moon, and the current incumbent, Antonio Guterres.

However, due to contrasting interests of different countries and diverse cultures, religions, and ideologies, UN reform cannot be achieved beyond cost-saving measures and peripheral changes. What is crucial is the reform of the UN Security Council, as in-depth communication and democratic consultation are needed in the face of accumulating threats and challenges, especially in the maintenance of unity in the UN.

Reforming the Security Council has been a subject of interest for many member states since the early days. Formal discussions began with the 1993 establishment of the Open-Ended Working Group (OEWG) on the question of equitable representation in, and increase of, the membership of the Security Council, and other matters related to the Security Council. The only progress, if one can call it that, was that after more than a decade of the working group's existence, the member states decided in September 2007, to move discussions to an intergovernmental negotiations process.

Security Council reform concerns the vital interests of all UN members and the future of the UN. While anticipating an expansion of the council and calling for full representation, several plans have been proposed by different coalitions of countries. This could lead to a major adjustment of the global governance system and international order. However, decades of attempts have remained comprehensively deadlocked. The evolution of China as a major economic and military power does not appear to have affected the current situation. The People's Republic of China won its seat as permanent member of the UNSC on October 25, 1971, and as a rising power is set to safeguard the authority of the select permanent members in the council.

The Security Council continues to offer a platform for intergovernmental negotiations, and remains the only option or legitimate forum for discussion among the member states on its own reform. The defining feature is the prioritization of increasing the representation of developing countries, especially African countries, considering a collective rise of the latter. The reform must increase the opportunities for small and medium-sized countries to sit on the council and participate in the decision-making processes, as that is the only way to make the council more democratic, transparent, and efficient.

Unfortunately, parties currently have serious disagreements on the general direction and approach of reform. Settling into a text-based negotiation, setting artificial timelines, or even trying to force through any premature reform proposal, only aggravates division and causes conflict, or even confrontation.

Besides the SC reform, the UN reform also covers other important aspects, such as management reform to increase efficiency, and the role of the UN in responding to broader humanitarian crises. The UN reform means the readjustment and distribution of interests and powers, and different member states and camps have their own demands. In this regard, reform should be based on enhancing the UN's capacity to address global challenges and to lead the world in sustainable peace and development. Member states should work in solidarity and cooperation to support the UN's cause of peace, development, and human rights, based on the consensus that the UN should play a central role in international affairs.

The bright side is that, in the face of multiple unprecedented challenges and threats, as well as snowballing difficulties of global governance, the vast majority of the UN member states are rallying around the lofty ideal: making the world a better and safer place.

Countless conflicts have ensued, with terrible consequences, some within just a few years of the San Francisco gathering to form the UN. Yet, for all the tensions and rivalries, not least during the Cold War era, a third world war has yet to erupt. And those few occasions that did take us to the brink—such as the Cuban Missile Crisis—were largely a result of accident and miscalculation, rather than any serious desire for world domination.

The UN should take credit for its role in evading a third world war thus far. Back at the height of the Cold War, the Security Council was frequently the forum where fevered tensions were calmed. The US and Soviet Union could deploy the veto to cancel each other out diplomatically, but also use it for face-saving purposes. This hardly gets the recognition it deserves in the peacemaking fraternity, but it should not be downplayed. It must not be forgotten when we discuss the organization's inglorious failings. One must also be candid about expectations of keeping peace across the world when so many conflict fault lines, historical grievances, and ancient antipathies prevail.

The other cautionary point is that any such body is only ever as effective as its members allow it to be. Rifts and division paralyze the UN, as we witness today over Syria, Yemen, Palestine, and Libya. The vetoes of the permanent five members of the Security Council can be viewed as a necessary evil to keep the UN from breaking up. These nations have protected their separate interests, but also their allies from censure or action. All too frequently, critics claim that the UN failed over, say, Palestine or Iraq, when really the individual states' involvement or position is to blame.

Palestine must rank as one of the UN's greatest failures. The UN General Assembly (UNGA) gave birth to the State of Israel with the 1947 UNGA 181, the Partition Resolution. More than seven decades later, the UN has yet to welcome the State of Palestine as a full member. The US, in particular, has, since 1967, gone to extraordinary lengths to shield Israel from legitimate charges of war crimes. But the other nations have not done enough to counter this, particularly US allies in the Middle East.

The UN Human Rights Council is not fit for its purpose. Member states are hardly going to be impartial judges and juries on their own behavior. Accountability in international relations remains weak to non-existent, with the International Criminal Court (ICC) being chastised for having only indicted African figures in its short history. Many will wait to see if the ICC dares to probe Israelis for war crimes.

Other notable failures include Rwanda and Darfur. Many are rightly still haunted by the failure of the UN and other parties to do anything to prevent these genocides. They are a stain on the UN's record that cannot be wiped away. The UN has suffered its fair share of humiliations, including during the wars that saw the breakup of the former Yugoslavia. In 1995, Bosnian Serbs held 400 UN observers hostage and used them as human shields. Even though Srebrenica was declared a UN safe zone, seven thousand men and boys were massacred in just a few days under the noses of UN peacemakers. The accountability of peacekeepers continues to be debated to date.

One would like to hope that serious effort will be made

to renew and reform this great body. Unfortunately, it will not happen within my lifetime. Past efforts have withered away. The permanent members are not going to give up their veto or risk diluting this golden power by offering it out to too many other states. Increasingly, the UN risks becoming an irrelevance as rival actors ignore international law and diplomacy in their nakedly raw quest for supremacy. Can the UN also handle the mega-threats of our age? Transnational terrorism and organized crime have proved too much. One can only hope that the UN can bring nations together to address climate change.

The UN also needs to address perhaps its greatest failing. The UN Charter itself memorably starts with, "We the peoples of the United Nations..." This remains a manifest falsehood. The peoples of the UN do not have a say. This is a body of states, whose leaders make the decisions. It serves their interests, not the people's, and in particular, those of the major powers. It is not remotely democratic, neither are many of its members.

The UN is in a difficult moment as the world faces climate crisis, a global pandemic, great power competition, trade wars, economic depression, and a wider breakdown in international co-operation. A failure of the UN is normally better understood as a failure of international co-operation.

Since 1948, the UN has helped end conflicts and foster reconciliation by conducting successful peacekeeping operations in dozens of countries, including Cambodia, El Salvador, Guatemala, Mozambique, Namibia, Liberia and Tajikistan.

To sum up, the main challenges for the post-Cold War world include control by and challenges from international capitals, legacies of the Cold War, asymmetrical threats such as terrorism, and regional and transnational conflicts. These challenges are diffusive, cascading, and unpredictable. Unfortunately, current decision-making powers—especially those given to the five nations with permanent status and veto power in the Security Council (China, France, Russia, United States, and United Kingdom)—affect fairness, truth, and lawfulness. The UN system suffers from the lack of a democratic process, which renders it unjust for years to come with regard to the population of Mother Earth as a whole.

High Commissioners During My Tenure

I was too junior to meet or interact with High Commissioner Poul Hartling, who served from 1978 to 1985. I simply knew him from the dull photos that were hanging in every UNHCR office in the country, at times next to that of the Ethiopian head of state.

Hartling was replaced by Jean-Pierre Hocké in 1986, who came to Ethiopia immediately following his assumption of office. I had the opportunity to meet him and brief him during the Sudanese refugee influx into Dimma. He also visited Itang camp. My first impression of him was positive, as he appeared to recognize local capacity, and supported our initiative to establish the camp using local experts. He was a decisive leader, in as much as he took decisions on the spot, which got our emergency budget submission approved with a speed I have not observed since then.

I had the privilege of driving with him and briefing him on the Mozambique refugee program in Central Malawi. We exchanged views and comments on all sorts of topics, during which I had also shared with him my observation that things in his country, Switzerland, were so organized that even the maize grew in line and with the same height. We laughed, comparing that to the African maize farms, where there was no line, and the size varied depending on the fertility of the location it grew in.

On a side note, I recall Hocké got along with the Ethiopian minister of the Interior, Endale Tessema, who took him around Addis Ababa and invited him for dinner at a local restaurant. I was on standby to assist if translation was needed by either one of them. To the contrary, the two had put all protocol aside and were enjoying Ethiopian food and whisky. A couple months later, Endale had led the Ethiopian delegation to the UNHCR Executive Committee Board, ExCom, and meeting in Geneva. I had also gone to Geneva to attend an emergency management training program.

Hocké had singled out Endale from the various governments' heads of delegations, and had invited him for Swiss dinner at an expensive Swiss chalet up in the mountains, where they served

242

Swiss food exclusively, and vintage wine. Hocké must have decided to pay back in-kind for the memorable cultural evening dinner he had spent in Addis with his host, the minister. I bumped into Endale the following morning, where he expressed his disappointment with the invitation, as he was served "red wine, as if I was a construction laborer." He went on to express his disappointment by observing that he was served "bread with boiling dough" (cheese fondue) to eat. From his point of view, he was not served quality food or drinks, as if he had not offered Hocké "a bottle of Dimple whisky and plenty of meat" in Addis. I did not know how seriously the minister was disappointed. However, the differences in culture and values between the two were glaring.

Thorvald Stoltenberg came in 1990 to replace Hocké, but left the same year without any visits to the field locations I served. I knew him through pictures sent to be hung on the wall that were removed when Madam Sadako Ogata assumed office in 1991. I have had several occasions to meet and discuss a variety of issues with Madam Ogata, whom I respected. Madame Ogata came into UNHCR with support team from Japan. During the early days of my first assignment to Geneva, I accompanied her advisor to South Africa, where Japan was trying to buy property to be given to the African National Congress (ANC) to help in skills training of returning refugees and ex-combatants. Japanese embassies extended her support, and I understood her to be part of that government.

Ogata had her preferred staff, such as Arnauld Akodjenou and Filippo Grandi, whom she had picked from the bureau, nurtured, and promoted. I never felt she liked me, even though she made me part of her Delphi Team. Upon visiting South Africa, accompanied by Filippo, who was staying behind, she requested my office to extend support to him. I reassured her that Filippo was my friend, and that "he will be treated as a person of concern to the high commissioner." To my surprise, she was upset and said, "Filippo is not a refugee," and walked away.

Madame Ogata expanded the organization in size, reputation, and influence. She also expanded the financial contribution and presence of Japan. The number of Japanese international staff in UNHCR grew from three to eighty-six during her tenure.

Ogata was replaced by Ruud Lubbers in 2011. He was hardworking, kept himself updated on the finances of the organization, and spent time trying to mobilize additional resources, including from his own country. As chief of PCOS, I and Roberto Meier, head of the finance section, were called regularly into his office to discuss finances and operational priority areas. He was a hands-on manager, and gave us homework which had to be completed in the evening for a meeting in the early morning the next day. He insisted we undertake a field operation review of major operations, distinct from the customary headquarters' review process.

When we were conducting such a review in Afghanistan, and we encountered some difficulties with the team on the ground, he would personally intervene and facilitate our work. He looked at all creative ways of mobilizing additional resources, and I accompanied him to Germany, together with Jean-Noel Wetterwald, head of the fundraising section, to negotiate additional funding from that country, where we agreed on a 7 percent overhead to GTZ-BMZ to be paid by UNHCR, on the understanding that the Government of Germany would increase its annual contribution to UNHCR by a fixed amount of €20 million.

Lubbers is one person I knew to shave regularly, as his hair and eyebrows would grow much faster than any I have ever seen. Because of the hair issues, he would also pick his nose regularly, which was uncomfortable at times.

The tragic manner in which he was removed from office, for an alleged sexual advance on a female colleague, remains a topic of discussion. The issue stopped being about what actually transpired in his office, and was overshadowed by the publicity it received. The recently announced UN zero-tolerance policy toward sexual harassment, coupled with various allegations of wrongdoings that suddenly mushroomed from his country of origin, the Netherlands, gave the allegation a life of its own. He also handled the case poorly, and his communication was not reassuring.

The day of his departure, I had gone to his office to bid him farewell with Marjon Kamara, where we met the only other person who had come to see him off, David Kapya. The absence of members of the Senior Management Committee was striking. I assumed that all stayed away out of fear of tarnishing their image. We took the lift down with him and walked him to his car, where Marjon jokingly said, "Some of us do not mind being hugged." And we hugged him farewell. That was the last time I saw him. He was replaced by Antonio Guterres.

High Commissioner Antonio Guterres is one I can call a friend, as I have gotten to know him over the years, and our relationship reached a stage that, at times, we communicated without talking. Mr. Guterres will be remembered for having come on his own without any supporters or assistance from Portugal or any other countries. He simply came and used UNHCR resources available in-house. He used the same secretaries, and even the same chief of staff, Athar Sultan-Khan.

Guterres was also one who did not single out his own nationality from amongst the staff or outside the organization. To the contrary, many Portuguese in the organization felt that he was ignoring them or did not support them at all.

Mr. Guterres was well-read on a variety of subjects and history. I was embarrassed on various occasions, as I had to concede that he had read more books on Ethiopia, Africa, and the Middle East than I. Traveling with him on official mission to Yemen, Sudan, and Kenya was tedious and educational as I learned a great deal from him on the history of those countries. He visited while I was representative in Liberia, and on several occasions in Pakistan. I assume it must have been his involvement with the Socialist International Movement earlier that must have given him the exposure and interest in regional geopolitical issues, which made him stand out in discussions during his visits and media encounters. He was a seasoned politician and a finance manager at the same time.

On the negative side, he came across as rude, as he would walk past without greeting colleagues, who took it as a sign of his lack of manners, coupled with arrogance. However, I know that usually mean his mind had locked in on one subject he wanted to discuss with a person. He became one-track minded and oblivious to his environment.

Guterres was constantly on a diet and would avoid sitting down for lunch or dinner with colleagues. However, he did not lose weight as much as he wanted because of his craving for chocolate. His love of sweets resulted in him spending time visiting the dentist regularly. He would avoid spending weekends in Geneva and would fly back to Lisbon, a practice for which he was criticized. He would have done more as secretary general of the UN had he been elected prior to Donald Trump's presidency, as he was not a supporter of multilateralism or the UN.

Transformation of UNHCR Over the Years

The Refugee Agency has grown in size and complexity over the years. It has also benefited from technological advances, particularly in the ICT and communications sectors. Some of the glaring changes include the continued growth of populations of concern, which has not been matched by an increase in resources. Because of diminishing resources, the quality of asylum continues to decline over the years. For example, when I joined the organization, qualified refugee students were sponsored by the organization to continue their studies up to graduate level at universities. Most refugee camps had secondary and technical schools. Given resource constraints, standards have been lowered and schools have gradually been downgraded to secondary, and now primary, level. The concept of refugee accommodation has also deteriorated over the years, with plastic sheeting being all too common in refugee camps. These plastic dwellings stand in sharp contrast to apartments built to house refugees in Southern Africa.

Improved communication has revolutionized the work of the organization. As field officers in the Hararghe Province, we used to submit our requirements to the suboffice in Dire Dawa once a week when we went there. That report was consolidated and sent to Addis Ababa by the next available pouch, which took a couple of days. From Addis, the diplomatic pouch to Geneva was arranged on a weekly basis. The return from headquarters to the field followed the same process. The introduction of the telex at the suboffice level was hailed as a significant progress. Coded messages were sent to Addis and then to headquarters. The transmitted messages were received by the registry at each level, as it had to be decoded, and a readable version was then forwarded to the concerned department or service. The gradual introduction of the personal computer, email and cell phone has revolutionized communication and made real-time exchanges possible. Gone are the days of carbon copying reports typed on a manual typewriter. Most UNHCR staff currently serving have not experienced making stencil copies of reports, which was the reality of staff members of my generation.

The various humanitarian coordination mechanisms and reporting requirements have become overwhelming to the extent that a significant number of staff being deployed to the field are primarily to perform such functions as distinct from directly working with and assisting populations of concern. What I observed in Liberia for the first time in 2005, became even more cumbersome and staff-heavy as country and province levels coordination mechanisms were introduced in Pakistan, which accounted for half the staff we had during the peak of the flood response.

With the increase of staff in the organization, the camaraderie and family-like spirit and relationships have been eroded over the years. Bureau directors used to act as village chiefs. Staff respected them, and they involved themselves in socialization activities in and out of the office. The directors served as counselors on both professional and personal matters.

The increase in the number of staff has resulted in the evolution of the culture and management style within the organization. Counseling and staff welfare are no more the purview of the directors, as specialist units have been established elsewhere in the organization. Staff rights have also improved, but so have staff demands. As a junior field officer, I recall that we did not have different rights compared to staff serving at A or B duty stations.

We had to wait for home leave to take a break from Category D and E duty stations. That has changed significantly. I remember being baffled in Pakistan, when the new generation of staff would insist on taking their six-week rest and recuperation leave at the peak of the flood response emergency, as it was mandatory. The compensation for hardship and security risk mitigation were non-existent during the early phase of my career.

For those working in the Africa Bureau, and indeed the whole organization, the sense of achievement and contribution toward the decolonization and final liberation of the continent in South Africa, Namibia, and the former Portuguese colonies of Angola and Mozambique, was a motivating and satisfying phenomenon. Currently, I do not think the return and reintegration activities could approach that sense of satisfaction.

I started working in the organization as a field officer and covered all sectors of protection and assistance. In the early days, field officers did almost everything from protection, collecting morbidity and mortality data at health posts, to measuring water outflow from taps, as well as engaging the refugee communities in discussions to assess the specific needs of groups and categories of refugees. A report covering all sectors of assistance was produced by the field officer and shared with the head of office. Gradually, health, sanitation, community services, protection, and various specialized functions were introduced at field level, eroding the central and prominent position of the field officer. The field officer is now the only function in the organization that has no support division advocating for it at headquarters, but instead lingers on without a clear definition of its functions.

The growth of the organization is not only in staff, but also an expanded management structure. When I joined UNHCR, there were only two directorates—Protection and Assistance—and a high commissioner with a deputy. Support services were limited mainly to personnel management and the finance section, with several regional desks. Upon my departure, the organization still had only one high commissioner and a deputy, but two assistant high commissioners for Operations and Protection at the Assistant Secretary General (ASG) level had been added at the top. Five geographic bureaus had been established, with six divisions. The number of services within each division had also expanded significantly. Overall, the staffing level had increased from around 1,000 to 15,500.

Life and Tragedies Continue After Retirement

Immediately following my retirement, I went to Los Angeles to visit my twin sister, who had been fighting cancer for some time. She was in the hospital, surrounded by friends and family, and in good spirits. I spent over a month with her. Given the kindness and warm personality of Turuye, she was surrounded and visited regularly by friends from Los Angeles and all over America. Her apartment mate and close friend, Aster Maherene, was a God-given supporter who nursed Turuye for a couple years to the end. The support she got from friends and their offspring made up for the lack of her own children.

Unfortunately, Turuye succumbed to her sickness and passed on February 19, 2016. In accordance with her will, she was laid to rest at Holy Cross Cemetery, next to her godfather and religious mentor, who had passed a couple years before.

By the end of February, I returned to Geneva to finalize my exit from the UN common system. The processes and procedures turned out to be protracted. Outstanding exit medical clearance, filling and submitting travel request for travel authorization to be issued, packing and shipment arrangements, after service health insurance, retiree UN security ground pass, return of car plates and petrol cards, return of assets, and so on. The UN Joint Staff Pension Fund had system-failure-related issues which delayed payment of my pension for a couple months. I did not suffer much, as I had well over sixty days of accumulated leave, which I could not use after retirement, so I took the sixty days in cash, which helped bridge the gap-pending pension payment. This problem has been so acute over the years that the Staff Council in November 2015, called for a more proactive solution by UNHCR on behalf of retired and retiring staff by suggesting the facilitation of a temporary loan to assist pensioners until they actually receive their regular pension.

The proposal foresaw that when the pension fund releases the pension, the lending entity could then deduct the full loan amount plus interest accrued based on a pre-signed agreement with the retiree. This proposal is worthy of consideration, given that the exit process takes time, even if the systemic issues are addressed.

I surrendered my apartment in Geneva, packed, and forwarded my personal belongings to Addis Ababa and headed back home to start a new chapter in my life. The new life back home starts with the initiation of reintegration, while finalizing UN exit formalities, including the submission of the travel claim and the submission of evidence of my relocation to Addis, which actually meant submitting a proof of residency from the local authorities. The receipt and clearance of the shipped personal effects also took more time and effort than anticipated.

I need to remind the reader that retirement does not mean that you wake up the day after and your memory, or your past experience and its impact on your future, has been erased. I have remained interested in humanitarian issues, and continue to follow developments around the globe pertaining to displacement and migration in all its forms. The topic has remained a centrepiece to my interactions with the world outside my immediate family.

I do realize that the UN was conceived and exists primarily to achieve and nurture peace. Achievement of global peace can only ultimately be fully realized when there is equitable distribution of wealth, knowledge, power, and access to social services. That remains an aspirational goal for the future. Displacement, be it due to natural causes or conflict induced, continues unabated. My commitment remains to do whatever I can contribute to alleviate the suffering of those less privileged than I.

UNHCR's Shortcoming of Not Using Retired Colleagues as Part of its Workforce

I am not favorable to the idea of retired colleagues returning to UNHCR as consultants doing more or less that same job they performed earlier. However, I do hold the view that the organization should keep a roster of retirees and call upon them to help bridge gaps for a limited period, in areas where they have proven to be competent. In fact, I wrote to Antonio Guterres following a mission to Nairobi, where UNHCR was frantically looking for staff to be deployed to South Sudan, while UNICEF and WFP had deployed former UNHCR colleagues to go help them out in Juba until they put a new team in place. The HC supported my recommendation and passed it on to the director of DHRM, who unfortunately did not see it as a priority. The current high commissioner, Filippo Grandi, also agreed, but his chief of staff, who was assigned the responsibility, was not able to do much.

In fact, Filippo invites retired former SMC members to join serving SMCs for dinner at his place. I have attended a few times, and the initiative is to be commended. He also seeks views of retirees on specific subjects. The Staff Council shares with retired staff, obituaries. The Staff Council would forward me selected communications they thought I could be interested in. I receive information on all major operations in Africa from a retired UNICEF colleague with whom I served in Liberia, Rozanne Chorlton, who has put me on her mailing list.

Finally, I need to underline that there was life before UNHCR, and there is life after UNHCR. The thread that binds one phase of life to the next continues to inform and shape one's interests and inclinations. I am blessed to be in good health, and gifted with two daughters and a granddaughter. I remain socially active with friends, relatives, and former colleagues. Suffice it to say, I continue to lead a fruitful and engaging life, which will be the topic of my next book, God willing, *Insha'Allah*.

AMHARIC TERMS

Afe Negu: "Mouth of the King" was originally the title given to the two chief heralds who acted as official spokesmen for the emperor. By 1942, this title was granted only to Justices of the Imperial Supreme Court.

Ato: Mister or the respected gentleman

Dejazmach: Commander or general of the gate—a military title meaning commander of the central body of a traditional Ethiopian armed force composed of a vanguard, main body, left and right wings, and a rear body.

Embumba: Women and girls

Etye: Elder and respected sister

Fit'awrari: Commander of the vanguard—a military title meaning commander of the vanguard of a traditional Ethiopian armed force.

Gashe: Elder and respected brother

Gesho: Rhamnus prinoides is a plant used for making Tej and Tela

Gugse: A pattern of a horse riding in time of war. Here, the horseman not only rides the horse but also harasses and fights the enemy. The riding is correlated with patriotic chants, coupled with scaring acts of the horseman to terrorize and rout the enemy.

Gra Azmach: Commander of the left wing – a military title meaning commander of the left wing of a traditional Ethiopian armed force.[3]

Iddir: Funerary associations have become such a widespread form of community social insurance throughout much of Ethiopia that they are commonly assumed to be traditional rural institutions.

Kegn Azmach: Commander of the right wing—a military title meaning commander of the right wing of a traditional Ethiopian armed force.

Weyzero: Madame

Hararghe: A province of Eastern Ethiopia until 1992, with its capital in Harar.

Dorro Wot: Spicy chicken stew, to be eaten with injera or Ethiopian pancake like bread

Gembo: Large clay container holding over fifty liters

Kitfo: Minced meat mixed with hot spices and butter

Acronyms

CCN: Council of Churches of Namibia

CROP: Country and Regional Operations Plan

EDU: Ethiopian Democratic Union

ODMS: Organizational Development and Management Service

OLF: Oromo Liberation Movement

IFLO: Islamic Front for the Liberation of Oromia

MCP: Malawi Congress Party

PLAN fighters: People's Liberation Army of Namibia

PTSS: Programme and Technical Support Service

RRC: Relief and Rehabilitation Commission

SLF: Somali Liberation Front

SWA: South West Africa

WSLF: West Somalia Liberation Front

INDEX

255